CRUSADERS OF THE JUNGLE

Many a good padre defended the Indians from exploitation by slave traders and adventurers

Crusaders of THE Jungle

By J. FRED RIPPY

and JEAN THOMAS NELSON

Illustrated by
WILLIS PHYSIOC

GREENWOOD PRESS, PUBLISHERS
WESTPORT, CONNECTICUT

11731

To the Memory of
JEAN THOMAS NELSON
an able and industrious young scholar
who died before his work was finished,
this volume is affectionately dedicated
by the author who survives

PREFACE

THE crusades did not end in the year 1291, nor were they confined to the attempts to rescue the Holy Land from the Mohammedans. In many respects the Spanish conquest and occupation of America was a crusade, and the term crusaders may certainly be applied to those zealous Catholic padres who entered the frontier plains, forests, and jungles of South America in search of souls for God and the Roman Catholic Church.

Their efforts were in considerable degree a failure; but if history should confine itself to the story of men who succeed, its pages would be greatly reduced. Explorers, diplomats, defenders of Spain's territorial claims, frontier boosters, and civilizing agencies, the missionaries confronted appalling obstacles almost everywhere: drought, famine, flood, epidemics of disease, depressing heat, insect and reptile pests, wild beasts, treacherous, ignorant, and hostile Indians, roving Spanish *encomenderos* looking for natives to exploit, Dutch and Portuguese traders in search of slaves. Spanish civilians and secular priests were ever prodding them from the rear and urging them to strike out anew into the untamed wilderness. The mission frontier advanced, receded, advanced, and receded again; but with almost superhuman patience and energy, and with a zeal which ran to meet martyrdom, the padres held on. The number of natives whom they converted and civilized will probably never be known, although it could hardly have been less than two millions in the heart of the southern continent. Even today, in some sections, the amenities of civilization have not yet reached the frontier blazed by their heroic enterprise. They carried the Spanish Catholic way of life to the natives of the jungle, and revealed the South American Indians and jungle to the modern world.

In this volume we endeavor to trace in broad outlines the origin, growth, and decline of the principal missions on the frontiers of tropical South America during the colonial period. We do not attempt a discussion of the Jesuit missions of Paraguay because we believe they deserve a book for themselves. A brief sketch of Portuguese missionary activity in Brazil is included, however, in order to show that the padres of Spain were not without religious competitors in the vast interior of the continent. We also attempt to reproduce the intellectual and emotional atmosphere in which the Catholic fathers lived and labored. The illustrations, although made after considerable research into the historical background of the period, are not intended to be exact representations, but rather the artist's conception of what might have been.

Professor John Tate Lanning and Dr. R. O. Rivera have contributed generously to the preparation of this volume; Dr. Ben Lemert spent many patient hours on the first draft of the map; and Mr. Willis Physioc, who sketched the illustrations, has labored with the enthusiasm of a genuine artist. To these gentlemen, as well as to Mr. Paul W. Porterfield, who made the final draft of the map, and to the staff of the University of North Carolina Press, the surviving author offers his most sincere thanks.

J. FRED RIPPY

TABLE OF CONTENTS

TABLE OF CONTENTS

BOOK I

/\/\/\

Setting

THE CHALLENGE

I

IN the year 1498, when Christopher Columbus first viewed the many-mouthed Orinoco as it emptied its yellow waters into
the Northern Sea,[1] * he gave free rein to
his fertile imagination. Realizing that the
land mass must be of huge dimensions to
supply water for so large a stream,[2] he
visualized the old maps that he had studied—charts that were
the distorted products of poorly informed and unscientific
medieval cosmographers. He recalled the mythical bronze
gates constructed in the Caucasus by Alexander the Great to
protect the civilized world from the fierce tribes of Gog and
Magog; the strange humans who lay on their backs shading
themselves with one great foot; the men with eyes in their
chests; that immortal bird, the phoenix; and, above all, the
earthly paradise. Surely somewhere in this great continent
near the headwaters of this mighty river was situated the
earthly kingdom of heaven surrounded by its high bronze
walls, a land of incomparable bliss. Perhaps hardy adventurers would blaze a way to its very portals, so that men

* All numbered notes indicate citations found in the back of the volume.

might enjoy the pleasure of a perfect Eden before their appointed time. Columbus felt himself to be the agent of the Almighty. When he spoke of his discovery, he said: "God made me the messenger of the new heaven and the new earth, of which he spoke in the Apocalypse of St. John, after having spoken of it by the mouth of Isaiah, and he showed me where to find it." [8]

In the decades that followed, bold adventurers forged their way into the interior of South America. Some perhaps hoped to view the burnished walls of the earthly paradise, but the majority were motivated by the desire for material gains— the carving out of principalities, the attainment of wealth, or the achievement of fame. Band after band of bearded men in helmet and cuirass, and armed with pikes, swords, and blunderbusses, sweltered in tropical heat, froze among the icy peaks of the Andes, and suffered hunger, disease, and grievous wounds as they advanced into the unknown in search of gilded men and fabled cities. These were the conquerors, no doubt cruel and selfish, but also strong and courageous, who carved out for Spain a new empire in South America. Conquistadores of the sword, they found no earthly paradise in the heart of the jungle. From ancient fortresses on rocky heights, or the darkness of the tropical rainforest, there issued no white-robed angels to welcome the wanderers. Instead they found proud Quechuas with death-dealing clubs, fierce Araucanians, man-eating Caribs, and sly Jíbaros who shot poisoned darts from woodland hiding places. Here, then, in the interior of this great continent were not divine beings to teach the Truth and reward the virtuous, but benighted souls who were themselves in dire need of the ministrations of the Holy Catholic Church.

II

The Spanish monarchs, while encouraging material conquests, felt that it was also their duty to promote the conversion of the natives of the New World. Ferdinand and Isabella, zealous Catholics as they were, initiated the plan of bringing the Indians into the fold of the Church Universal. "Scarcely was the new world discovered, when they gave the most evident proofs of having sought it and undertaken its conquest in order to subject it to the mild rule of Jesus Christ. The first gold that was presented to them, instead of making it shine upon their Crown, they placed at the feet of the Redeemer."[4] The conquest of the Americas became for the Catholic Kings more than the acquisition of lands and wealth. It assumed the form of a crusade against the ignorance, the idolatry, and the peculiar superstitions of the savages of the western hemisphere. Subsequent Spanish monarchs attempted to carry out the plan initiated by the Catholic Kings, so that the Spanish crown became the champion of the enlightenment and the protection of the Indians.

Hardly had the news of the discovery of America reached Rome when Pope Alexander VI issued the bull *Inter caetera* (May 3, 1493), urging the Spanish monarchs to undertake the conversion of the natives:

We exhort you very earnestly in the Lord and by your reception of holy baptism, whereby you are bound to our apostolic commands, . . . that . . . you . . . lead the peoples dwelling in those islands to embrace the Christian profession; nor at any time let dangers or hardships deter you therefrom, with the stout hope and trust in your hearts that Almighty God will further your undertakings. . . . Moreover, we command you in virtue of holy obedience, that . . . you should appoint to the aforesaid countries and islands worthy and God-fearing, learned, skilled, and experienced men to instruct the aforesaid inhabitants and residents in the Catholic faith, and to train them in good morals.[5]

As a symbol of the fact that they were proceeding in the name of and under the protection of God, explorers and conquistadores carried with them emblems of the Church. The little vessels of Columbus had emblazoned upon their sails the sign of the cross. The gold-embroidered standard of stout Cortés exhibited the royal arms between two crosses, with the encouraging Latin motto, "Comrades, let us follow the sign of the holy Cross with true faith, and through it we shall conquer."[6] It was in the name of the Carpenter of Nazareth that salvation was dispensed and kingdoms were despoiled from the *mesas* of Arizona to the arid plains of Patagonia.

America was a virgin field of opportunity for the Church militant, which, "like a city built in the form of a square, has four corners facing the four parts of the world, and desires to gather them [the heathen] within its Catholic walls in order that they may be a flock subject to its Shepherd, the Roman Pontiff."[7] Perhaps the Divine Father, who had laid the heavy hand of His wrath upon the ancient civilizations of Egypt, Palestine, Greece, and Rome, was consciously opening up this new world in order that its inhabitants might have the opportunity of embracing the true religion which those ancient peoples had rejected. It was also evident that in recent times the Jews and Moors of Spain, because of their hardness of heart, had been justly visited with God's displeasure. The Almighty would not give those depraved people another chance, but beyond the ocean were other millions who were entirely ignorant of the divine law. He was now prepared to extend to the Indians the infinite boon of His love, and it was to be the duty and the privilege of Spain to carry to them the good tidings.[8]

In 1508 Pope Julius II granted to the sovereigns of Spain

*As a symbol of the fact that they were proceeding in the name of God,
explorers and conquistadores carried with them the emblems of the church*

the *patronato,* or royal patronage, which virtually allowed them the exercise of the papal prerogatives in the Spanish dominions. By this grant it devolved upon the kings of Spain to exercise the powers and fulfill the duties which the pope exercised in Italy and many other parts of Christendom. One ninth of the tithes were to go to the royal treasury together with the money collected by the sale of bulls of crusade and indulgences. The king was given the right to nominate high church officials, to grant and revoke licenses of missionaries to the New World, and to issue ordinances for the erection of ecclesiastical buildings. No papal bulls were to be circulated in America without the consent of the sovereigns of Spain.[9] The Spanish monarchs, besides being the political heads of the empire, were now the highest ecclesiastical authority as well. While the patronato gave them great powers, it also imposed upon them grave duties. Upon the shoulders of the Spanish Hapsburgs and Bourbons rested the burden of millions of copper-colored souls, and it was their task to make them white.

Shortly after the discovery of America the Spanish monarchs wrote letters to the heads of the religious orders in Spain commanding them to come to court for a personal interview. They asked these ecclesiastical officials for godly men to accompany the explorers and conquistadores into the western world. With the second voyage of Columbus, missionaries began to go out to the Indies. Alonso de Ojeda, Juan de la Cosa, Amerigo Vespucci, Cortés, Pizarro,[10] and many other adventurers had priests or friars with them. The first missionaries, seeing the vastness of the field and the great number of heathen, realized that more laborers must be trained to gather this great harvest. They appealed to the temporal authorities in the colonies or sent commissioners

8

back to argue the need for more padres before the Supreme Council of the Indies and the king himself.[11]

The first order presented by the king to the Council of the Indies stated:

According to the obligation . . . under which we are Lord of the Indies and States of the Ocean Sea, nothing do we desire more than the publication and amplification of the Evangelic Law, and the conversion of the Indians to our Holy Catholic Faith. . . . We command . . . our Council of the Indies that . . . they have special care for matters relative to their Conversion and Teaching, and above all that they . . . use all their powers and knowledge in providing sufficient ministers for that purpose, making use of all other necessary and convenient means that the Indians and natives of those parts be converted and conserve the knowledge of Our Lord God to the honor and praise of his Holy Name.[12]

While the Catholic Kings were making plans for converting the Indians by the saintly method of persuasion and example, they also published laws specifically declaring that it was to be the duty of the American natives to accept the Christian teachings. The very first item of the *Compilation of the Laws of the Indies* strikes the keynote of Spanish policy in regard to the spiritual welfare of the Indians:

In order that all may universally enjoy the admirable benefit of Redemption through the Blood of Christ our Lord, we pray and charge the natives of our Indies who have not received the Holy Faith that, since our motive in sending them Teachers and Preachers is the profit of their conversion and salvation, they shall receive them and hear them kindly and give entire credit to their teaching. And we command the natives and Spaniards and any other Christians of the different Provinces or Nations—dwellers or inhabitants in our said Kingdoms and Seignories, Islands and Mainland—who, having been regenerated by the Holy sacrament of baptism, have received that Holy Faith, that they firmly believe and simply confess the Mystery of the Holy Trinity— Father, Son, and Holy Spirit, three distinct Persons and one single true God—, the Articles of the Holy Faith, and all that the Holy Mother Roman Catholic Church holds, teaches, and

9

preaches; and if with pertinacious and obstinate spirit they err and become hardened in not holding and believing all that the Holy Mother Church holds and teaches, may they be punished with the punishments imposed by law.[13]

Viceroys were ordered to put an end to idolatry and cannibalism among the Indians and were authorized to punish offenders with great vigor.[14] Viceroys, audiencias, and governors were specifically commanded to see to it that the Indians were converted to Christianity and that there were enough ecclesiastics to teach, baptize, and administer the sacraments to the natives within their jurisdiction. In case of shortage they were to make known the fact to the religious prelates of their districts and to the king.[15] False native priests and witch doctors were to be separated from the other natives so that their influence might cease to contaminate the superstitious savages. Indians who went so far as to teach idolatry should be placed in convents where they should be given instruction in the faith.[16]

A royal *cédula* (decree) of 1522 designated the mendicant friars as the ones who should preach and administer the sacraments to the Indians, while a cédula published in Granada on November 17, 1526, gave to the religious orders a virtual monopoly of the preaching of the gospel to the natives in America.[17] At first there had been some doubt in the minds of many Spaniards as to whether the Indians were men possessing souls capable of attaining salvation. These doubts were dispelled by a bull of Paul III, published on June 9, 1537, declaring that the Indians were indeed true men, capable of receiving the faith of Christ, and that "the said Indians, and all the other people, are to be brought and invited to the said Faith of Christ by the preaching of the Divine Word, and with the Example of the good life."[18]

III

With what profound emotions the humble friars in the safe, though often austere, environment of their monasteries in Spain * must have learned of the vast stretches of land, the great kingdoms, the multitudes of peoples beyond the Atlantic who waited in spiritual darkness for those who might come to teach them the true way to everlasting life! What various motives must have stirred them to leave the land of their birth to spend years, possibly a lifetime, in the inhospitable environment of the New World!

The restricted life of the monastery with its rigid discipline must have been irksome to those friars who were inclined to dissoluteness. They now saw an opportunity to escape from the watchful eyes of their superiors and enjoy more fully the pleasures of this world while at the same time participating in the privileges of ecclesiastical office.

For the person of adventurous inclinations was opened a door to a wider range of activity where he could allow freer play to his audacious temperament. Such a friar might become a crusader not greatly different from the men of former times who rode before the walls of Jerusalem in armor of Toledo steel beneath their monkish cowl and cassock. To such people of honorable intentions, who lacked the contemplative turn of mind, the American mission field must have offered a welcome escape from the drab monotony of existence within stone walls.

After the first years of discovery and conquest had passed and monasteries had been built in America, the monkish life offered a career in the New World to the poor man whose capacities and inclinations may not have suited him for a

* The Catholic missionaries to the Indians of America came also from Germany, Italy, and other European countries.

soldier's life and whose pride may not have permitted him to remain in Spain as a farmer or tradesman. In a religious house in Peru or elsewhere in the colonies he might achieve some prestige among his brothers and be respected by the natives of the district; and, if he were of an intellectual disposition, he might write books on archaeology, native languages and customs, or the flora and fauna of his new home.[19]

There were also persons in the monasteries of Spain whose aspirations were more exalted than these, men who forgot themselves in a vision of unselfish devotion to the cause of religion. In bare cells of great stone cloisters on the bleak Castilian plateau what inspiration must have come to solitary men keeping lonely vigils during long winter nights! In the light of a flickering candle the face of the Christ upon the crucifix may have assumed a lifelike expression of agony; and the kneeling friar may have heard in a state of spiritual ecstasy the command to carry the message of Christ crucified to the Indians. And perhaps he remembered the warning, "Go your ways: behold, I send you forth as lambs among wolves."[20] To such men as these there came a vision of service to others—

to those in sorrow that they may be comforted, to those laboring under the burden of poverty that they may not be overcome by their tribulations, to those who are sick that they may get well again, to all upon whom God, for one reason or another, has laid a heavy hand, that it may please Him to allow the sunshine of life to bless them once again with its joyous rays.[21]

To such men America presented the challenge of selfless consecration to a great cause; and the annals of their achievements contain accounts of struggle, heroism, and martyrdom.

The deeply religious were likely to have dreams or visions, and at times the scene of their dreams was America, and the principal characters Indians. Father Antonio Ruiz de Montoya, a Jesuit, one night when praying found himself, while in a state of ecstasy, in a plain where three Jesuits dressed all in white drove with some difficulty a number of hogs. He perceived that the venerable fathers were trying to guide the swine into a church. After exercising much care and patience as well as expending considerable energy, they finally managed to herd them within the sacred walls. Father Montoya entered to determine what they were doing with hogs in a church. After his eyes had become accustomed to the darkness, what was his astonishment to find, not hogs, but many Indians, all kneeling, with their faces toward the great altar! When Father Antonio awoke, he felt that this vision had been sent to him from above as a sign that even the lowest of men might be brought to salvation, and that God loved the Indian even as the Castilian.[22]

The padres had received the challenge. Armed with breviary and crucifix, and inspired by an undying faith, they would go forth to conquer the legions of Satan beyond the Ocean Sea.

THE REPLY

I

URING the entire colonial period, priests and friars went in increasing numbers to the New World. They carried with them more than religious instruction, for they became the teachers of the natives in letters, agriculture, music, and the manual arts. They became the champions of the Indian, the defenders of his rights against the aggrandizement of individual Spaniards, and occasionally against the oppression of the secular authorities as well. The first missionaries to the American natives were usually men of high character. They established schools as well as churches, workshops as well as chapels; nor did they permit their crucifixes to interfere with their farming or their breviaries with their stock raising. It was largely through them that the amenities of

European civilization were disseminated to a fairly large degree among the indigenous population of the Spanish colonies. Such men as Bartolomé de las Casas, the "Apostle of the Indies," and Juan Zumárraga, the first archbishop of Mexico, have become famous in history as defenders of the native races; but more humble men, such as Juan Rivero in New Granada, Father Samuel Fritz in Peru, and hundreds of other self-sacrificing missionaries gave years of devoted service on the frontiers of Spanish America.

The missionaries, on leaving their homeland, realized that they were perhaps giving up forever their old friends and kinsmen. That they could be fully aware of the sacrifices they were to make is indicated in the letter of a Jesuit written on the eve of his departure for America:

> We know, my dearest brother, our fortune, which I say is the greatest that God can concede to his chosen ones. And what? By chance is it a thing of little account to live unknown and, if I have to tell the truth, despised by everyone, or at least held in slight esteem? Oh, fortunate we, if in such a great enterprise we are participants! Courage, my beloved brother! Courage! We go, we go, but where? To the Indies, that is, to Calvary. To what end? To crown ourselves, indeed, but with thorns; to rest, yes, but on a cross. . . .[1]

This particular Jesuit was drowned along with forty-three other members of the Company of Jesus when their ship foundered.

Nor did the superiors, in sending out the missionaries from their religious houses, have to cajole them with false promises and descriptions of a life of ease among friendly natives. When a group of padres on the point of going into the *montaña* (territory east of the Andes) of Ecuador, asked their superior what he meant by his statement, "I see blood," he replied:

You wish to know? Well then, know that the Lord has wished to make me see what one day will become of my sons. They will have to labor much in America, and they will also see their apostolic labors blessed. But accompanying the blessings will go thorns and blood.[2]

II

The activities of the missionaries were closely regulated. On May 23, 1539, a law was issued prohibiting friars and clerics from going to the Indies without royal permission. If they should manage to reach America without having received such permission, the royal officials in the colonies were to return them to Spain. The same act provided that no newly converted Jew or Moor, nor the children of either, should be allowed to proceed to the Indies.[3] Bishops and archbishops were in 1552 expressly charged to prevent priests and religious * who had gone to America without royal permission from saying Mass, administering the sacraments, or teaching the natives, and were ordered to compel them to return to Spain.[4] In order that there should be as little opportunity as possible for heresy to creep into the colonies by way of Spain, reconciled heretics, sons and grandsons of persons who had been burned for heresy, or who had worn the *sambenito,*** or had ever been condemned for heresy, might not go to the Indies. Violation of this law was punishable by confiscation of goods or, if the guilty person possessed no property, by a hundred blows.[5] Colonial officials were not to permit anyone who was not a native of Spain or the Indies to hold an ecclesiastical office.[6] The officers of the *Casa de Contratación* (House of Trade) at Seville were not to allow foreign religious to go to the Indies: such persons applying

---

* Namely, members of the religious orders: Franciscans, Dominicans, and the like.

** The garment having a yellow cross on front and back which was worn by penitents by order of the Inquisition.

for permission to proceed to America were to be referred to the Council of the Indies, which would decide the matter.[7] Religious going to the American colonies even with permission might not disembark in the Canary Islands, nor could religious dwelling in the Canaries proceed to America without a royal license.[8] The officials of the Casa de Contratación were ordered to keep missionaries from carrying any of their relatives with them either as companions or as servants.[9] Religious voyaging to the Indies at the expense of the royal treasury must go where they were assigned. If they failed to land at the place designated, they were to be returned to Spain.[10] Laws of 1588 and 1601 provided that missionaries should not depart for the colonies except by special consent, unless there was at least one convent of their order there. Governors of ports in the colonies were to return to Spain any religious who violated this provision.[11]

During the early colonial period it was the custom, when additional religious were needed in the colonies, for representatives of the orders to go to Spain, visit the monasteries, and choose as many new missionaries as were needed in the districts from which the emissaries came. There seems to have been some competition at times between the representatives of different houses in America, so that one might try to seduce the religious that another had collected. A law of March 11, 1553, prohibited missionaries from leaving one commissioner for another who was conducting padres to a different location in America, unless the permission of the commissioner who had first enlisted the religious was obtained.[12] This custom of sending commissioners back to Spain to secure new workers proved so unsatisfactory that in 1574 an act was passed providing that the provincials of the religious orders in America, instead of sending representatives to Spain, should simply forward a list of such missionaries as were needed to the king, who would see that the required religious were sent to the colonies.[13]

Members of the religious orders going to America to serve as missionaries to the Indians were employees of the monarchy. Their income began when they left their monasteries in Spain. For their journey to the coast they were given a sum of money proportionate to the distance of their monastery from the port of embarkation. This amount was supposed to be enough to pay their living expenses en route, the hire of a mule, and the transportation of their baggage. The principal ports of embarkation were Seville, Cádiz, and Sanlúcar.[14] The president and judges of the Casa were specifically ordered to see that all religious arriving at Seville under the arrangement to go to the Indies at state expense actually left Spain. They were to make a list of the missionaries, which should later be checked by the officials at the colonial ports.[15] Each missionary was given free passage to America; and in the case of the Dominicans, passage was also given to one servant for each friar. The padre was allowed funds for clothes, bedding, and food.[16] At Seville the money to be used in buying clothes and equipment for the missionaries was turned over to a "Commissary of Religious," who made the necessary purchases, which were then checked by the factor of the Casa.[17] The amount of cash furnished for clothes varied. The Franciscan friar was allowed 15 ducats, the Dominican 24½ ducats, the Augustinian 400 reales, the Jesuit 500 reales, the Barefooted Carmelite 20 ducats, and a member of the order of *La Merced* 24 ducats. In 1607 these money payments were commuted to payment in goods. The royal treasury also furnished the missionaries with food for the voyage and clothes necessary for the first year's residence in America.[18]

III

The hardships of the missionary friar began almost at the moment when he left his monastery. With what feelings of sadness must he have reined in his mule on reaching the summit of the hill from which he could have one last view of the familiar landscape that he had come to love! Only for a moment would he stop. Then, prodding his mount, he would make his way down the slope that led to a new life in a new world. The journey to Seville, particularly if the padre came from Navarre or Aragon, was long and tedious; although when he stopped at night at a wayside inn, a house of his religious order, or the home of some hospitable person who was willing to exchange a night's lodging for the blessings of a holy man, the traveler might tell with pride that he was going to the Indies, and bask in the admiration of the less adventurous folk who listened to him. For long hours as his mule ambled along the dusty road he must have envisaged himself preaching to multitudes of Indians, who, hanging upon his every word, asked with one accord to be baptized. Perhaps he even allowed himself the luxury of contemplating the reward that would be his in heaven for this sacrifice that he was making. Such reveries in part compensated for the many discomforts—the hours in the saddle, the glaring heat of summer or the chilling cold of winter, the dust and mud, the danger of being waylaid by some robber along a lonely mountain pass, and the racking aches that come to one unaccustomed to riding—suffered by the missionary friar as he followed the *camino real* to the busy city on the Guadalquivir.

Months of waiting at Seville may have been necessary before the annual fleet, *los galeones*, was ready to sail for Cartagena and Porto Bello. A group of religious that Father Hernando Cabero once gathered at Seville had to tarry three years before they could secure passage to America.[19] While waiting for the fleet to sail, the padre had an opportunity to meet new people and make new friendships. The bustling activity of the principal port of Spain must have been extremely interesting to the man who for years had lived in the quiet of the cloister. While mingling with the sailors, soldiers, and adventurers who were engaged in maintaining and expanding the dominions of His Catholic Majesty, the man of God could feel himself to be identified with the great movement of empire. He was alive. He was now an integral part of the scheme of things, a man of action, no longer like a tedious and uninspiring volume hidden in some forgotten corner of a great library to gather dust while uncut pages became yellow and brittle with age.

At last the fleet of merchantmen and huge, clumsy men-of-war would be ready to sail. The officials of the Casa had checked and rechecked each ship to see that no foreign goods nor foreign persons were on board, that each vessel was in good condition, that all passengers had the required passports, that the friars were on the right vessels; and then the unwieldy flotilla finally dropped down the Guadalquivir. On the way to the open sea the fleet would be joined by other vessels that had loaded some miles downstream from the city and, soon after reaching the Atlantic, by still other vessels from Cádiz and Sanlúcar. Some miles out from land the fleet was again checked by the officials of the Casa, who then returned to Seville, and the galleys finally ploughed through the green waves toward the southwest seeking the zone of the northeasterly trade winds. The intrepid padres were definitely on their way, if not to the Holy Land to wrest the sepulchre of Christ from the infidel, at least to a new land to free the souls of men from the clutches of the Prince of Darkness.

The accommodations for missionaries on board ship were probably better than the average. Yet even the ship's officers and prominent state officials going to the colonies lived in quarters that would be considered wretched by voyagers of today. Experience had shown just how much food a friar should take with him. A member of the Mercedarian order, besides his vestments, shoes, slippers, blanket, pillow, and clothes, carried with him the following supplies: a barrel containing a hundred-weight of biscuits cooked hard and dry so that they would not easily spoil; two hams weighing twenty pounds; twenty-five pounds of rice, raisins, and vegetables; half a jar of capers; two jars of olive oil and one of vinegar; twelve gallons of wine; eight jars of water; preserves; eggs and live chickens; and one live sheep for every two friars. Since there were no common meals on board and since passengers had to prepare their own food, each member of the order of *La Merced* carried copper pots for cooking, as well as glassware and other utensils. If the voyage was very long, the food might spoil, so that it was highly advisable to have some live animals on board which could be slaughtered during the latter part of the journey. When a group of missionaries traveled together, they often carried with them a lay brother or a servant to do their cooking. Three or four padres were sometimes crowded into one small, poorly lighted, and inadequately ventilated cabin.[20]

The missionaries did not wait until their arrival in America to begin their ministrations. They held services on board ship. They confessed the sailors, soldiers, and other passengers. They called down the blessing of God upon the vessel. In times of danger, as when a tempest threatened destruction or when a vessel was attacked by pirates, they raised their voices to heaven in supplication for the intercession of the Almighty. Moreover, on those long and difficult voyages there was opportunity for heroism, courage, and self-sacrifice even during fair weather, for stale water and salt meat caused passengers to sicken and sometimes to die. There was need for the comforting words and the kindly ministrations of the padres. The voyage to America was enough to test the mettle of the hardiest. After weeks, or perhaps months, on the rolling, tossing back of the Atlantic, the inspiration of even the most saintly must have become dulled. "Many left the decks in order to fall on the bed, and some became sick and died during the voyage." [21]

Upon arriving in the Indies, the missionary again felt the force of the law. The port authorities investigated as to whether he had received permission to come to America, and if so, to this particular port. If his entrance papers were all correct, the missionary was permitted to disembark.

He had overcome great difficulties in order to reach the New World; and now, as many a friar discovered to his sorrow, it was nearly impossible to return to Spain. Under the provisions of a law of June 17, 1563, priests and religious in America must obtain permission from their prelates and the viceroy before returning home. The prelates were ordered not to give such permission to those religious who had gone to America for the purpose of preaching to and teaching the Indians until they had resided in the Indies as long as ten years. Officers in charge of the fleets were discouraged from attempting to aid dissatisfied missionaries to return to the Peninsula by a penalty of 50,000 maravedís and loss of office if they permitted them to embark on the homeward bound fleet without proper credentials. [22] A law of October 17, 1575, provided that generals, admirals, or captains carrying clerics or religious to Spain from the Indies when they did not have licenses from the viceroy were to be fined from 200 to 500 pesos for each cleric or religious. [23] The restriction was further intensified in 1610 by the provision that no religious who had gone to the Indies at public expense should be permitted to return to Spain except for urgent and particular cause after examination by the president and *oidores* of the audiencia, and that these should not permit his return unless "the need is so public and urgent that it cannot be remedied." [24]

Although the missionaries in the colonies were under the jurisdiction of the superiors of their orders, general regulations respecting their government came from the Council of the Indies.[25] Religious in the Indies were ordinarily not permitted to move from one administrative division to another. The Jesuits, however, according to a law of 1572, were allowed, by permission of the superiors of their order, to move about freely throughout the American colonies. Royal officials in America were ordered to give them what aid they might need.[26]

If after having spent the required ten years in the colonies, a missionary managed to obtain permission to visit his aged parents in Spain, he might go to Europe with the intention of spending a few months before returning to his adopted home. Leaving his few belongings, including the little library that he may have managed to collect, he would make the long journey home through the Straits of Florida and across the North Atlantic with the prevailing westerlies. Once more amidst the scenes of his youth, he would find it impossible for him to go back to his charge in America without again securing royal permission.[27] Thus did the insidious incubus of red tape follow the missionary throughout his career.

IV

The religious who went out to the colonies to labor for the salvation of the heathen Indians were often doomed to bitter disillusionment. In Spain the more enthusiastic of them had dreamed of bringing into the fold of Mother Church huge tribes of benighted redskins, but, for many, life in the Indies turned out to be as drab as life in the monastery at home. During the later colonial period especially, when the religious orders possessed numerous houses in the more densely settled parts of the colonies, the newcomers were often detailed to service in these places. They frequently became teachers in the colleges, preachers, or managers of farms, or were placed in even more prosaic niches in colonial monasteries. Jorge Juan and Antonio de Ulloa, in their report to the king on the condition of the colonies during the early part of the eighteenth century, wrote: "There are many who ask to be included in the missions; but as it does not happen thus, they find themselves laughed at when they arrive there, seeing how different is their exercise from what they thought, and they find it impossible to return." [28]

Great as was the chagrin of the enthusiasts who were not permitted to go out to the frontier to bring the savages into the fold, it was surpassed by the disappointment of many who did undertake such work, for they found that there was much vexation of spirit connected with the propagation of the faith in the wilds of America. Juan Rivero, one of the greatest of the Spanish missionaries in South America, wrote:

Those who are in Europe think, and are so influenced to go to the Indies to convert infidels, that it is only necessary to disembark and tread the sands of these shores in order to find at the first steps cities inhabited by heathens, or very numerous towns as in China and Japan; they go then to the imaginary place and, holding a crucifix and with the gift of tongues, they begin to perform miracles, converting and baptizing in a very few days innumerable people. Consequently it happens that when they actually come to these places and see the difficulties, and find that in order to form a settlement of wild Indians the invincible constancy of many years is needed—that it is necessary to learn their language at the cost of much study, that it is necessary to take the Indians out of the forest by entering and hunting them like wild beasts, that it is necessary to clothe them and support them at the beginning until they cultivate their farms, that indeed some flee . . . , and that scarcely do they have the exterior appearance of rational beings—their spirit fails; they sigh for Europe, their native land, or begin to turn their attention to other enterprises as those of China and Japan, as if there were not difficulties to overcome in those places, and perhaps greater ones than present themselves here.[29]

In all parts of the Indies, whether in the principal ports and viceregal capitals or in some miserable Indian village on the headwaters of the Amazon, the Orinoco, or the Paraguay, the sincere friar found opportunity for service. One man who spent more than four decades in the colonial ministry achieved lasting fame, though he lived and worked practically all of the time in the port of Cartagena. He was Father Pedro Claver, known as the "Apostle to the Negroes." For forty-one years he labored among the blacks who were shipped from Africa to this port for distribution over the tropical part of Spanish South America. When a cargo of slaves arrived, he would go to receive them, embrace them, and give them nourishment bought with alms that he had collected from charitable people in the city. If he was unable to give them freedom in this life, he could at least offer them hope for salvation in the life to come. No matter what horrible and loathsome disease infected the blacks while they were confined in the dungeons of Cartagena, he did not hesitate to go among them. One godly man who accompanied him was said to have fainted at the sight of so much misery and because of the sickening odors of the prison. Many times Father Pedro allowed some wretched Negro to sleep in his bed. He continually preached to the unfortunate slaves, making use of interpreters, for the Guinea Negroes spoke some thirty dialects. He went about the city with a saddle-bag collecting alms for the support of the hospitals of San Sebastián and San Lázaro. Although the latter, a hospital for lepers, was shunned by both doctors and priests, Claver fearlessly entered, aiding the sick, bringing the consolation of religion to the dying, burying the dead. He went among the diseased unharmed. He was said to have baptized some 400,000 people. Shortly before his death on September 8, 1654, he asked to be taken to San Lázaro in order that he might embrace the lepers and tell them that he loved them.[30]

In time, many of the missionaries acquired an affection for the land of their adoption, and came to glory in their sufferings and disappointments as well as in their triumphs. The hard life of the frontier had for them its attractions, while the artificialities of civilization came to seem useless and burdensome. The letter from which the following extract is taken was written in Spain by a Jesuit who had spent years in Paraguay. He is congratulating a fellow Jesuit who is on the verge of departure from Lisbon for that province. He refers to Paraguay as his country and to Lisbon and Madrid as places of exile:

The letter of Your Reverence I received with very great pleasure and with not a little envy at seeing Your Reverence depart for my country while I continue in this exile. This noise and hand-kissing, these polite speeches, this loss of time, and, above all, this preoccupation with business cares and projects . . . are not for me. Finally, my Father, I remain like one exiled.[31]

V

In America there was for the earnest and spirited friar always the call of the frontier. From the beginning to the end of the Spanish-American colonial period there roamed beyond the margin of civilization many Indians who had hardly been touched by civilizing influences. As the generations passed, the frontier line in South America was pushed farther and farther into the interior, but the frontier never vanished. Always there was opportunity for men who feared nothing but God to find wandering tribes somewhere in the vast tropical lowlands east of the Andes. These infidels constantly presented a challenge to the brave friar to meet dangers greater by far than those that he had encountered in his journey to the Indies.

And he knew how to answer the challenge.

> Behold him on his way! the breviary
> Which from his girdle hangs, his only shield;
> That well-known habit is his panoply,
> That Cross, the only weapon he will wield:
> By day he bears it for his staff afield,
> By night it is the pillar of his bed;
> No other lodging these wild woods can yield
> Than earth's hard lap, and rustling overhead
> A canopy of deep and tangled boughs for spread.[32]

Whatever may have been the devious plans of pope and curia or the king of Spain,—although they may have used the missionary friar as a tool in the effort to achieve a great dream of empire—the padre himself was usually sincere, courageous, self-sacrificing, and long-suffering, even though he may also have been intolerant, superstitious, and not averse to cruelty if he thought it would help him achieve the end desired, the conversion of the natives. It was owing to the work of the members of the religious orders, mainly the Jesuits, Franciscans, and Dominicans, that the authority of the Roman Catholic Church was extended throughout the remote regions of South America, and that hundreds of thousands of naked savages heard the story of the Child of Bethlehem.

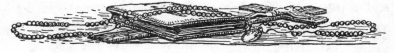

SHEEP WITHOUT SHEPHERDS

I

HEN Columbus sailed on that memorable voyage which made known a new world and inaugurated a new age, the seven million square miles of South America were occupied by a large number of tribes and cultural groups ranging in stages of civilization from the dull and dwarfish savages of the Amazonian forests to the comparatively highly civilized inhabitants of the Inca empire. It is impossible to determine accurately the population of the continent in the year 1492, or in the year 1800 for that matter.* The plateau regions which are now a part of the national domains of Colombia, Ecuador, Peru, and Bolivia were most densely settled; but the Indians along the Amazon were sufficiently numerous to cause a Portuguese Jesuit to declare that if a needle were dropped among them it could not fall to the ground through the press of bodies.[1] This statement was no doubt an exaggeration, although there must have been two or three million natives roaming

---

* The population of America in 1500 has been variously estimated at from twenty-five to forty million. Except for the Valley of Mexico, North America was not thickly populated.

through the tropical forests and over the savannas of the vast interior of this immense portion of the earth's surface. In the north, near the mouths of the Orinoco, lived the Caribs; the Arawaks occupied the Guianas; the Tupi Indians inhabited the region from the Amazon to southern Brazil; there were Guaranís in Paraguay, Araucanians in Chile, Quechuas and Aymarás in the Inca empire, Caras in Ecuador, and Chibchas in Colombia.[2] But these were only a few of the major groups. If one should list all the Indian tribes, such as the Chiquitos, Mojos, Chiriguanos, Tunebos, Guayras, and the rest, the number would run into the hundreds. These native races possessed a variety of religious beliefs, observed different customs, and spoke a multitude of languages. While a group of less than a thousand persons might be found speaking a tongue completely foreign to that of the Indians living about them, similarities of languages, customs, and beliefs might be discovered among tribes dwelling thousands of miles apart. Apparently the nomadic tribes east of the Andes had at some time wandered great distances, such migrations being facilitated by the numerous navigable waterways of the vast interior of the continent.

II

The question of the origin of these millions of Indians was not long in presenting itself to the Spaniards.[3] Had they originated in America or had they migrated from some other part of the world? If they had immigrated, whence had they come? How? When? Had the hand of Divine Providence guided them to these regions for some reason known only to Omniscience? Could an explanation of their existence here be found in Holy Scripture? It was the opinion of some that the American aborigines were descendants of the ancient Carthaginians, who reached America on one of their extended voyages and found it too beautiful to leave. Father Alonso de Zamora argued that if this were the case, then, since the ancient Carthaginians had conquered and enslaved the inhabitants of the Iberian Peninsula, it was only the "equity of Divine Justice" that the Spaniards should now enslave the descendants of the Carthaginians.[4] It was Father Alonso's opinion, however, that the Indians were the descendants of one of the sons of Noah, very likely Japheth, and that they, together with the lower animals, had crossed over on dry land at some time before Asia and Europe were separated from the Americas. He pointed out that since in the single year of 1603 the Magdalena River had changed its course for a distance of eight leagues, it was not unreasonable to suppose that in the distant past even greater changes had occurred, not only in rivers, but in oceans and great land masses. He says:

From the boundaries, then, of Tierra Firme with Asia and Europe there passed the first men to the lands of New Spain, multiplying so much that not being contained in that Mexican part, they came by the land of Florida, whence some . . . populated the islands of Barlovento. Others reached and settled Panama, and from there they passed to this part called Peruvian, which is all the Tierra Firme, inundating it with various nations, to the Strait of Magellan.[5]

Father Joseph de Gumilla suggested that the Indians might be the progeny of the lost tribes of Israel, and pointed out the similarity of certain Indian and Hebraic rites, such as circumcision.[6] He personally believed that the Indians were the descendants of Ham, the second son of Noah. It was his opinion that the forefathers of the American Indians had come to South America from Africa. As an additional argument to prove this point, Gumilla asserted that since Noah told Ham he should be the servant of the slaves of his brothers, and since the Indians were noted for their greater willingness to serve

Negro slaves than white masters, they were certainly the offspring of Ham.[7]

Father Joseph de Acosta was of the opinion that the Indians were neither descendants of the Jews nor of the inhabitants of the lost continent of Atlantis, as some averred. He maintained that if they were of Hebraic origin they would not have forgotten their laws, ceremonies, and language. According to Acosta, the Indians came from Asia, Africa, or Europe, either by water, being blown thither by storms, or on dry land before the continents were separated.[8]

The reason that inforceth us to yeeld that the first men of the Indies are come from Europe or Asia, is the testimonie of the holy scripture, which teacheth us plainely that all men came from Adam. We can therefore give no other beginning to those at the Indies, seeing the holy scripture saieth, that all beasts and creatures of the earth perished but such as were reserved in the Arke of Noe, for the multiplication and maintenance of their kinde; so as we must necessarily referre the multiplication of all beastes to those which came out of the Arke of Noe, on the mountains of Ararat, where it staied.[9]

III

The missionaries in South America often reported religious beliefs and practices among the Indians of sufficient similarity to Christian teachings to serve as a foundation for the Catholic structure which they intended to build in the minds of the natives. The Incas had the confessional. They confessed when their relatives or chiefs were sick or on a dangerous expedition; and when the Inca became ill, there was widespread confessing. The Inca customarily confessed to the sun. The sins which were laid bare on these occasions were stealing, killing when not at war, adultery, poisoning, sorcery, and failure to observe feasts.[10] At Cuzco was a great stone cross which was venerated by the Indians.[11] The Incas believed in a heaven, *Hanacpacha*, for the good, and in a place of punishment, *Hucupacha*, for the wicked. They told of a great flood which at one time had covered the land, during which certain people had saved themselves by hiding in caves, whose entrances they closed with stones. Finally they sent out dogs, which returned wet and clean, proof that the flood had not subsided. Later they sent out the dogs again; and this time the animals returned muddy, an indication that the deluge had passed. After the Indians emerged from their hiding places, they had to contend with huge serpents which crawled about in the slime of the primeval forests.[12] In various places in America the natives had stories of the Flood, the Garden of Eden, the construction of a Tower of Babel, of punishment of adultery by stoning, of baptism, and circumcision.[13] The missionaries did not try to stamp out these beliefs, nor even many other superstitions which were not at all similar to Christianity, provided they did not contradict the Catholic teachings. The result was that conversion of the Indians was much less difficult than it would have been if the padres had attempted to destroy the native religions entirely. Bartolomé de las Casas reported that in many parts of the mainland of South America the natives believed in the true God, Creator and Lord of the world.[14]

The Indians of the lower Orinoco valley believed in the immortality of the soul, though there was a difference of opinion as to what happened to the soul after death. Some held that souls, instead of going to some distant dwelling place, remained in the vicinity of the abode where the deceased had lived. Some imagined that they journeyed to a distant land where their relatives awaited them and where they would live in the eternal enjoyment of sensual pleasures. Others maintained that the souls of deceased people would go to some lake to enter the stomachs of huge snakes which would transport them to a land where they would spend an eternity in dancing and drunken orgies.[15] The tribes of the Orinoco region were not idol worshipers, though some of the Indians, who believed that the sun was a god, had to be taught that "It is not; because it is fire that God created in order to give us light."[16] In a lake on the plain near the river Tame was supposed to be a huge snake which the Tunebo Indians consulted and from which they received advice as from an oracle.[17]

Only a few of the tribes had gods of a high order. The Caribs believed in a god whom they called *Quiyumocon,* or Our Great Father. The Salivas believed in a divinity whom they called *Puru,* who lived in heaven, and whose son had once come down to earth to kill the great Serpent that preyed upon mankind. The Betoyes called the sun god, or *Theos.*[18] The Airicos of the Venezuelan llanos believed in two gods, who were brothers. The elder of these had once destroyed all the inhabitants of the earth; but afterward the younger brother came down to propagate a new race of men. The younger god was the cause of earthquakes. The Indians did not attribute to these gods superior moral qualities, but thought that they were great drunkards and had fierce quarrels. The Airicos believed in the existence of a devil who reigned over the wild hogs of the forest.[19] The Achagua Indians of New Granada, besides worshiping a supreme Lord or Creator, worshiped *Jurrana-minari,* god of tillage; *Baraca,* god of riches; *Cuisiabirri,* god of fire; *Pruvisana,* god of the earthquakes; and *Achacató,* the foolish god. They also had a story of a great flood, which they called *catana;* and they believed that while it destroyed most of the human race, one wise man with his family went up to a high mountain, so that they were saved.[20] When Father Gumilla asked a Saliva

Indian whether he had ever thought of God, the savage replied:

No, Father, only one night, very clear and cloudless, I was contemplating the Moon and the Stars; and while considering their movement, I wondered if they were people: afterwards I thought about the plagues that we suffer here of mosquitoes, hornets, snakes, and the like, and I said: "There those people are well off, free from these plagues and dangers; he who placed those people there, why should he not place me there also?" [21]

The Indians of Peru worshiped jaguars, bears, lions, snakes, lightning, thunder, the rainbow, storms, crossroads, and occasionally a deformed tree. While the Indians of the high, cold plateau made sacrifices to the sun, those of the coast worshiped and sacrificed to the sea. They also worshiped the bones or the entire bodies of their deceased ancestors, a custom which perhaps explains why they mummified the dead. One chief had an emerald that he exhibited to his people several times a year in order that they might worship it, and make gifts and sacrifices to it so that it would answer their prayers. [22] The Indians of Peru also had a supreme god, *Pachacamac*, creator of the earth and all that is upon it. To the Incas, the sun was not a good god, but a demon, powerful as an aid in war, and who therefore must be propitiated. [23]

The Maynas of the upper Amazon region had some idea of God, whom they called "Our Father" and "Our Grandfather." They said that he had created heaven, the earth, and all that is on the earth, and that he continued creating food for his children here on this planet. They had other gods too, such as a god of the river. One of their gods, they told the padres, had in ancient times descended to earth, where he had lived in a cave with a huge snake for a spouse. When the missionaries first came among them, the Maynas feared that

35

the good men were bringing a powerful and brave god who would destroy them. They had a story of a great flood that had in olden days covered the whole earth so that all were drowned except a man and woman who had climbed a very tall tree. God had once taken the form of a man, who had come down to earth to teach mankind. These Indians believed also in the devil; occasionally they would be disturbed by the fear that some animal, bird, or noise of the night was Satan, and they would flee frightened from their villages. They believed in another life, for when Father Figueroa told an old dying Indian that, having accepted Christianity, he would go to heaven, the old fellow replied, "Yes, Father, I indeed desire to go there, because my parents are there waiting for me with yucca and ripe bananas." The Maynas thought that in the future life they would have a happy existence, eating, drinking, singing, dancing, and cutting off the heads of their enemies. They thought that the souls of the people whom they decapitated here on earth passed into jaguars or other animals. They knew nothing of the idea of hell and punishment in a future life for the sins committed in this. When a missionary told one old Indian that he was in danger of going to hell, the Indian replied, "You lie in what you say, for there is no such thing." [24]

Among the Mojos of the *oriente* (area east of the Andes) of Bolivia were a multitude of gods, some being common to many settlements while others had jurisdiction over limited areas. Some of their gods were single, others married. There were different gods to preside over the fields, fish, clouds, and jaguars. The jaguar gods were worshiped with the greatest ceremony, since the Indians were afraid of being killed and eaten by these animals while they slept on the ground in the forest.[25] Some of the Mojos worshiped the sun, moon, stars, invisible jaguars, and small idols of ridiculous form. Among these savages were sorcerers to heal the sick and priests to appease the demon gods.[26] The religious dances of the Mojos must have been shocking to the good padres. After the savages had become thoroughly drunk, it is asserted, "they begin to jump about in a Sort of Cadence, and throw their Heads indolently from Side to Side; making at the same Time indecent Motions with their Bodies, and this is all their dancing. The more extravagant and ridiculous a Person is on this Occasion, the more religious he is thought." [27]

As for the Chiquitos, who dwelt in what is now eastern Bolivia, "They live . . . like beasts, without knowledge of another life, having no God but their belly, and limiting all their happiness to the pleasures of the present life." [28] The Chiquitos did, however, have some beliefs in regard to a future life and supernatural beings. They called the moon "Mother," and thought that eclipses of the moon were caused by the moon's being bitten by dogs. On such occasions they would shoot their arrows into the air, hoping to kill or frighten away the ferocious beasts. They were particularly afraid of devils, and looked upon the noises made by wild beasts as being omens of good or evil portent. They may have believed in immortality of the soul since they buried arms and provisions with their dead. They thought that thunder and lightning were departed spirits quarreling with the stars,[29] or perhaps that the deceased souls were angry with their brothers who remained on earth.[30] The Chiquitos had a practice similar to the suttee. If the witch-doctors were unable to cure a sick man, the entire blame for his illness was placed upon his wife, whereupon she might be executed. This practice was a convenient method whereby dissatisfied husbands, by pretending illness, might get rid of undesired wives! [31]

37

The average South American Indians had little idea of religion and were almost incapable of understanding what the missionaries were trying to explain

IV

The average South American Indian was by no means an ideal neophyte. While some of the more highly civilized tribes had religious beliefs and customs similar in part to those taught by the emissaries of the Roman Catholic Church, others had little idea of religion and were almost incapable of understanding what the missionaries were trying to explain. While some of the South American aborigines possessed a semblance of that nobility so often attributed to the Red Man of the United States, others, particularly those in the unhealthful, moist, continuously hot lowlands, were but little removed in mental development from the lower animals with which they fought. In speaking of the Indian of Venezuela, the French traveler, Depons, said:

His heart, shut against pleasure as well as hope, is only accessible to fear. Instead of manly boldness, his character is marked with abject timidity. His soul has no spring, his mind no vivacity. As incapable of conceiving as of reasoning, he passes his life in a state of torpid insensibility, which shows that he is ignorant of himself and of everything around him. His ambition and desires never extend beyond his immediate wants.[32]

Father Joseph de Gumilla described the wild Indian as "a monster never before seen, who has a head of ignorance, a heart of ingratitude, breast of inconstancy, shoulders of laziness, feet of fear, stomach for drink, and inclination to get drunk." Nevertheless, he justified the padres' efforts to convert these savages by saying that "this coarseness may be overcome by force of time, patience, and education; . . . in the savage Indians are discovered the precious pearls of those souls which our Redeemer bought at so dear a price." [33]

The ceremony of naming children among the Guaranís of Paraguay was particularly repulsive. A prisoner of war was royally entertained with food, drink, and women for some days prior to the celebration. On the day set for the christening, his throat was cut with elaborate ceremony. When he was completely dead, the whole tribe filed by, each member touching the body with his hand or a stick, at the same time giving a name to the children in his family who had not yet been christened. This having been done, the body was cut up into small pieces so that every member of the village could have some soup. Everyone partook of this broth, "not excepting children at the breast, whom their mothers took care to make partakers of this hellish repast." [34]

Several tribes of the Ucayali River region observed the practice of circumcising girls. When a girl reached the age of eleven or twelve, a great festival was held attended by numerous friends and relatives. For a period of seven days preceding the ceremony the Indians celebrated with dances and drinking sprees. On the eighth day, just after sunrise, the child was made to drink an intoxicating beverage until she became drunk, whereupon the operation was performed by two women. The girl was then carried from house to house while the Indians danced and sang mournful songs. [35]

There were numerous savage practices among these lost

39

sheep of the South American wilds that had little or nothing to do with religion. The Jíbaro and Munduruká Indians of eastern Peru and Ecuador were head hunters and head shrinkers.[36] Cannibalism seems to have been quite common, although there are people who believe that the stories of cannibals were invented by the Spaniards to justify their exploitation of the natives.[37] According to Father Figueroa, famous in the annals of the missions of Ecuador, the Roamaynas not only ate the enemies whom they had killed in battle, but their own relatives and even their own children. When a person died of disease, his friends might place the blame on someone else in the tribe, whom they would proceed to kill and eat. In this procedure, the Roamaynas were chivalrous enough to send a message to the supposedly guilty man informing him that they were coming after him and advising him to be prepared. He then proceeded to clear the members of his family out of the house so that they might hide in a place of safety; and, arming himself with lance and shield, he awaited the arrival of his would-be murderers. Since the aggressors were often several in number, they usually managed to do away with him; but occasionally the tables were reversed, and the attackers served to replenish the larder of the hunted.[38] Father Juan Lucero, writing from Laguna in the Marañón region on June 3, 1681, reported that there were Indians in his vicinity who ate such of their relatives as died of sickness:

Others there are who bury them neither in the church nor in their houses, because they say it is a pity that their relatives should have to eat dirt; whereupon they cut them up and, together with all their kindred, they eat them. The bones, very well roasted, they grind and, putting them in their wine, they drink with great lamentation. They then get on a great drunk, which lasts eight days, . . . and mourn their dead with loud outcries.[39]

The Chiriguano Indians of the oriente of Bolivia were among the most ferocious of all the South American tribes. They would frequently attack the neighboring tribes and capture several hundred at a time, selling some, enslaving some, and fattening others to play the passive rôle in savage banquets.[40]

The various tribal groups had ingenious ways of mutilating themselves. The Omagua Indians along the Marañón flattened the heads of their small children by tying a board tightly against their foreheads. The pressure exerted on their soft skulls over a period of many months gradually produced the desired result. The Omaguas said that this custom had originated when their forefathers had seen the devil with his head flattened.[41] Some of the savages of the Ucayali River region slit the ears of their children and hung weights to them, so that in the course of time their ears reached down almost to their shoulders. These Indians were known as Orejones or Big Ears.[42]

The practice of infanticide seems to have been fairly common among the more backward tribes. The Mojo Indians buried children alive if they were ill or deformed, if they cried much, or simply to avoid the burden of rearing them.[43] The native mothers of the Orinoco valley were so accustomed to killing their children that the missionaries appointed spies to watch them during the month of childbirth to see that they did not extinguish their offspring. These mothers insisted that it was their duty to kill their daughters as an act of mercy, since the female children could look forward only to a lifetime of slavery to the men, caring for their physical needs, making chicha for them, being beaten by them, and in the end growing old and seeing their husbands take younger wives whom the older ones were required to serve. A woman who

had killed her daughter at birth defended herself before
Father Gumilla as follows:

> Father, if you will not become angry, I shall tell you what is
> in my heart. . . . My Father, I wish that when my mother bore
> me she had loved me well and had had pity on me, freeing me
> from so much work as hitherto I have endured and shall have to
> suffer until death. If my mother had buried me as soon as I was
> born, I should have died; but I should not have felt death, and
> with it I should have been freed from the death which is to come,
> and I should have escaped so many tasks as bitter as death. . . .
> The Indian woman can not do better by the daughter that she
> bears than to free her from these labors, to take her from this
> slavery worse than death.[44]

A practice among the Indians of the lowlands of tropical
South America which caused the missionaries much worry
was that of going with little or no clothes. To the missionaries, this was the height of indecency even though the temperature may have been above ninety and the relative humidity
close to a hundred. The Carib woman, for instance, wore
little except a band about two inches wide, called a *guayuco*,
around the waist, and she considered this of less importance
than the pigment with which she covered her body.[45]

V

It was among such people as these—drunkards, murderers,
and cannibals, who were guilty of polygamy, superstition,
cruelty, inconstancy, infanticide, and who were the victims of mental dullness and ignorance—that the Spanish padres
went for the purpose of making heathen savages civilized
Christians. There were those who believed that the condition
of the Indians was hopeless and that, since it was impossible to
make rational human beings of them, the Spaniards were justified in enslaving them. But the good friars, while seeing as
well as anyone the many shortcomings of the natives, could

better than others perceive their finer qualities. Father Joseph
de Acosta says that the purpose of his book, *The Natural and
Moral History of the Indies,* is to

confute that false opinion many doe commonly holde of them,
that they are a grose and brutish people, or that they have so little
understanding, as they scarce deserve the name of anie. So as
many excesses and outrages are committed vpon them, vsing them
like brute beasts, and reputing them vnworthy of any respect;
which is so common and so dangerous an errour. . . .[46]

Father Francisco Figueroa made the statement that the

Indians, beneath their coarseness and crudeness, are good timber,
and that behind their brutal actions they conceal a docile, obedient, and humble nature. . . . And above all they have within
them the preciousness of their souls, which were redeemed at infinite cost by the blood of Christ our Lord.[47]

Father Juan Rivero was of the opinion that the

Indians are not so incapable as one might think, nor is the barbarous and rustic genius with which they resist the Christian faith
and customs so common. . . . In truth, there is no nation, however barbarous and backward it may be, provided it is of a docile
nature, which is not capable, and very capable, of being subdued
through wise and tactful treatment, and of being cultivated with
much improvement in the Catholic faith, if the missionary has
properly equipped himself and if he applies himself with determination and fervor to its culture and education in its own
language.[48]

Not only did the points of similarity between the native
religions and Roman Catholicism serve as a basis upon which
to build the Catholic structure; conversion may also have
been aided by the fact that some of the Indian tribes had
legends that in ancient times missionaries such as these had
come among them. From Mexico to Paraguay stories were
current of white men who had exerted great influence or
power over the native races. In Mexico there was Quetzal-
coatl, the Fair God, who was some day to return to rule his

people. In South America the stories of white missionaries of olden times may have been legends which were current among the Indians before the conquest; but on the other hand the natives may have made up these stories after they had heard the preaching of the Spanish friars, or at least connected the friars' descriptions of Biblical characters with legends originally having Indian actors.

In New Granada the Indians related how, some fourteen hundred years prior to the arrival of the Spaniards, there had come among them an old man whose beard reached to his waist and whose hair was tied with a ribbon. He was barefoot; he wore a tunic reaching to the calves of his legs, and over this a blanket tied at the right shoulder. He visited many villages, where he preached to the natives, to each tribe in its own language. Besides imparting to them the mysteries of the Holy Faith, he taught them to spin. After dwelling among them for some time, he disappeared. According to the story of the Indians, his tracks were still visible in some rocks near Guane. Father Alonso de Zamora suggested that this ancient missionary was the apostle Thomas, who was supposed also to have preached in the East Indies and to have left signs on the rocks there. The natives of the valley of Ubaqué in New Granada attributed miraculous powers to a rock on which were marks apparently made by a human foot, and they were accustomed to put dust from the rock into beverages to give to the sick. The ancient apostle was said to have had the same appearance and dress attributed to St. Thomas by the Christians. He taught the immortality of the soul, the resurrection of the dead, reward and punishment in a future life, and the existence of one supreme God.[49]

In Peru impressions of the soles of a man's feet and knees, and of a pilgrim's staff, all believed to be those of St. Thomas, were said to have been found on a great rock in a village of the province of Chachapoyas. Other similar signs were said to have been discovered about fifteen leagues from Lima. At another place the apostle was said to have lain down on a rock and stamped there his back, his head, and the calves of his legs. At still another he left the imprint of his left foot and some letters that he drew in the rock with his finger. He was said to have taught the natives the way to heaven, to have silenced devils, and to have abolished the vices of adultery, polygamy, and drunkenness. This good man was so basely persecuted by the Indians, however, that he, like the apostle to New Granada, disappeared from among them.[50] The Indians of the Peruvian seacoast had a tradition of a bearded man with curly hair who had come up out of the sea to preach against the worship of the moon, sun, and other false gods, and to warn the natives that they should sacrifice to and worship only the great and supreme god, *Pachacamac*. This apostle, according to tradition, had been driven from the village of Hilavaya. When the Indians pursued him, they were made permanently dumb; and their village was soon afterward visited by pestilence and famine.[51]

The Guaraní Indians of Paraguay told the missionaries that in olden times there had come among them a holy man called *Pay Luma, Pay Tuma,* and *Pay Abara,* or "father who lives in a state of celibacy." He had preached the true faith to them so effectively that many had been converted. But he had left them, predicting that they would forget his teachings and fall away from the worship of the true God, only to be reconverted after the passage of centuries. They told of a rock near Asunción, where the footprints of this holy father might be seen.[52]

Such stories as these caused the Spaniards to believe that the Indians had at one time been Christians and that subsequently they had abandoned the true religion. Hence, when the padres went out to convert the wild Indians, they said that they were "reducing" them to the faith that they had formerly had; and the settlements of converted Indians were called "reductions." What a noble work it would be to return the lost sheep to the fold, to restore these backsliders to the religion of Christ! The fields were white, awaiting the harvest. Father Gumilla, laboring in the forests and llanos of the Orinoco valley, prayed:

Oh good Jesus, most lovable Redeemer of souls! Well do you know, Lord, what spacious, immense, and abundant harvests of innumerable Nations are being lost in that New World, only through lack of Workers who may gather them and guide them with the light of your Gospel. You, Lord, command that we pray to you. . . . Humbly and affectionately I beg you, that you send many and very fervent Missionaries, who in full hands may gather the fruit of your copious Redemption. And I pray also to all the true and faithful Sons of your Holy Church, that every day they make to you repeatedly this same supplication, for they know that it is your will.[53]

WARDS OF THE CROWN

I

 ENERAL extension of the Catholic faith to the New World interested the Spanish monarchs as much perhaps as conquest of territory. The expeditions against the American natives "were undertaken and accomplished in the name of Religion; the warriors fought, conquered, and died like soldiers of the Cross; the missionaries always marched at their side. . . ."[1] No matter what cruelties may have been perpetrated upon the Indians by the conquerors, the policy of the crown of Spain toward the natives was friendly. A cédula of August 6, 1555, permitted the Indians to keep their "just and good" laws.[2] It was the wish of the monarchs that the indigenous inhabitants of the Indies should be won over to the Christian religion and to the acknowledgment of Spanish suzerainty by peaceful means, and that force should be employed only as a last resort. If possible, the Indians were to be converted to Christianity before they were completely subjected to the secular authorities. Of course, in the last analysis, the Indians either accepted Christianity and Spanish

47

authority of their own accord, or had them thrust upon them. But once they had submitted, they became the wards of the crown, enjoying special privileges and exemptions, for which they paid well in the form of tribute.

II

The policy of the crown went further than conversion. The Indians were to be settled in towns; they were to be taught Spanish manners and customs, reading, writing, arithmetic, art, music, and superior methods of agricultural and industrial production. They were to be made sober, industrious, peaceful, and intelligent citizens.[3]

A law was promulgated as early as August 14, 1509, requiring that as soon as the pacification of the natives should be completed, the *adelantado* or governor should apportion the Indians of his locality for service among the Spanish settlers, provided that each Spaniard (*encomendero*) agreed to aid and defend them and to furnish ministers of the gospel to teach them the Christian doctrine and administer the sacraments.[4] A law of October 20, 1545, specified that the encomenderos should be "meritorious" individuals.[5] During the early colonial days the Indians thought that "Christian" and "Spaniard" meant the same thing. Since most lay Spaniards who went to America were far from being meritorious individuals in the moral and ethical sense, the natives came to think of Christians as being persons who were haughty, selfish, and cruel. Indians would sometimes say to priests, "We welcome you, but do not bring any Christians with you." In complaining of an evil priest, they would say that he acted like a Christian. Said Friar Rodrigo de la Cruz: "Thus, among the poor Indians, when a friar happens to approach, someone says, 'Here comes a Christian,' but another who sees better says, 'No, he is a priest.' And if one asks an Indian, 'Are you

48

a Christian?' he replies, 'No'." [6] In 1528 priests and members
of religious orders were designated to teach the Christian
doctrine and administer the sacraments to Indians and slaves
working in the mines. Such laborers were to be permitted to
attend Mass on Sundays and feast days.[7]

Since it soon proved to be quite difficult to teach Christianity to nomadic Indians roving about in search of fish and
game, the governors and viceroys were ordered to persuade
the natives to live together in communities in order that they
might be instructed more advantageously.[8] The Council of
the Indies, on March 21, 1551, "resolved that the Indians
should be reduced to Towns, and should not live divided and
separated by mountains and forests, depriving themselves of
all spiritual and temporal benefit, without the aid of our
Ministers. . . ." [9] The natives were to be reduced without
the use of force and in a kindly manner.[10] Bishops and archbishops were urged to facilitate the settlement of the Indians
within their jurisdiction.[11] When they had settled in the
places designated, their former lands were not to be taken
away from them.[12] The village sites were to be located where
there were plenty of lands, wood, water, and pasture for the
grazing of the natives' flocks so that their animals might not
get mixed with those of the Spaniards.[13] In the new settlements the native chiefs remained in direct control, although
higher Spanish officers were placed above them. The Indians
were required by an act of June 26, 1523, to pay to the
government a part of the product of their lands as tribute.[14]
A law of 1578 specified that only natives between the ages of
eighteen and fifty must pay tribute,[15] and in 1607 those Indians who had accepted the Catholic religion and received
baptism were exempted from the payment of tribute for ten
years.[16]

On December 10, 1566, the king of Spain sent a cédula to

the audiencia at Bogotá commanding that no impediment be placed in the way of missionaries in their efforts to convert the Indians:

> Know that we, desiring . . . the conversion of the Natives of those parts and that they may be brought to the knowledge of our Holy Catholic Faith to the end that they may be saved, have tried and each day do try to send Religious and Learned persons who are God-fearing, in order that they may endeavor to bring the said people to the true knowledge of the Faith; and although in many parts they have accomplished and each day do accomplish . . . great results, . . . we are informed that [the labor of said Religious and Learned persons is being hindered] because of the impediments that they have had from some Spaniards who have resided and do reside in those parts, especially from those who have held and do possess enslaved Indians. . . . We therefore command that no person nor persons . . . dare to impede any Religious of whatever order that there may be who shall be traveling with the permission of the Prelate. . . .[17]

Any individual violating this order was to lose half of his possessions, and, if he were an encomendero, all of the Indians that had been assigned to him.

The churches where the Indians were to worship were to be constructed with funds furnished equally by the royal treasury, the Indians, and the encomenderos of the diocese.[18] Since the revenue of the government and the income of the Spaniards came almost entirely from the labor of the Indians, the burden of erecting the great cathedrals which until today stand as a monument to Spanish ecclesiastical enterprise in America, rested mainly upon the shoulders of the native races. Indians were ordered by an act of July, 1622, to aid in the building of churches by making adobe and cutting wood.[19] The Indians of each town or suburb were commanded to erect houses for the priests.[20]

Once having accepted the Catholic religion, the Indian convert thus discovered that he had incurred obligations. If when at the point of death he did not confess his sins and receive the sacrament of the Eucharist, half his goods were confiscated. If he should die, however, under conditions where it was impossible for him to confess to a priest and partake of the sacrament, the penalty did not apply.[21] He found that he had to give up old customs that may have been dear to him. Polygamy, which had been practiced by many tribes, was not permitted under the Spanish régime.[22] The Indian was required by law to wear clothes.[23] He might not ride horseback nor use firearms.[24]

While he incurred obligations, the native convert at the same time acquired privileges and exemptions not accorded to wild Indians nor to the Spaniards themselves. The viceroys, presidents, members of audiencias, and ecclesiastical prelates, were ordered to favor and protect the Indians in the maintenance of their prerogatives, "for we desire that the injuries that they suffer be remedied, and that they live without molestation or vexation."[25] In 1589 special protectors of the Indians * were provided for.[26]

The Inquisition, which during the colonial period burned sixty men and women in Lima, and in Cartagena subjected heretics to the tortures of the "Iron Maiden,"[27] did not apply to the Indians. An act of February 23, 1575, stated: "It is hereby prohibited to the Apostolic Inquisitors to proceed against Indians, their punishment being intrusted to the Ordinary Ecclesiastics, and they ought to be obeyed, and their commands fulfilled; and against witches who kill with enchantments, and use other kinds of witchcraft, our Royal

---

* The law recited that protectors had existed before but had been suppressed. Shortly after the beginning of the Conquest the Spanish government evinced concern for the welfare of the Indians. The laws of Burgos, 1512, were designed to shield them from exploitation; three Jeronymite fathers were sent to America in 1516 with the same purpose in view; the New Laws of 1542 were intended to emancipate them from slavery and gradually to free them from serfdom.

51

The exemption of the natives from punishment by the Tribunal of the Inquisition was at times opposed by both ecclesiastical and secular officials

Judges will proceed." [28]   This exemption was at times opposed by both ecclesiastical and secular officials.   One padre, Juan Rivero, thought that Indians should be punished by the Inquisition, though not so severely as Europeans.   Serván de Cerezuela, who arrived at Lima in 1670 to open a tribunal of the Inquisition, was advised by some of the townsmen to disobey the law and subject the natives to the tribunal.[29]   It need hardly be said that the Spaniards in the colonies could, if they wished, find ways of accomplishing the ends desired without going through the formality of trying Indians before the Holy Office.

While some theologians approved the enslavement of Indians, and while the religious orders sometimes owned slaves,[30] the laws prohibited the enslavement of the natives of America. Any Spaniard, Negro, mestizo, or mulatto convicted of gambling or trading in Indian slaves was by a law of 1618 to be condemned to the galleys for six years, or to equivalent service.[31] Indians carried from Portuguese Brazil into Spanish territory to be sold as slaves were automatically freed,[32] and the colonial governors were ordered to prevent the Portuguese from enslaving Spanish Indians.[33] There were certain exceptions, however, to this law. Spaniards might enslave the fierce and warlike Caribs, provided they were of male sex and over fourteen years of age.[34] During the first years after the conquest, Spaniards were permitted to enslave Indians who took up arms against them. But a cédula published on September 16, 1639, provided that "no Indian, of whatever quality he may be, even although an infidel, may be held captive nor placed in slavery in any manner, or for any cause or reason, nor may he be deprived of the natural dominion that he has of his goods, children, or wife. . . ."[35] While some laws prohibited the enslavement of the Indians, others were quite similar to those passed by Virginia prior to 1860 for the purpose of regulating slavery. To cite one case, Indians were forbidden to go from one village to another under penalty of twenty lashes.[36]

Persons employing Indians were not to hinder them from attending church on Sundays and feast days for the purpose of hearing Mass, under penalty of a fine of two hundred thousand maravedís.[37] Indians, Negroes, and mulattoes were not to work on Sundays and feast days.[38] An act of October 10, 1618, required persons with heathen natives in their employment to send them to church each morning at the sound of the church bell in order that they might learn the Christian doctrine. Any employer violating this statute should lose the services of his employee, besides paying a fine of four pesos for each day that the Indian failed to attend church.[39]   Encomenderos were commanded both to defend the Indians and to see that they were taught the Christian doctrine.[40]   Encomenderos who failed to make provision for the spiritual education of the natives under them should be deprived of their encomiendas and banished from the province.   "And we declare that the Encomenderos ought to ask for and solicit with all diligence such Religious Ministers, or Clerics, as are needed, and provide them with convenient stipends for their sustenance, and with whatever is necessary for divine worship: ornaments, wine, and candles. . . ."[41]   No person might take a neophyte away from a mission without the permission of the governor, his lieutenant, or the corregidor; and these officials were not to give permission except in case of great necessity.[42]   The laws went into such minute matters as prohibiting Spaniards from requiring native mothers to leave their villages to act as wet nurses for the children of the Spaniards if the mothers had infants of their own,[43] and providing that baptized Indians might keep their long hair if they wished, even though the priests tried to carry out St. Paul's advice on this subject.[44]   A cédula issued on August 5, 1701, addressed to the governor of Venezuela, directed him to keep encomenderos off the missions "because of the injury that they do to the reduction of the Indians, for enemies make use of that pretext to say that the Missions are no more than a means to carry the Indians to the slavery of the haciendas."[45]

Hospitals were to be established in all the Indian towns, "where the poor sick people may be cured, and Christian charity exercised."[46]   Bishops and archbishops in the Indies were to see that deceased natives should be interred in churches or monasteries if this were possible;[47] and for the benefit of those Indians who were far from a house of God, some place of burial was to be blessed "in order that the Faithful may not lack Ecclesiastical burial." [48]

An act of June 7, 1550, ordered that schools be established among the natives for the purpose of giving them instruction in the Spanish language. [49] A royal cédula of August 27, 1692, directed that teachers of the Castilian language should be placed on all missions to teach the converts to read and write. [50] Laws of 1578 and 1603 provided that no ecclesiastics, whether secular or regular, should be given appointments to work among the Indians unless they had learned the native tongues. [51] Religious going to the Indies from Spain were urged to learn the indigenous languages carefully. [52] An act of March 17, 1619, required that all members of religious orders not knowing the languages of the Indians among whom they were working should be removed and others who were acquainted with them substituted. [53] While learning the native tongues, priests and teachers of the doctrine among the Indians were to instruct the natives in Spanish "and in it to teach the Christian doctrine in order that they may be made more capable in the Mysteries of our Holy Catholic Faith." [54] A royal cédula published in 1584 ordered that in Peru the catechism and doctrines of the Roman Catholic Church, which had been translated into some of the native languages by the Jesuits, should be printed in those tongues for circulation among the Indians. [55]

Legislation was enacted for the purpose of protecting the natives from exploitation or oppression by priests and members of religious orders. Prelates and other ecclesiastical judges were not to impose money fines upon Indians for any cause, [56] nor condemn them to be sold for service. [57] Religious were not to use Indians to carry burdens without paying them what they deserved. [58] They were not to require other services of the natives except in necessary cases. [59] Prelates, clerics, and religious houses were not to be made encomen-

55

deros of Indians.[60] Indians were not to be required to make clothes for priests.[61] Religious were prohibited from requiring Indian women to come to their houses under the pretext of teaching them and then compelling them to work for them without pay.[62] Exceptions to the rule of exempting Indians from working for priests and religious without receiving wages were permitted in Tucumán, Paraguay, and Río de la Plata, where each padre engaged in teaching the Indians the Catholic doctrine was allowed the services of two boys between seven and fourteen years of age, one Indian man, and an old Indian woman for kitchen work. He was to give them clothes and food; and, if he demanded other services of them, he was required to pay them.[63] On the other hand the religious were ordered not to shelter or hide Indians who had fled from work in the mines.[64] The colonial audiencias were ordered to correct the practice sometimes followed by priests and religious of taking food from the Indians without adequate compensation.[65] Prelates were required to punish friars who should kill or mistreat the natives, violate their wives and daughters, or rob them of their property.[66] Religious who were guilty of leading evil lives were not to be punished by simple fines, since such light penalties would furnish a bad example to the Indians. They were instead to be removed from office or otherwise severely punished.[67] Prelates were commanded to investigate, during their visits over the territory under their jurisdiction, the treatment of the natives, and "solicit that they be taught and instructed with care, charity, and love convenient to our Holy Faith, and treated with gentleness and temperance."[68] In 1543 Charles V directed the Dominicans of Nueva Granada to see that the royal decrees for the protection of the Indians be observed, for "all provisions in them are dedicated to the

56

service of God and the conservation, liberty, and good government of the Indians." [69] *

III

The ambition of both Church and crown was to convert every person throughout Spanish America to the Catholic faith. Most of the natives of the more highly civilized sections of South America, such as the Incas in Peru and the Chibchas in New Granada, were forced or persuaded to accept a nominal Christianity during the early days of the conquest. But beyond these regions there wandered over several million square miles of the interior of the continent, mainly to the east of the Andes, hundreds of thousands of savages, some of whom still lived in the Stone Age. During the first sixty years after the conquest these wilds were traversed by adventurers in search of "other Perus," of El Dorado, and of Manoa, the fabled city of gold. When these men found there were no other kingdoms to despoil, but only impoverished natives who possessed little more than a few weapons and were but slightly advanced beyond the beasts of the forest in their manner of living, they lost interest in further exploration and conquest. But the ambition of the crown was never satiated. Aside from the religious motive, there was always the desire for imperial expansion simply for the sake of acquiring more square leagues of land, while the constant encroachments of the Portuguese upon Spanish territory made advisable the establishment of permanent settlements to the east of the Andean cordillera. In founding settlements, constructing fortifications, erecting churches, and converting and civilizing the Indians of the great river basins of the interior of South America, Church and State worked

---

* This reference is probably to the well-known New Laws of 1542, which were never effectively enforced.

hand in hand. The missionary friars were the instruments with which a new civilization, an Indo-Latin civilization, was to be created in the heart of the great continent.

Three general types of work were carried on by the Church in America, corresponding to three stages on the road to civilization through which the natives were passing. First, there was the work among the Indians of the towns. These people were presumably completely civilized. A goodly number of them spoke Spanish. They engaged in farming, grazing, or mining. They went to church and attended schools. They possessed a considerable degree of local autonomy under their own *caciques* (chiefs). These settlements were known as *doctrinas*, and they were usually under the spiritual care of the secular clergy. The priests were commonly called *curas* or *doctrineros*. Second, there were the missions, or reductions, occupied by natives who had but recently been taken from the forests and persuaded or forced to settle down in order that they might be more effectively controlled and Christianized. These reductions, varying in size from a few dozen to several thousand Indians, were under the control of members of religious orders. Usually there were one or two friars in each mission, but in sparsely settled areas on the far frontier one missionary might have charge of several reductions. Finally, there was the activity of the friars among the wild Indians whom they had not yet succeeded in persuading to settle upon a reduction.

The Spanish mission, then, was merely a step in the complete Christianization and civilization of the Indian, an intermediary stage between the wild, nomadic savages beyond the frontier and the Europeanized Spanish towns. The mission (with a few exceptions) was not meant to be permanent. It was a training school organized to make "rational men" out of irrational savages. The Spanish crown never dealt with the American Indians as independent states, as was done in the English colonies. All natives living west of the Line of Demarcation established in the Treaty of Tordesillas in 1494 were deemed to be subjects of the Spanish crown. They must be made to recognize their masters, both secular and ecclesiastical. This was the duty of the padre.[70]

Having founded a mission by persuading a group of savages to settle in one locality and by going through the formality of baptizing them, the padre began the task of teaching them the rudiments of the Catholic dogma and ritual, and tried to persuade them to give up their more heinous savage practices. Finally, when he had changed them into some semblance of civilized beings, he turned them over to the care of the secular clergy and pushed farther into the wilderness in search of new fields to conquer. Alexander von Humboldt described the process:

As the missionaries advance towards the forests, and gain on the natives, the white colonists in their turn seek to invade in the opposite direction the territory of the Missions. In this protracted struggle, the secular arm continually tends to withdraw the reduced Indian from the monastic hierarchy, and the missionaries are gradually superseded by vicars. The whites, and the castes of mixed blood, favored by the corregidores, establish themselves among the Indians. The Missions become Spanish villages, and the natives lose even the remembrance of their natural language. Such is the progress of civilization from the coasts towards the interior; a slow progress, retarded by the passions of man, but nevertheless sure and steady.[71]

According to Father Francisco de Figueroa, a year was ordinarily required to establish a new mission on a firm basis, during which time land would be cleared, houses built, and crops planted and harvested;[72] but naturally this initial period varied widely. The life of a mission was usually about ten years, although in some cases the Indians were kept for twenty or more years on a reduction before being turned over to the secular clergy. During this period the Indians were looked upon as little children, so that their shortcomings were not so severely punished as were those of Indians in the older settlements. In determining the age of a mission there was the question of when to begin reckoning the time. The padre might find a tribe of Indians temporarily settled in a crude village in the neighborhood of a good fishing site and sprinkle them with some water from a stream. Did this constitute the founding of a mission? Was a mission founded when the natives consented to be baptized, or when they moved to a new location designated by the missionary, or when they had built their new village and cleared the land for crops? In the Orinoco valley the reduction of Tupuquén was being planned in 1743, although it was not formally founded until five years later. The mission of Cunuri was begun a year before its formal foundation in February, 1744. The mission of San Joseph de Leonisa (Guiana) was formally founded in February, 1755, although it had been pronounced to be "in a very good state of restoration" in June, 1754. The date of founding was in practice usually the date when the church was formally opened after having been furnished with equipment at government expense.[73] A Capuchin prefect, writing in 1788, stated that the consent of the colonial governor was not necessary for the founding of new missions and that the choice of sites was entirely in the hands of the friar, although the governor might give advice.[74] Some of the secular officials, however, disagreed with this view. An act of 1618 ordered that reductions, once founded, were not to be moved without the express order of the king, viceroy, president, or audiencia.[75]

There was also the question of how to determine when the converts were ready to be turned over to the secular clergy.

According to Father Domingo Muriel, "he will not be misguided who says that they begin [the doctrina] from the time the Indians accept correction; and the correction, considering the disposition of the people, is not made but by means of corporal punishment. While the docility for this is lacking, the town and doctrina are without foundation."[76] Some tribes readily accepted corporal punishment, while others who were more fierce, such as the Chiriguanos of eastern Bolivia, could never be beaten without danger to the padres.

The missionaries on the frontier were ordinarily independent of the local secular authorities. In case of interference with their activities by the civil officials, they might appeal directly to the king over the head of the viceroy himself. They determined the location of new villages, and governed the Indians of their reductions.

Favorite sites for their pueblos were often far distant from the settlements of the Spaniards: upon the banks of a navigable stream, or in a pleasant valley, or upon a protected plain. Missionaries of the Catholic faith in Spanish America were frequently pioneers of civilization. Agents of the State as well as of the Church, they were chroniclers, preachers, teachers, colonists, and explorers.[77]

IV

Since the missionaries were instruments of state policy in the expansion of empire, it behooved the government to give the padres what aid and protection it could. Sometimes the friar proceeded alone into the wilds far beyond any possible effective support, where he subsisted on wild fruits and herbs or upon the crude fare of the native, defenseless against the attacks of wild animals and ferocious savages. It was the policy of Church and State, however, to keep in sufficient communication with him to be able to give him some assistance. Garrisons were often placed on the missions for their defense, but they were frequently used for other purposes. The government furnished the missionary with wearing apparel and other equipment, including bells, vestments, and tools. A law of 1587 ordered the prelates of religious orders to provide the necessary clothes and food, particularly wine, to the padres; and, if possible, a horse should be given them so that they might hasten to administer the last sacraments to sick Indians living at a distance.[78] Special grants of money were occasionally made for particular purposes, such as the construction of a new church. The missionaries were paid annual salaries, called *sínodos*, which varied from one colony to another. They were supposed to be in direct ratio to the difficulty of the mission and its distance from the older European towns. In New Spain the sínodos of missionaries on the northern frontier were as much as $450.[79] The Jesuit fathers of the upper Amazon region received 200 pesos a year for food, but they spent most of their stipend on their Indian wards.[80]

The Spanish monarchs could never forget the depopulation of the islands of the West Indies at the hands of the early conquerors, and they were determined that the horrible story of cruelty and bloodshed should not be repeated on the continent. It was of course impossible to enforce laws for the protection of the Indians in regions where the civil authorities were themselves interested in the indiscriminate exploitation of the natives. The missionaries, rather than the secular officials, became the principal agents for the enforcement of the laws in the regions where they had jurisdiction. As early as 1536 a law provided that no traveling Spaniard might remain in an Indian town more than two days, under penalty of a fine of fifty pesos for each day that he should remain beyond this time.[81] In 1563 Spaniards, Negroes, mulattoes,

Philip II

His Catholic Majesty encouraged religious work among the natives

and mestizos were prohibited from living on reductions and in Indian towns, since such persons were usually

unquiet individuals of bad life, thieves, gamblers, vicious and depraved men, and because the Indians, fleeing from molestation,

63

leave their Towns and Provinces, and the Negroes, Mestizos, and Mulattoes, besides treating them badly, are served by them, teach them their bad customs and idleness, as well as certain errors and vices which will corrupt them and pervert the fruit that we desire: . . . their salvation, increase, and tranquillity.[82]

Provincials of the religious orders were charged not to remove from their reductions without necessary cause religious engaged in the pacification and conversion of the Indians.[83] The viceroys, audiencias, and justices were ordered to aid, honor, and favor the missionaries,[84] and no one should impede them in freely teaching the Christian doctrine to the Indians, under penalty of loss of half his goods.[85] When a religious order had once entered a region, the religious of other orders were not to attempt to found monasteries or teach the Indians there.[86] The viceroys were to inform the king every three years of the state of the religious within their viceroyalties.[87] With the view of encouraging religious work among the natives, Philip II ordered that persons who had been engaged in converting and teaching the Indians, particularly if they were well acquainted with the native languages, should be given preference in appointments to ecclesiastical benefices in America.[88]

IN QUEST OF THE FLOCKS

I

EALOUS vanguard of the church, the missionary friars were the "light horse" [1] who preceded the main body of the ecclesiastical army in the conquest of souls. While they needed ability and courage, the principal attributes of the successful missionary were, in the opinion of Father Joseph Parras, love of God and zeal to save souls.[2]

The ideal way to convert the savage Indians of the South American forests, the method thought practicable by many of the inexperienced missionaries, was for the padre to go into the wilds among natives who had never before seen a white man, unless it were an adventurer intent on robbing them, and armed with a crucifix and a breviary, and moved by the Holy Ghost to a marvelous eloquence, persuade the savages to give up their manner of living in order to accept Christianity and Spanish domination. A number of padres did employ this method; and if they knew the Indian languages or had good interpreters, if they possessed powerful

Many a friar went into the wilds armed only with a crucifix and a breviary

as well as pleasing personalities, and if they were adepts at showmanship, they sometimes succeeded. Father Monroy and a lay brother Jesuit, Juan de Toledo, were quite successful in reducing some of the Omaguaca Indians by this method in the closing years of the sixteenth century. One cacique, who had once accepted Christianity, but who had renounced it and become a sworn enemy of both the gospel and the Spaniards, refused to be reduced. Father Monroy is said to have gone to his village, entirely unarmed, and thrown himself upon the mercy of this chief, saying: "You cannot expect much honor by taking away the life of an unarmed man. If, contrary to my expectation, you will consent to listen to me, all the advantage of our conversation will be yours; whereas if I die by your hands, an immortal crown in heaven will be my reward." The cacique was so much impressed by the boldness of the padre that he presented him with a kind of liquor made by the Indian women from corn ground between their teeth, and agreed to make peace with the Spaniards.[3] Father Cyprián Baraza was also very successful in ingratiating himself among savage natives. He would take up his residence in an Indian hut and live as the Indians lived, influencing the savages more by example than precept. Lockman says of this good padre:

He would sleep in the midst of 'em, exposed to all the Inclemencies of the Weather; and without regarding the Stings of the Moskitoes. Tho' these *Heathens* eat in so distasteful a Manner, he yet always took his Meals with 'em. Finally, he made himself a *Barbarian* with these *Barbarians*, the easier to lead 'em into the Paths of Salvation.[4]

But in many cases the padres accomplished nothing more by this peaceful and kindly method than an untimely martyrdom. Some of them indeed went alone among savage tribes for the very purpose of becoming martyrs, confident that they would receive their reward in heaven.

The heroism and sacrifice of these brave soldiers of the cross are worthy of admiration, but it is likely that they accomplished less than the more coldly calculating missionaries who planned their conquests in advance, taking into consideration the intelligence, customs, religious practices, and beliefs of the natives, their mildness or ferocity, and their attitude toward Spaniards. The successful missionaries adopted methods which were suited to local conditions rather than those which harmonized with an impractical idealism. If the cutlass were needed as well as the crucifix, the long-headed padre would take with him those who knew how to wield it.

II

Incursions into the country beyond the frontier for the purpose of reducing the natives came to be called *entradas* or *conquistas de almas* (conquests of souls). The details of the entrada varied in different parts of South America and at different times. Ordinarily it was an expedition consisting of one or two missionaries, a body of converted Indians from the older reductions, and several Spanish soldiers to protect the padres in case of unprovoked attacks upon them by the savages. Father Ricardo Cappa of the Society of Jesus, after citing examples of failure to convert Indians in South America without the support of arms, stated:

I well know that there were very zealous Missionaries who without human aid conquered for God entire provinces and kingdoms, but this happened in civilized countries that already had their religion, although it was false, and customs more or less restrained, for it was only a matter of teaching them to know the true God. As for savage Indians without any culture or religious ideas, it is necessary to subdue them with a good armed force.[5]

The Jesuits in Paraguay were among the most skillful in reducing savage Indians, just as their missions, once organized, were among the most successful on the continent. The padres, having decided to bring a certain body of Indians within the pale of the Church, would send out a few picked converts from the older reduction as emissaries to their brothers beyond the limits of civilization. These ambassadors of religion carried with them inexpensive but serviceable gifts which they distributed to the greatest advantage among the prospective neophytes, explaining that they came from a Jesuit father who loved them greatly and who wished to come to live among them and serve them. The padre was pictured as being a most extraordinary man, the source of every good gift, and possibly endowed with the ability to perform miracles. He would bring to them iron for their tools and weapons, cattle, beautiful clothing, and other useful articles. He would furnish them with food, construct their houses, and heal their sick. The native emissaries would perhaps not even mention the Christian religion, and they would certainly refrain from emphasizing the possibility that the savages would be expected to do any work. Such proposals were evidently attractive. If the Indians consented, as they usually did, to the missionary's coming among them, he soon arrived, accompanied by a number of converts, who went armed, but also carried additional gifts, especially food. The wild Indians were given a great feast, and plans for a new town were made. The town site having been selected, streets were laid out, locations for fields and pastures determined, and construction begun.[6] In the meantime the padre would probably make a speech similar to the following:

Sons of my heart, the love of God and the desire for the salvation of your souls brings us through these dense forests, suffering a thousand wants, labors, and miseries. For your spiritual welfare we leave the comfort of our provinces to come to teach you the way of salvation, to instruct you in the light of the Catholic truths. Know then that there is an Omnipotent God, Creator of the Universe, whose Most Holy Son is Jesus our Redeemer and Sovereign Master, beneath whose Banners I desire that you live, detesting Idolatries and diabolical falsehoods, with which you worship the devil, seducer and father of lies. To this end I come as a Delegate of God and his Minister, resigned to remain among you if happily you embrace his most Holy Law, which is an easy yoke, and to teach you the Divine Mysteries and the road to Heaven, where I desire you to go to enjoy an eternity of glory.[7]

Although the Indians might not understand what the good padre was talking about, they were so filled with food and in such an amiable state of mind that they would very likely consent to be baptized; whereupon the missionary would then proceed to sprinkle them with holy water, and henceforth they were deemed Christians. Toward the end of the colonial period it was considered necessary that prior to receiving the sacrament of baptism the Indian should admit that drunkenness, uncleanness, fornication, adultery, and incest were sins, and that idolatry, superstition, and falsehood were mortal sins.[8]

The Indians of the older reductions often participated wholeheartedly in founding these new missions, furnishing to the missionaries from their own stores peas, beans, corn, oxen, horses, and so forth.[9] For their services in founding the new settlements they not only were assured an extra allotment of bliss in the life to come, but they might be given petty positions which, though not allowing them sufficient power to interfere in the government of the mission, gave them an opportunity to wear on occasion ostentatious uniforms. While the new mission with its church and other buildings was being constructed, the neophytes were drawn into the work as though it were a game. Finally they were firmly informed that the privileges of this new mode of life were accompanied by obligations and that they, as well as the older converts, would have to work.

This method of establishing new reductions was fairly successful among the Guaranís, but some of the more warlike tribes of Paraguay, such as the Mbayas, had no desire to abandon the chase and settle down to agricultural pursuits. Nor did the caciques look with approval upon the proposal that they should be deprived of their authority in favor of a few palefaced men clad in black. The Jesuits dealt with these obstinate chiefs by enticing them to the older reductions and there throwing them into prison, where they remained for years. This method, however, was unusual, force being used by the Jesuits of Paraguay only as a last resort.[10]

In Quest of the Flocks

When a group of Indians had been converted and reduced to a settled form of life, they were expected to swear an oath of allegiance to the king of Spain. One of the governors of Chile, in his letter of congratulation (April 8, 1704) to two Indian caciques who had just accepted Christianity wrote:

'Twas a great Pleasure to me to hear, by your Letter and the Testimony of your Deputies, the kind Treatment which you gave the Jesuits; and the Resolution you have taken to embrace our holy Religion. Having therefore returned the most solemn Thanks to God, the supreme Lord of Heaven and Earth, for this happy News; I am to assure you, that you could not have done an Action more pleasing to the great Monarch of *Spain* and *India*, Philip V, my Lord and Master, on whom Heaven bestow long Life, Prosperity, and Glory. For this Reason, as I represent his Person in the Employment which he has pleased to confer upon me; I offer and promise in his Name, for ever, his kindness and Protection to yourself and all who shall follow your Example; observing, at the same Time, that you must oblige all your Vassals, after embracing the *Catholic* Faith, to take an Oath of Fidelity and Obedience to the King my Master; who will ever be your Support, your Protector, and Defender, against all your Enemies.[11]

In the region of the Marañón River, gifts of tools, axes, machetes, and knives were used to attract the Indians to the faith. These implements eased the labors of the natives so much that they were inclined to accept Christianity and consider the bargain a good one.[12] The missionaries were so anxious to bring the heathen natives into the fold, and so confident of the efficacy of a few drops of water to purge the soul of sin, that they were greatly tempted to buy with trinkets or other articles the permission to baptize the Indians. The viceroy of Peru, Don Francisco de Toledo, complained of this in a memorial presented to the king at the end of his term of office in 1582, and asked that the king give orders that no Indians be baptized until they were taught the Christian doctrine, because, this not having been done, and the padres . . . being very desirous of saying that they have baptized many thousands of Indians, without teaching them first to be men or catechizing them as they ought, the natives have remained as idolatrous as before, neither understanding what is taught them, nor having capacity nor dispositions to be Christians.[13]

Moreover, the missionaries, eager to be considered successful by their superiors, were inclined to report the foundation of missions before they were actually established. It was sometimes the practice of the padres to erect huge crosses at the place designated for a new mission village. Here the Indians would kneel while the father explained to them the efficacy of the cross in cleansing them of sin,[14] and since the secular authorities as well as the missionaries wished to make it appear to the king and the Council of the Indies that rapid progress was being made in the conversion of the Indians, reports were apt to go to Spain containing maps showing reductions which in reality consisted of little more than these crosses, which had perhaps fallen into decay before the report reached the king.[15]

Father Joseph de Gumilla describes the method of making an entrada in the Orinoco region as follows: After the converts of an established reduction have informed the padre of the location of a heathen nation somewhere in the vicinity, the missionary finds out if they are enemies or friends, pacific or warlike, brave or cowardly, sedentary or nomadic. Having gathered this information, the missionary does not immediately go among them, for they may attack him or flee into the forest where it will be difficult to find them. Instead, two or more Christian Indians who know the language of the savages whom it is proposed to convert are sent to them well laden with gifts for the chief and old men of the tribe. The ambassadors are not to inform the savages outright that the padre wishes to visit them, but are to say that the missionary is taking care of the mission Indians and is sending these savages gifts as an indication of his regard for them. Having aroused curiosity, the ambassadors answer questions relative to why the friar came to them, when he came, and what he does. If the messengers deliver their sales talk well, several of the heathen Indians return with them to the mission to look it over. They are well entertained so that they will carry back a favorable description of the reduction. These embassies are sent several times, and finally carry the message that the padre would like to visit the heathen tribe if he were not so busy taking care of his own people. The strategy is to allow them to become so curious that they will invite the missionary to come to see them. If the distance is great, a second missionary is left in charge of the mission. The padre starts out accompanied by a number of friendly Indians to carry burdens, row the canoes, and gather food. A few soldiers go as escort to protect the religious, who carries such gifts as glass beads, knives, pins, and fishhooks. A day or two before the group reaches the settlement of the savages, two Indians are sent ahead to inform the tribe that the father will arrive soon.

On reaching the village, the padre finds that the Indians have crowded in from the surrounding country to see the strange white man. The missionary is given the use of the guest house, which is usually maintained in the Indian villages for the comfort of strangers. Here the cacique and his captains come, salute the padre, and sit down, the other men of the village following their example. The wives of the cacique and the chief men each bring a cup of chicha and a plate of meat and bread, after which the wives of all the other members of the tribe do the same. If the padre does not taste every cup and dish, the Indians are insulted; but after tasting, he may pass them on to the other members of his company.

73

Having eaten, the missionary retires to his hammock, and the chief approaches and makes a long speech telling him how happy they are to have him visit the village. The friar responds with a lengthy harangue telling how glad he is to be with them, what great love he has for them, and that he desires only to promote their welfare and to defend them from their enemies. Then he gives out the presents, first to the chief, then to his wife or wives, next to the captains, and so on down the line until the last baby has received something, if only a pin.

So far the missionary has remained silent about the real object of his visit. The converted Indians of the expedition, having been instructed in what to do, gradually open the subject of Christianity and explain the advantages of mission life. They answer questions, letting it be known that the missionaries seek only the welfare of the Indians, to care for their sick, to bring them tools to lighten their labor, and to teach their children to look at paper (*i.e.*, to read).

While in the Indian village, the padre visits the sick and pleases the parents by paying special attention to their children. The children become fond of him and beg their elders not to let the padre leave. The missionary now begins to baptize the infants and youth, giving each a string of brightly colored beads. By this time almost the whole tribe are begging him to remain with them. The chief offers him a wife and is astonished when the friar answers that his love is placed above in heaven, and that he looks upon women merely as his children. Thus it is that the padre insinuates himself into the good will of the savages and is able to persuade them to accept the Christian doctrine.[16]

Some of the companies that went on great entradas, often both exploring and proselyting expeditions, carried along sufficient supplies and merchandise to stock a fair-sized modern

While in the Indian village, the padre pleases the parents by paying special attention to their children

store. One entrada into the country along the Apure River in Venezuela carried balls, powder, gun matches, weapons, cotton coats, hemp shoes, crude lead for making balls, biscuits, salt beef, cassava, salt (a delicacy greatly desired by the Indians), flour, corn meal, cacao, cheese, sugar, machetes, meat knives, ordinary knives, oil, wine, vinegar of Castile, candles and ornaments for Mass, combs, mirrors, needles, pins, silk, ribbons, axes, hatchets, strings of coral, glass toys, fishhooks, linen, hats, woolen blankets, medicines, bandages, knives and needles for treating wounds, cakes, preserves, honey, and ham.[17]

III

It is sad to relate that the methods used in reducing the Indians to a settled life and to the Catholic faith were not always so humane as those hitherto described. When one reviews the first years of the conquest and the colonial epoch, one cannot overlook the accounts of brutality of the Spaniards, of Indians beheaded simply as an example to others, of how they fed Indians to their huge mastiffs.[18] Humboldt wrote of the early entradas:

> The soldiers, excited by the allurement of gain, made military incursions (entradas) into the lands of the independent Indians. They killed all those who dared to make any resistance, burnt their huts, destroyed their plantations, and carried away the women, children, and old men, as prisoners. . . . This violent manner of *conquering souls*, though prohibited by the Spanish laws, was tolerated by the civil governors, and vaunted by the superiors of the society [Society of Jesus], as beneficial to religion, and the aggrandizement of the Missions.[19]

One of the colonial bishops wrote of the secular clergy engaged in missionary work during the first years of the colonial epoch, that they "had busied themselves more in the conquests, serving less as Chaplains than as Soldiers, and reducing Evangelical preaching to dagger thrusts and blows." [20]

In certain sections of the montaña of Peru, where the natives were so wild and ferocious that they were exceedingly dangerous, and where the missionaries had no converts who knew the language of the savages, it was customary to send an expedition to capture a few of the unconverted Indians. These savages were brought to the reduction, where they were well treated, taught the language of the converted Indians or perhaps of the Spaniards, and induced to accept baptism. The missionaries, having made friends of these captives, sent them back to their fellows to tell them the advantages of living in a mission. There some of their savage acquaintances would be persuaded to go to the mission on a visit. They would be well treated and loaded with gifts, and the wild tribe would be sufficiently impressed to permit the padres to make them a visit, which they would do, usually accompanied by soldiers.[21] The statement of Enrique Torres Saldamando, that the Jesuits of Peru converted Indians entirely by example and teaching "without there being employed other arms than the manifestation of the eternal truth"[22] is hardly correct.

Don Eugenio de Alvarado, writing from the Guiana missions on April 20, 1755, gave his opinion that for the savages in Guiana "government is more necessary than the gospel, for the savages respect more the gun than the Holy Christ, and they are as ignorant of the Divine word as Europeans are of their vernacular." In this region the missionaries contemplating an entrada would prepare salt beef, cassava, and other food for the journey, get together gifts of nanking, calico, knives, hatchets, and cutlasses, and select a few Christian Indians who were acquainted with the tribe to which they were going, and who could be counted on to vouch for the attractiveness of mission life. A few soldiers from the garrison (*presidio*) of the settlement of Santo Tomás de Guayana would accompany the expedition. The company would proceed to the country of the wild tribes, and with a combination of kind words, promises, gifts, and threats, attempt to cajole the savages into accepting the Christian religion and giving up their semi-nomadic way of living.[23] On such entradas force was occasionally employed. The following letter, written by Fray Mariano de Cervera to Fray Jaime de Puigcerdá (December 9, 1787) sounds more like the letter of a slave catcher than of a humble man of God:

Greeting, peace and grace in the Lord.—Last year I went to the mouth of the Orinoco to an "entrada" among the Guaraunos. I took but two soldiers and Guayanos from Caroni. The "entrada" was short and successful because in a very few days I made my haul and returned with 149 souls and every one arrived here except eight who escaped from us in San Antonio, though after-wards they were caught.[24]

The civilized Indians of Venezuela participated in these entradas with enthusiasm, since they were often rewarded if the expedition was successful. In the upper Orinoco region women and old men, as well as the younger Indians, took part in the conquistas de almas; and, under the pretext of recapturing converts who had fled from the missions, they seized children for the purpose of making them their *poitos,* or serfs.[25]

Occasionally useless acts of cruelty were perpetrated during the entradas. A missionary could too easily permit his apostolic zeal to outrun his humanitarian sentiments. In his mind the latter might justifiably be repressed when a lost soul was at stake. The following story was told to Alexander von Humboldt by a priest in Venezuela: [26] In 1797 the missionary at San Fernando on the upper Orinoco led his Indians on an entrada to the Río Guaviare. Perceiving a hut near the bank of the river, the missionary ordered several of his assistants to examine the place. Finding there an Indian woman and her three children, her husband being away from home, they seized the four of them, bound them, forced them into a canoe, and took them back to the mission of San Fernando. The mother repeatedly fled, but was captured and beaten with straps made of the hide of the manatee. As further punishment she was finally sent to the mission of Javita, twenty-five leagues from San Fernando, while her children were kept at San Fernando. Later she managed to escape from Javita and to find her way back to her children through the dense forest, which was traversed by crocodile infested streams. This time she was sent to an even more distant mission, where she starved herself to death. Her husband very likely never knew what had become of his family.

Such procedure as this on the part of the less worthy friars caused trouble for those who did not resort to similar dishonorable methods. Many of the Indians thought that the missionaries were in league with Spaniards who wished to exploit them, and looked upon the entradas as slave-hunting expeditions, so that there was real need for the soldiers who accompanied the missionaries. The story was spread abroad in the Orinoco valley that the padre at the Betoye mission habitually ate Indians, and that his bedroom was decorated with the skulls of these poor unfortunates. He was also supposed to have a store of Indian flesh salted down against a rainy day. It was with the greatest difficulty that the missionary persuaded the Indians that he was not a cannibal.[27] The Indians in general had a decided and well-founded fear of the lay Spaniards, which caused many of them to move farther into the depth of the forest to avoid being seized for labor on the plantations and in the mines.

While persuasion was used in many cases in reducing the Indians, and while force or the threat of force was resorted to when it was deemed advisable, there were times when the Indians themselves asked that padres be sent to them. This was most commonly the case with those Indians who had once had good and kindly missionaries among them, but who had been deprived of their padres because the friars had died or had been transferred to other territory. According to Padre José Amich, the Indians of the mission of Santa Cruz (in Peru), who had lost their padre, asked with tears in their eyes for a new one, saying, "Why did they teach us about God if they leave us in the power of the devil? If they had not taught us, we should not have the pain that we now feel." [28] Don Carlos de Sucre, governor of Cumaná, wrote on March 23, 1735, that many nations send me their Caciques to swear obedience, recognizing His Majesty as King and Master, and asking for Missionary Fathers, so that if I now had five hundred Missionary Fathers I could employ them all, and my greatest sorrow is that I have not a single priest to give them; and it is the most pitiful thing in the world to see these poor wretches asking for fathers and not a father to give them.[29]

The Indians who so anxiously desired missionaries among them very likely had either heard of the gifts that they carried in their baggage or had discovered that the padres were in the habit of defending their converts from excessive exploitation by the lay Spaniards.

IV

The opinion of ecclesiastical and secular writers in colonial South America, from the viceroy down to the simple friar in charge of an Indian village of a few dozen families, was that force might rightfully be resorted to for the purpose of reducing and converting Indians. What better justification could there be for killing a few natives than that by so doing the souls of thousands of other heathen would be saved! The soldiers who accompanied the padres were the sword in the hand of the Almighty, whereby he conquered the Prince of Darkness in the jungle.

Father Manoel Joachim, writing from Turiri in the Peruvian oriente on November 6, 1752, expressed the view that "This barbarous people does not hear the voice of the Gospel if the sound of exploding powder does not precede it." Father Francisco de Figueroa listed four causes for the relative lack of success of the Jesuit missions on the Marañón: (1) the superiors of the order did not consider the region worth a great expenditure of money and effort; (2) there was a lack of missionaries; (3) the devil was working against the missionaries; (4) there were not enough soldiers to support the padres. He thought that with twenty to thirty soldiers paid by the state to act as convoy the Jesuits would achieve marked success in these missions. He suggested that the state should compensate itself for the expenditures required to maintain this force by collecting tribute from the Indians after their reduction. Thus the Indians would bear the expense of their own conversion.[30] The soldiers of the escort, besides furnishing armed protection, were to aid in teaching the Indians how to work as well as to set for them a good example by regular attendance at church and in the classes where the doctrine was taught—"in short, serving as a bridle in order that they may not dare any incivility, nor be so inconstant and ready to return like beasts to their haunts and hiding places."[31] Father Francisco asked those who opposed the conversion of savages with the aid of soldiers, "What would a lone priest manage to accomplish with such a people without great labor, as of fighting with wild beasts, if he did not make use of convenient means to dominate them, which are the rod and forces of Justice?"[32] Father Juan Rivero, one of the mildest and most sincere of the missionaries, approved the use of force where it was absolutely necessary, and where it was certain that the Indians were being reduced for the sole purpose of converting and civilizing them. On the other hand, he objected to the "tyranny and disorder with which many, abusing their power and arms, go on these conquests in order to serve their own interests, at the cost of piety and contrary to liberty."[33]

Moreover, there were Spaniards of a practical turn of mind who emphasized the fact that the reduced Indians would add to the material wealth of the empire by the fruits of their labor and the taxes and tribute which they paid to the royal exchequer. Their conversion was for their own benefit, and would amply offset any disadvantages arising out of their becoming profitable units in the economic life of the colonies. Since both State and Indians profited by their reduction, severe methods might justifiably be employed to reduce them.[34] The king at times permitted missionaries to withdraw at their own discretion from frontier garrisons as many soldiers as they needed, within a fixed limit, for use in their entradas.[35] The higher colonial authorities also granted the missionaries armed protection when they thought it advisable.[36] Hipólito Villaroel, favoring the use of force, argued that

it is necessary to give thought to their conversion, and subject them by punishment to the acknowledgement of their social obligations; otherwise they will be lost both to God and to the State. . . . For experience teaches that the more gently and suavely these people are dealt with, the more insolent do they become, the more insubordinate, and the more deeply are they rooted in their abominations, vices, and evil habits.[37]

Father Baltasar de Lodares, a modern Venezuelan writer, says that while peaceful methods of conversion were the ideal, they were often dangerous and impractical; and he cites the failure of the efforts of Bartolomé de las Casas to Christianize the natives of Cumaná.[38]

Father Juan Rivero thought it was not surprising that the Indians often had a horror of becoming Christians, since conversion was frequently the first step to ultimate actual, if not legal, slavery. The zeal of Spaniards to reduce the natives was frequently "born not of any desire for their welfare but of greed and deceit."[39] On the other hand, Father Gumilla claimed that the Indians had nothing whatsoever to fear from the Spaniards. He held that the very fact that some Indians fled to the forests proved that all the reduced Indians could flee if they wished. The fact that many remained on the reductions and later in the Indian villages under the secular clergy was for him sufficient proof that they were well treated.[40] Juan Nuix maintained that there was no single case where Spaniards made war on the natives because of their heathenism.[41]

It was the duty of the missionary friar to restrain the Indians and the Spanish soldiers who accompanied him on an entrada, for often they were motivated by ambitions far different from the desire to save souls. This was sometimes difficult to accomplish, for occasionally the company that went on an entrada consisted of several hundred armed men. Father Guillelmo D'Etre went on an expedition taking with him three hundred Indians armed with lances, bows, and arrows under the command of six Spanish officers carrying firearms. Since the savages among whom they were going had killed a Spaniard, the good padre, fearing that his soldiers would exceed the bounds of Christian decorum in their desire for revenge, called the captain aside and

begged him that he should not permit the blood of the miserable Indians to be shed: that he should cause them terror in order to repress their ferocity, but that he should use kindness and clemency in order to tame their nature and gain them to Jesus Christ; and not by means of arms, but by the virtue of the Cross, should the Christian Law be announced to them.[42]

It has been charged that the Indians were compelled to accept the Catholic religion. It would be more nearly correct to say that they were sometimes forced by arms to give up their nomadic and warlike form of life and to settle down in villages to peaceful pursuits. This having been done, the padres proceeded to bring them into the Catholic fold by persuasion, example, and the use of gifts. While the missionaries were doing this, the soldiers sometimes remained on the mission, not to punish those who refused to admit the truth of the padre's teachings, but to keep order and protect the friar. Doubtless some atrocities were committed on entradas during the three centuries of the colonial period, but it is difficult to find mention of them, since the accounts were usually written by the padres themselves.

For purposes of state, the missionary was plainly an instrument of imperialistic expansion as well as an agent of the Church. If we criticize the use of force on the entradas, we should remember that in the process of pushing the frontier line farther into the interior force would have been used in any case when needed, whether the element of Christianity entered or not. The reduction of the savages to a settled form of life was no doubt accomplished with much greater facility and less cruelty when missionary fathers were with the conquering forces than would have been the case if the reduction had been intrusted entirely to the civil and military authorities. While some missionaries may have been moved by such religious fanaticism as to advise the generous use of firearms on occasion, they were at least usually free from the desire to secure economic gains for themselves through the personal exploitation of conquered and enslaved natives. And when we remember that one padre and five or six soldiers often entered unexplored country inhabited by tens of thousands of savage Indians, the demands of the situation appear to be greatly in favor of the armed entrada.

THE REDUCTION

I

OT long were the Spanish secular and ecclesiastical authorities in the American colonies in discovering that it was impracticable to attempt the Christianization and civilization of the hordes of nomadic savages without first persuading them to accept a settled form of life. Once the Indians were reduced, or induced to settle in permanent villages, a friar could teach, catechize, direct, and control a much larger number of them than he could if the natives were repeatedly abandoning their crude settlements for new fishing and hunting sites. There was also a psychological value in transferring the Indians to a new location chosen by the padre, for they would feel less at home here than in a place to which they had become accustomed, and could consequently be more easily dominated.

The missionaries in the moist interior of South America usually located their missions on the banks of streams, in places where they would escape all but the most serious of the frequent floods. The farming lands reached back into the forest behind the village. Since in low, level regions the

85

banks of streams that are subject to overflow are usually higher than the land one or two miles from the main channel, these sites combined the advantage of good drainage with those of proximity to a transportation route and a fish supply. While reduction sites were usually chosen because of natural advantages, other considerations might be influential in determining their location. The padres sometimes moved a reduction simply because they preferred the view of the landscape from another position. New missionaries arriving at established missions to take the place of friars who had died or had been transferred, were inclined to have the Indians pick up their baggage and move elsewhere because of real or fancied shortcomings of the old site.[1]

The reduction was more than an institution for making peaceful citizens and Roman Catholics of the natives. It was also an agricultural and industrial school where the natives were taught to raise crops introduced from Europe and to manufacture a variety of commodities both for use on the missions and for export.[2]

The mission was a miniature benevolent despotism rather than a communistic institution. In theory the padre was to bear all the responsibility and decide all questions of material as well as spiritual importance. He should in reality be a padre (a father) to the Indians, caring for them and, if advisable, chastising them even as the father of a family cares for and punishes his children. The ideal relationship between missionary and neophyte is described by Robert Southey in *A Tale of Paraguay:*

> Content and cheerful Piety were found
> Within those humble walls. From youth to age
> The simple dwellers paced their even round
> Of duty, not desiring to engage
> Upon the busy world's contentious stage,

Whose ways they wisely had been trained to dread:
Their inoffensive lives in pupilage
Perpetually, but peacefully they led,
From all temptation saved, and sure of daily bread.

They on the Jesuit, who was nothing loth,
Reposed alike their conscience and their cares:
And he with equal faith, the trust of both
Accepted and discharged. The bliss is theirs
Of that entire dependence that prepares
Entire submission, let what may befall;
And his whole careful course of life declares
That for their good he holds them thus in thrall,
Their Father and their Friend, Priest, Ruler, all in all.[3]

Most of the frontier missions were small. The synod of
the bishopric of Quito stated that from two hundred to four
hundred Indians were enough for one missionary on the
Marañón River, the number varying according to whether
the Indians lived in compact villages or were scattered through
the forest.[4] In 1679 the sizes of some of the llanos missions
were as follows: Tunebos, 300; Macaguane, 350; Tame, 800;
Pauto, 600; Casanare, 1,200, "all Christians and dressed with
decency."[5] The great majority of the reductions in South
America had populations of less than one thousand, although
the Paraguay missions were much larger than this. In some
cases one missionary cared for several reductions, while in
other instances two or more padres were assigned to one
mission.

The Spanish missions of South America in 1804 were in
the jurisdictions of the following archbishoprics: Charcas,
Lima, Caracas, and Santa Fé de Bogotá. The archbishopric
of Charcas contained the dioceses of La Paz, Tucumán, Santa
Cruz de la Sierra, Paraguay, Buenos Aires, and Salta. The
archbishopric of Lima embraced the dioceses of Trujillo,
Arequipa, Quito, Cuzco, Guamanga, Panama, Santiago de

Chile, Concepción, Maynas, and Nueva Cuenca. The archbishopric of Santa Fé de Bogotá contained, prior to the creation of the archbishopric of Caracas in 1803, the dioceses of
Popayán, Cartagena, Santa Marta, and Mérida. The bishopric
of Maynas was created in 1802.[6] Bishops and archbishops
were frequently interested in the success of the frontier missions. The archbishop of Bogotá in 1794 suggested that colleges should be established for the specific purpose of training
missionaries.[7] On the other hand, high ecclesiastical officials
sometimes opposed the frontier missionaries, particularly if
they were Jesuits.

In addition to these divisions, Spanish America was parti-
tioned by the important religious orders into provinces, over
each of which was an officer known as a provincial, who was
ordinarily elected for a three-year term by a "provincial
chapter." These provincials made reports direct to the papal
curia as well as to the viceroys. Over each of the great missionary orders was a general, elected for a period of six years,
except in the case of the Dominicans and Jesuits, whose general was elected for life. The "provincial chapter" also
elected an officer known as a procurator, who was sent to the
"general chapter" in Europe when it met for the election of
a new general. Here he would present a report and make
suggestions relative to possible changes in his province.[8]

II

The central architectural feature of the reduction village
was the church. Ecclesiastical structures of some pretension
and beauty were frequently constructed on the frontier five
hundred or a thousand miles from the centers of Spanish population. During the early days of missionary activity in Paraguay, the padres could not find any lime with which to make
mortar for the construction of stone buildings. In lieu of

cut stone and mortar, the church builders used for each wall two rows of wooden pillars placed close together, filling the space between with small rocks and bricks cemented with dirt. Church towers several stories high were constructed in this fashion.[9] Later the Jesuits in Paraguay began to use for construction purposes large blocks of *Tacurú* stone, which was soft enough to be easily carved when first quarried but hardened gradually with exposure. Adobe was also used, as were the woods native to the region. The buildings were roofed with tile.[10] Some of the churches were elaborately ornamented. A French traveler, Frézier, gave the following description of the interior decoration of a Paraguayan church in 1716:

> The Facing of the Altar is very sumptuous. In the first place are three large Pictures in Frames of massy Gold and Silver. Above them are carv'd Works and Bass Reliefs in Gold; and higher yet, quite up to the Roof, is a Sculpture of Wood enrich'd with Gold. On the two Sides of the Altar are two Pedestals of Wood cover'd with Plates of Gold engraven, in which stand two Saints of massy Silver. The Tabernacle is of Gold. The Pyx, wherein the Holy Sacrament is kept, is made of Gold, and set round with Emeralds and other precious stones. . . .[11]

In the Maynas territory the churches were usually made of adobe or "French mud." They were whitewashed and frequently adorned with paintings. By the sale of wax, vanilla, and such other commodities of high value per unit of weight as could be transported to the markets of Lima and Quito, the padres purchased furniture and decorations for their churches. These edifices, like those of Paraguay, frequently contained articles of gold and silver.[12] They usually had bells to call the converts to worship, bells whose strokes were "hard blows to all hell, for they gather in the sheep of the flock of Christ."[13] Father Francisco de Figueroa gives us a picture

89

of the devotion with which the converts cared for their temples:

The church which they have built is famous and attractive, not only for the excellence of its materials, the richness and beauty of the art of its paintings, but for the . . . cleanliness and neatness with which are kept the altar, ornaments, and paintings, which are red over white, renovated each week by persons who are detailed for this work, taking away every spot that may be on them and shining every part that may be dull. Because of this, the church always seems new and always agreeable. . . . On the altar is placed a very beautiful sculptured image of our Lady of the Immaculate Conception. . . . This is placed in a prominent niche with its cornices decorated with shells and bespattered with gold.[14]

In New Granada many of the churches and other mission buildings were made of bricks manufactured by the Indians under the direction of the padres. While most of the churches were decorated with paintings of the Crucifixion, of the Virgin and Child, of berobed saints and haloed cherubs, the church at Arenas in the Orinoco valley had in 1800 a border of pictures of armadillos, jaguars, caymans, and other animals indigenous to the region.[15]

In building the churches, men, women, and children, working in gangs, carried on the construction as a coöperative enterprise. It is astonishing that Indians who had never built anything more elaborate than a hut of poles and palm leaves could construct huge adobe, brick, and stone buildings which would have done credit to European artisans. The will and enthusiasm with which they worked is delightfully described, perhaps with a touch of exaggeration, by the missionary fathers. Padre Juan Rivero tells of how little children hardly able to walk carried clay for Father Neira's church among the Achaguas. According to Diego de Eguiluz, the Mojo Indians, while building one of their churches, "did not leave a forest that they did not investigate to find where to cut

With enthusiasm the Indians constructed huge stone buildings which would have done credit to European artisans

beautiful and incorruptible joists, bringing them with joy as if it were a matter of play, without feeling hunger, the sun, nor fatigue, though some timbers came from so far that they dragged them more than a league; which seems unbelievable to one who knows or has notice of their natural laziness." [16] This writer tells of how, when some Indians were building the mission church of San José de los Maharenos in eastern Bolivia in 1695, and the missionary told the chief of the village to stop work for a few days in order to hunt and fish so that his children might have food, the cacique refused to suspend his labor, saying that God would give them plenty to eat. These Indians were said to have risen early each morning in order to begin their work by moonlight. This building, 36 by 150 feet in size, was made of adobe and covered with tile.[17]

The church having been completed, dedication services were in order. Sometimes the dedication was simple, consisting of little more than a sermon by the padre. Sometimes the little children would perform dances taught them by the missionary.[18] At the dedication of a new church at Kourou, Guiana, on December 12, 1728, the ceremony began with a procession of both Indians and Spaniards singing the *Veni Creator*. When they reached the church door, the friar prayed and blessed the outside of the building. As he threw some holy water on the wall, a cannon was fired. The blessing of the church completed, the crowd entered, Mass was said, and the padre preached a sermon. Choirs of Indian converts sang religious hymns. The whole ceremony, including several salutes of the cannon, must have impressed the natives, and it gave the padres "a feeling of great tenderness to see a holy joy traced on the countenances of the Neophytes." [19]

III

About the church, which was usually on a plaza near the center of the mission village, were the arsenal, the padre's house, workshops, storehouses, granaries, and the homes of the natives. Where possible, the streets were wide and straight, laid off in checkerboard fashion, the principal thoroughfares terminating in the plaza. In Paraguay the central square was large enough to serve as a field for the exercise of the militia. The tendency was to make the church as pretentious as possible and the other buildings as comfortable and durable as was consistent with the climate and materials at hand, but not ostentatious. The houses of the converts were built almost identically alike in order that no one might be envious of his neighbor.[20]   In the upper Amazon valley the villages were constructed on the same general plan as those of Paraguay, but they were smaller, and the huts were cruder, often being made of wood and thatched with palm fronds. The mission villages of Guiana were also laid out in the form of a square. Each Indian family had its own house substantially constructed of clay or bricks. The roofs were made of tile or palm leaves, the latter being as effective as the former in keeping out water, although less durable and more attractive to scorpions and snakes.   In front of the houses the roofs extended for some distance beyond the walls and were supported by poles so as to form a convenient porch.   Humboldt spoke of these settlements as being extremely neat, reminding him of villages of Moravian Brethren.[21]   Governor Diguja of Cumaná described the Capuchin mission villages of Guiana:

The houses of all the towns are built with symmetry, with sufficient size and comfort for the Indians; the churches, although poor, are well adorned and large enough, and the same is true in the case of the house of the padres adjacent to the church; and near this house is a large tower made of wood and clay and covered with straw, where they have placed two or three small cannon.   A circle of stakes defends this tower, house, and church, a sufficient wall for defense from Caribs, together with the cannon, if there is someone to manage them, for the noise of these frightens these Indians, and they do not dare come to the town, much less to the stake fence that defends the tower, where the women and children and even the Indians take refuge if the enemy forces are superior and do not allow sufficient time for the use of arrows in their defense.[22]

IV

Outside the village lay the fields of the mission, some of which were farmed by the community while others were the personal holdings of the natives. Some of the missions may have had mineral resources sufficiently near to make mining profitable, but it was commonly necessary to import metal ware from the Spanish settlements. Iron and steel were so scarce on the Paraguay reductions that the Indians often used tools made of stone or of wood hardened in fire. Their bell metal came from Coquimbo, Chile. The missions, like the medieval manors, were based primarily on agriculture.[23]

Work on the reductions was required of the Indians both as a means of production and as a disciplinary measure. On the Jesuit reductions in Paraguay each Indian family had a plot of land for its own use. Near the tropic of Capricorn they produced corn, cotton, wax, and honey, while farther to the south they grew wool, hemp, and wheat. The products of the field were supplemented by fish and game. The Indians carried on a small trade among themselves by barter. In addition to the individual holdings, each mission had community lands, the harvests of which were deposited in public warehouses. These stores were used for the maintenance of the missionaries and the civil and military officers (who were usually Indians); for the support of the sick, infirm, widows, orphans, and the poor; and to supply expeditions sent out from the mission. Any surplus was sold in order to secure funds to pay the tribute of the Indians and to buy supplies which could not be produced on the reduction, such as iron, steel, copper, firearms, and some of the decorations for the churches. If there were a crop failure and danger of famine on one reduction, the other missions supplied it with the necessary food. The Paraguay missions carried on commerce in wild honey, wax, and especially Paraguay tea, which was shipped as far as Peru.[24]

On the communal lands, work was carried on according to a specific routine. There were definite times for rising, going to bed, attending church, laboring in the fields, and working in the town. In going to work in the fields, groups of converts marched from the village square carrying a statuette and accompanied by musicians who made the morning air tingle with their music.[25] *Yerba maté* being distributed each morning and evening in the Paraguay missions, the Indians took with them to the fields a supply of this tea to help soothe their weary muscles as the day wore on. The Indians on the Paraguay missions do not seem to have been overworked. A mission Indian did about as much in a day as a laborer in Spain would accomplish in three hours. The laborers stopped work in the morning to hear Mass and in the afternoon for prayers. After each recess they had tea. While working in the field, they habitually kept a pot containing yerba maté boiling over a fire so that they would never be without a fresh supply.[26]

In Guiana the mission Indians, when not needed for labor on the reductions, were permitted to work outside the missions for the lay Spaniards. They were paid wages in either money or goods, being frequently employed in agriculture and carpentry, or in rowing boats. The missionary's control of the neophyte followed him beyond the mission. Each laborer was required to show to the padre the pay that he had received. If it was deficient, the missionary demanded that the employer make up what was lacking. It was customary for the missionary to keep the money of his wards to prevent them from squandering it, using it to buy commodities for them as the need arose.[27]

V

Life on the mission was a combination of study, work, religious worship, and recreation. The ancient amusements were suppressed as much as possible. The Indians found a partial expression of their love of recreation in religious processions and exercises, which were sometimes accompanied by dancing and singing. The songs tended to be elementary in character, emphasizing some idea that the missionary wished to impress upon his converts. The following eulogy was sung on the Píritu missions of Venezuela:

> Thou art divine, Mary,
> Like the dawn, the moon, and sun,
> Fountain of all the lights;
> Thanks to God, thanks to God.
>
> Daughter art thou of the Eternal Father,
> And of His kingdom
> Thou art queen;
> Thanks to God, thanks to God.
>
> Of the Sacred Trinity
> Thou art the greater temple,
> And the ark of its treasures;
> Thanks to God, thanks to God.
>
> Thou art a virgin, and thou art a mother
> With the greatest perfection
> That God himself can make;
> Thanks to God, thanks to God.
>
> . . . . . .
>
> All men then sing
> With great joy and love
> On seeing that thou art so good;
> Thanks to God, thanks to God.
>
> Holy, holy, holy,
> Oh holy Mother of God,
> We sing to thee; and we say:
> Thanks to God, thanks to God.[28]

In Venezuela in 1800 the burden of Catholicism rested less heavily upon the shoulders of the Indians than upon the Spaniards. The natives were required to attend Mass on

Sundays, New Year's Day, Christmas, and on the days of the Ascension, the Nativity, the Purification, the Assumption, Corpus Christi, and St. Peter. The Spaniards had to hear Mass twice as many days if they wished to avoid conviction of mortal sin. Nor did the natives have to fast so frequently as did the white Christians, their fast days being limited to Holy Saturday, Christmas Eve, and the Fridays of Lent. So conciliatory did the theologians become toward the Indians that they decided that the natives might eat human flesh without sinning.[29]

In their efforts to impress their neophytes, the missionaries sometimes resorted to methods not greatly different from those employed by Protestant evangelists of a later day. While on the one hand they pointed out that eternal bliss is a reward for virtue, on the other they threatened the sinner with the agonies of hell. Nor were they ignorant of the value of visual instruction in emphasizing their religious precepts. Some of them were said to be guilty of constructing huge statues with movable arms and rolling eyes which by their hideous aspect were more efficacious than the most vivid word picture in driving home a description of the occupants of hell." [30]

Since a bull published by Leo X on April 25, 1521, conceded to the religious who were to convert infidels the right to administer the sacraments,[31] the missionaries were able to perform the functions which were ordinarily in the hands of priests in the older communities. On the Paraguay missions Indians might be found engaging in religious exercises in the temples of worship at almost any time of the day from sunrise to dusk. The children were required to assemble at the church at daybreak to sing until sunrise. Then came the women and men to hear Mass prior to going to work. In the evening the children went again to church in order to

*The children were required to assemble at the church at day-
break to sing until sunrise*

learn the catechism, after which the whole population attended prayers. This was followed by the rosary. On
Sundays and holidays all the people on the reduction were
required to be at the church by daybreak. After the singing,
marriages were performed, and perhaps an infidel or two who
had recently arrived from some savage tribe were baptized.[32]
In the Guiana missions about 1740 the Indians assembled each
morning at the church for prayer and to hear the padre
explain the doctrine in the native language. The Indians
were often permitted to take an active part in the divine
worship by singing or playing the guitar, harp, trumpet, flute,
or the violin. Sometimes they also gave mystery plays, and
on holidays they engaged in dances.[33]

Father Juan Rivero says of these religious celebrations:

But what is most admired, and causes the greatest tenderness, is to see the solemnity with which they celebrate their fiestas and give thanks to the true God, with the skill of their song and of musical instruments, there being heard in our villages the concerted music of many voices. The forests and barbarous solitudes, a little before inhabited by wild beasts, are now converted into choirs as of angels praising God.[34]

On the reduction special care was taken in the instruction of children, for the missionaries well knew that it was easier to train young minds in the Catholic faith than to abolish entirely the superstitions, fears, and prejudices of the older Indians. The children were used as a means of converting the adults. They acted as little missionaries to their own families, and helped the padres by spying on their elders and by reporting when anyone was sick or when a child was born so that the missionary might baptize it. The Indians born on the missions or brought there at an early age must have been much more tractable than those who remembered the freedom of the forests. Father Joseph de Gumilla says of the relationship between the Spanish padres and their little wards:

I know that they love that innocent flock more than do the mothers who bore them; and when one of them dies, I have seen the Missionaries cry more tenderly than the parents of the deceased child themselves; and with reason, because each well instructed child among them serves afterward as a firm column to maintain our Holy Faith in that Town; and ordinarily the fruit does not cease there, because those children well brought up are afterward instruments of which God makes use to continue gathering new peoples to the mild yoke of Our Law. . . . These, I say again, are the inestimable treasures hidden in those difficult and intricate forests; these the precious pearls that after having cost our Beloved Jesus all His blood yet go lost in those dense forests.[35]

On the missions the Indians attended schools where they were taught reading, writing, arithmetic, Spanish, music, manual arts, and agriculture. The more adept might also be taught painting and sculpture. The general plan was to teach the natives enough to make them intelligent, constructive, orderly, and religious members of the community, but not enough to make them dissatisfied with their condition or to desire to supersede the padres in the control of the missions.

The missionaries objected to the settlement of Spaniards, other than the soldiers of their escort, on the reductions, maintaining that they would interfere with the management of the missions, and that they would corrupt or exploit the Indians, "experience having convinced them, that all the new Christians of America, who have fallen from their primitive fervour, fell merely in consequence of their having conversed too freely with the old Christians from Europe; or even having only taken too near a view of them." [36] Spaniards who wandered into the missions were given hospitable treatment for a few days and then kindly told to move on. [37]

The padres had complete charge of the internal administration of the missions, not being subject to the local civil and military authorities. They were not only ministers of religion, but judges, civil administrators, and military chieftains. Frézier in 1716 estimated that the Paraguay missions could on eight days' notice assemble a force of sixty thousand fighting men armed with swords, guns, bayonets, and slings with which they could throw stones weighing five pounds. [38] The missionaries were subject, however, to the commands of their superiors within their religious orders, to the bishop of their diocese, to the archbishop, to the viceroy, and to the king. There were occasions when they appealed directly to the king over the heads of all subordinate officers.

The statement of du Dezert relative to the Jesuit reductions is perhaps generally applicable to the South American missions, particularly in regard to the intellectual life of the Indians:

Life on the missions was pleasant, but it hardly permitted any progress. It was organized for the *status quo*. The conservative and pessimistic spirit of the Fathers seems to have considered superfluous all idea of evolution. The famous axiom, "Let sleeping dogs lie," was the fundamental rule of Jesuit wisdom in the Indies.[39]

BOOK II

/\/\/\/\

Crusade

Chapter VII

THE CUMANA MISSIONS

I

UMANA, one of the first provinces to be the field of the apostolic labors of the missionaries among the South American Indians, was bordered on the east by the Atlantic Ocean and the Gulf of Paria; on the north, by the Caribbean Sea; on the west, by the Unare River; and on the south, by the Orinoco, extending to the southernmost mouth of that great river so as to include its entire delta. This region had the advantage of proximity to the seacoast and was readily accessible to the first explorers who navigated the waters of the adjacent Caribbean.[1] It consists of forested hills and low plateaus in the northwest, and of plains and jungle in the south and southeast.

Two Dominican padres, Francisco de Córdova and Juan Garcés, went from Spain to Cumaná in the year 1514. Here they seem to have been regarded by the Indians, who were of a mild disposition, as beings of a divine nature. In this same year, apparently, two Franciscans also arrived. At first the padres were successful; but after Spanish slavers from Santo Domingo kidnapped and carried into slavery a chief, his wife,

Bartolomé de las Casas, "Apostle to the Indies"

and seventeen other natives, the Indians revolted and killed Córdova and Garcés. In 1516 Friar Pedro de Córdova, with the assistance of a group of Dominican and Franciscan padres, founded the first missions on the coast of Cumaná. Four years later the natives attacked the Dominican monastery and killed two more padres, but the revolt was soon suppressed with the aid of Spanish soldiers, and the Dominicans rebuilt their house.

The most noted of the early attempts to convert the natives of this region was that of Bartolomé de las Casas, the great "Apostle to the Indies." Shocked and depressed by the behavior of the Spaniards toward the natives of the islands of the Caribbean, he proposed to found in Cumaná a white settlement entirely different from those which had been based upon the ruthless exploitation of the natives. The colonists were not to be adventurous cutthroats, but peaceful individuals, farmers, artisans, missionaries, and the like, who would devote themselves to tranquil pursuits. Las Casas hoped to convert and civilize the Indians entirely by peaceful methods. After he had been granted the legal right (May, 1520) to establish his colony, he traveled through Castile gathering recruits. In a short time several hundred colonists joined his enterprise and set out for America. They went first to Puerto Rico, where the majority of them remained while the good padre proceeded with the rest to Cumaná in order to make preliminary arrangements for the establishment. A few months after they arrived in the new country, however, the Indians, who had been further antagonized by the Spanish slave-hunting expeditions, rose in revolt and made a general attack on the Spaniards in the region. Most of the settlers were killed, and the survivors fled to other Spanish possessions in America (1521). Thus failed, largely because of the avarice and cruelty of the Christian subjects of His Most Catholic

Majesty, one of the noblest experiments in Spanish colonial history.[2]

II

From this time until the middle of the seventeenth century the region was neglected by the missionary friars. When other padres finally arrived in Cumaná in 1650 they found the country very sparsely populated with Spaniards who were continually at war with the Indians.[3]

The man who is given credit for the permanent foundation of the Franciscan missions in Cumaná was Friar Francisco de Pamplona, whose career was in some respects similar to that of Ignatius Loyola. Born on August 11, 1597, of noble parents, his original name was Tiburcio de Redin. His father, who was an officer at the battle of Lepanto, died when Tiburcio was a boy. At an early age the son entered the army, and so distinguished himself while fighting in Milan that he was made a knight of the order of Santiago shortly after reaching the age of twenty. In 1623 he made his first voyage to the Indies as a "captain of sea and land." He was later a captain in the war against Portugal, and he spent eight years altogether in the Royal Armada, four of them in voyaging to America. He was impetuous to the point of rashness. In Seville on one occasion a subordinate of his, who had committed homicide, was condemned to death by the local judges, whereupon Don Tiburcio forced the court at the point of his sword to turn the condemned man over to him for punishment. In Madrid he and some friends put to flight a justice of the peace and other officials whom they encountered on the street. In order to free the capital of his molestations, the king made him chief commander of the Barcelona squadron. Later he went to Panama, where he became captain of one of the galleons and, on his return voyage, captured a Dutch ship. Once while he was resting in a deck chair on a vessel at sea, two soldiers began to quarrel near him. He commanded them to desist, and when one of them continued his ranting, the hot-blooded knight attacked him with a dagger. The soldier jumped overboard, but Don Tiburcio followed him into the water and killed him. Subsequently, in Madrid, Redin participated in a street brawl, during which he was knocked from his horse with a stone. Carried to his house by friends, his first words on regaining consciousness were, "Most Holy Mary, protect me!" He soon recovered, but the experience caused him to change the course of his life. He went to his mother's home in Pamplona, where he dedicated himself to prayer and the sacraments, and during this period he became convinced that God was calling him to join the order of Capuchin Franciscans. In 1636 he went to a Capuchin monastery to ask admission, but was advised that there was a place for holy men in the army and that he should ponder the matter longer. He was finally permitted, however, to join the order, taking the habit in the convent of Capuchins of Tarazona on July 26, 1637, with the name of Friar Francisco de Pamplona.

He soon became noted for the assiduous performance of his monastic duties, and was even known to walk long distances barefoot over rocky roads. Once while leading a procession in Seville, he came to a place where he had formerly killed a man. He began to cry and wail so loudly that it was necessary to take him out of the procession. In 1645 he went with a group of missionaries to the Congo. Returning shortly afterward to Spain, he was sent in 1647 with four other padres to Panama, where he established a mission among the Indians of Darién.[4]

In 1650 Pamplona led an expedition of three other friars to the island of Margarita with the intention of exploring the

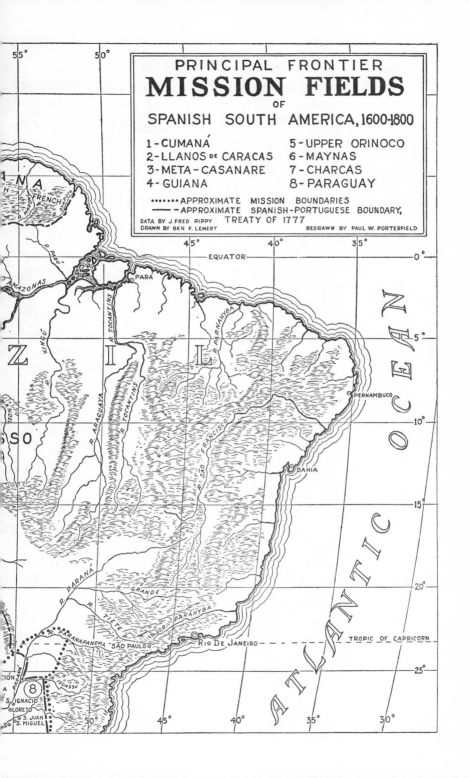

PRINCIPAL FRONTIER
MISSION FIELDS
OF
SPANISH SOUTH AMERICA, 1600-1800

1 - CUMANÁ   5 - UPPER ORINOCO
2 - LLANOS DE CARACAS   6 - MAYNAS
3 - META - CASANARE   7 - CHARCAS
4 - GUIANA   8 - PARAGUAY

•••••• APPROXIMATE MISSION BOUNDARIES
——— APPROXIMATE SPANISH - PORTUGUESE BOUNDARY,
DATA BY J. FRED RIPPY   TREATY OF 1777
DRAWN BY BEN F. LEMERT   REDRAWN BY PAUL W. PORTERFIELD

adjacent mainland for suitable places to establish missions. The group reached Cumaná the same year, and learned that the Cumanagoto Indians, some eight thousand in number, were in need of conversion. With the permission of the governor of Cumaná, they proceeded to the port of San Cristóbal de Cumanagotos, and from there went a few miles into the interior to the country of the Píritus. The Indians received them in a friendly manner, and the missionaries erected a chapel. From here they advanced into the country of the Cochismas, where they baptized many natives, and during the next two years founded three reductions: San Miguel, El Salvador de Guanape, and Purísima Concepción de Píritu.

The missionaries soon became involved in a dispute with the governor of the territory, and Friar Francisco decided to return to Spain to report on the possibilities of this new field and to defend the missions against the accusations of the civil authorities. He died (1651) on the way, at the port of La Guaira.

In 1652 the Capuchins were forced by royal decree to retire from Cumaná, and the field was granted to another order of Franciscans. But Father Lorenzo Magallón, one of the Capuchins, returned to Spain, where he presented the case of his brothers before the Council of the Indies.

III

A royal cédula was issued in 1654 ordering six Observant Franciscans to proceed to Cumaná. Leaving Spain in July, 1654, they soon took charge of the missions of Píritu or Cumanagotos.[5] In 1656 another group of eight religious of this order arrived in Cumaná and advanced among the wild Indians of the interior, accompanied by soldiers and by interpreters who told the savages that the missionaries had been sent by the king of Spain to teach them the laws of God and to make them Christians.[6]

A cédula dated November 20, 1656, however, permitted Magallón, who was then in Spain, to return with five Capuchin missionaries to Cumaná, where he was to place them under the orders of the governor. Father Lorenzo and his friars—José de Carabantes, Francisco de Tauste, Agustín de Frías, Lorenzo de Belmonte, and Lay Brother Miguel de Torres—reached Cumaná in January, 1658; and the governor commanded them to work among the Indians of Cumaná and Maturín.[7] Indeed, the province of Cumaná had just been divided (1657) between the Capuchin Franciscans and the Observant Franciscans. Píritu, which was the section between the rivers Manzanares and Unare, was given to the Observants, while the rest was placed in the care of the Capuchins, the mission areas of each reaching south to the Orinoco.[8]

A royal decree of May 21, 1658, ordered that six other Capuchins be sent to Cumaná. At that time the Spanish king wrote to the president of the Casa de Contratación as follows:

There was also seen in my council a letter of Padre Agustín de Frías, who writes from the missions of Cumaná and asks for more religious and clothes to dress the Indians, for those who need the lights of the Catholic Faith are many and the spiritual laborers few. Considering all this, we command that you see to it that in the armada which is being prepared there shall go six religious . . .; and you will spend up to the sum of four or five hundred ducats on clothes and other things Father Agustín . . . asks. And you will give all the orders for the provisioning of the said religious, in such manner that they shall go well provided for.[9]

Instead of going immediately into the territory of the Indians, the Capuchin missionaries began preaching in Caracas and other towns of Venezuela, where they soon aroused the ire of a "certain person of influence who was living a wicked life."[10] This individual wrote to the Council of the Indies complaining that the missionaries were not working among the natives and advising that they be recalled to the convents of Spain. At the same time Father Magallón played into the hands of his opponent by addressing a letter to the council requesting that permission be given the padres to move to the province of Caracas because the Cumanagoto Indians were at war with the Spaniards. The result of all this was a royal decree ordering the Capuchins to return home; but when the cédula reached Venezuela, the governors of Caracas and Cumaná took the side of the friars, disobeyed the royal order, and advised the missionaries to remain. Fathers Tauste and Frías were sent to Spain to report to the Royal Council, and in consequence another decree was issued on October 26, 1662, directing the governor of Cumaná to keep the padres on the missions and ordering twelve additional Capuchins to be dispatched to the area.[11]

In the meantime the Capuchins had established their first mission—Nuestra Señora de los Angeles de Guáchero—in the area of Cumaná assigned to them, and five missions had been founded in the Píritu area. The great era of apostolic enterprise in northeastern Venezuela had at last been initiated. By 1700 the Capuchins had founded seventeen reductions and the Observant Franciscans twenty-five.[12]

IV

Despite French and Carib attacks and occasional revolts of the converts, the eighteenth century was on the whole a period of prosperity for the Cumaná missions. By 1760 the Observants of Píritu had established forty-three reductions, and the Capuchins had founded forty-one in their portion of Cumaná.[13]

The governor of Cumaná gave a favorable report of the Capuchin missionaries in 1754. "These clergy," he said, "live

'These clergy live exemplarily, devoted and attentive to the purpose of their ministry'

exemplarily, devoted and attentive to the purpose of their ministry. They maintain peace and union among themselves, without causing any disquiet to those outside. Their watchful care they devote to the conversion and preservation of the Indians and to the propagation of our holy faith." After telling how the missions provided food for the aged, the infirm, the widows, and the orphans among the Indians, the governor continued: "These missionaries try always to keep the Indians under obligation and grateful by means of their generosity, in order that, finding themselves contented thereby, they may not think of going off." [14]

Another Cumaná governor reported in 1761 that the Capuchins of his province had in charge thirteen mission towns and seven doctrina towns, with a total population of a little less than five thousand, and with nearly four hundred haciendas and eighteen churches. [15] This estimate was probably too conservative, for two years later another official reported that the population of the villages of both the Observants and the Capuchins was between twenty-six and twenty-seven thousand. [16]

Writing in 1779, Father Caulín asserted that since the beginning of the missions of Píritu, one hundred and ten missionaries of the Observant Franciscans had labored in that field, that they had baptized in all more than fifty-eight thousand Indians, that sixteen doctrinas and fourteen missions with a population of above twelve thousand converts were then in existence. [17] In the following year Padre Simón Torrelosnegros, prefect of the Capuchin missions of Cumaná, wrote that up until that time the Capuchins of this section had founded forty-four missions without any other aid than that of the Indians, and an additional two missions in an adjacent region. A total of nearly fifty-three thousand had been baptized and 14,496 married, while 26,674, "who . . . [had] died in the communion of our Holy Mother Church," had been buried. In the year 1780 there were 12,013 persons in these missions and doctrinas, and perhaps there were others which Torrelosnegros does not mention.[18] Thus there appears to have been more than twenty-four thousand converted Indians in the entire Cumaná area in 1780.

Already the missionaries were approaching the end of their task in this region. They had advanced step by step from the Caribbean to the Orinoco, and in the course of less than a century and a half, had established some eighty-seven reductions. During the next twenty years they were to found only two or three missions in the Cumaná field.[19] They had encountered great hardships. At least a dozen of them had become martyrs and as many more were believed to have been poisoned by the natives. More than two hundred altogether had worked among the Indians of the area.[20]

They had done much to promote agriculture and stockraising. Father Caulín writes of "innumerable ranches of horses, mules, and cattle . . . ; and of broad valleys in which the [native] inhabitants cultivate and produce abundant crops of sugar, honey, brown sugar, bananas, maize, cassava, rice, beans, and other things." He referred to the Observant Franciscans of Píritu.[21] Largely as the result of the efforts of the Capuchins, cacao, coffee, and sugar plantations were established in the valley of the Guarapiche River, with irrigation projects for supplying them with water during the dry season. And they promoted the livestock industry so successfully that one of the ranches was said in 1810 to be occupied by a million head of cattle—an evident exaggeration, but the ranch must have contained immense herds to furnish a basis for such a statement.[22]

Gradually, however, their wards were being taken over by the secular authorities—the civil officials and the priests.

"With forced fingers rude" these functionaries would fain pluck the fruit before the "mellowing year." The padres struggled with them constantly, but were never able for long to resist their impetuous haste. As early as 1699, Don Joseph Ramírez, civil governor of the area in which the Píritu missions were located, proposed to place corregidores over these reductions and to compel the Indians to pay tribute. He also attempted to impose "other obligations unendurable at the time in such new establishments, which it had cost so much to transplant from the forest of Infidelity to the pleasant garden of the church." Fearing that the change would cause the Indians to flee their settlements, Father Ruiz Blanco went to Spain to appeal to the king. Arriving in Madrid in September, 1701, he placed before the Supreme Council of the Indies a memorial objecting to the direct control of the Indians by the civil government. As a result of this petition, the Spanish monarch dispatched an order commanding that the corregidores be removed and that Ramírez should not interfere with the government of the missions without a special order from the Council of the Indies.[23] But the civil authorities were not held in check for many years. In 1717 the secularization process began in Píritu, and by 1779, as already noted, more than half of the mission reductions were doctrinas, many of the latter under curas and all of them paying tribute. The Capuchin establishments encountered a similar fate. Of the thirty-six in existence in 1761, twenty-three were doctrinas, sixteen of which were subjected to the oppressive rule of the corregidores.[24] In both Píritu and Cumaná proper the native population was declining, the Indian families having on the average no more than two or three children.[25]

During the war for independence, which was a death blow to these missions, the cavalry obtained many of its horses from this region. The missionaries were forced to leave

Cumaná in 1812, and according to tradition, their residence in the town of Cumaná was converted into a military barrack. The fate of the Píritu area was probably not essentially different. The Indians of this mission field supplied the rank and file of the armies of both sides. At the beginning of the war with Spain there were said to be some eighty thousand inhabitants in the region, but within a few years the population declined * to about forty-one thousand.[26]

* It is not clear whether our authority, Lodares, refers to the population of the mission fields of both Cumaná and Píritu, or merely to the inhabitants of the Capuchin area. It would seem more reasonable to include both in the total. They embraced two civil provinces: Nueva Barcelona, or Cumaná, and Nueva Andalucía.

THE MISSIONS OF THE LLANOS OF CARACAS

I

THE Llanos of Caracas comprise those great plains that stretch southward across central Venezuela from the mountain ranges which border the Caribbean coast to the rivers Orinoco and Apure. Even today these plains are a *terra incognita* to the average Venezuelan of the highlands about Caracas, although on them graze the herds of immense *hatos* (ranches) under the care of picturesque *llaneros*, or cowboys. In the seventeenth and eighteenth centuries this was far from being a delightful region in which to seek and convert savage Indians. It is an area of rivers and lakes, of level grasslands broken here and there by clumps of trees, with strips of thick forest along the waterways. Much of the land is only a few feet above the streams even during the dry season; for while the temperature is high throughout the year, there are two distinct seasons: the wet season which comes during our summer months, and the dry season which corresponds to our winter, when the prevailing winds are from the north and northeast. During the latter, no rain falls for weeks or even months. The plains become parched, the smaller streams dry

up entirely, and the llanos become a veritable land of death. Thousands of head of cattle and other animals perish from thirst or starvation. Then comes the season of rainfall, and the landscape lives again as the withered grasses drink up the welcome gift of the rain gods. But soon the streams become swollen and begin to overflow their banks along the lower levels. And before the rains have passed, thousands of square miles of lowland will have become flooded. The livestock and wild animals take refuge on the *mesas* and *médanos*, areas of low tableland which stand out above the flood like so many Ararats. The llaneros, who have almost lived on horseback during the dry season, discard their mounts in order to wield canoe paddles. The Cossacks of Venezuela now become sailors of inland seas.[1]

In going from one mesa to another during their entradas in the Llanos of Caracas, the padres often had to wade water up to their chests and even their necks.[2] Lurking in these turbid streams and lagoons, were huge ungainly caymans (alligators), which were utterly incapable of distinguishing a man of God from the basest sinner. And almost as dangerous as these alligators were the fierce *caribes*, fish that were capable of doing great damage with their sharp teeth. Whole schools of them would sometimes attack a man and cut him to pieces. The electric eel, which according to Humboldt could paralyze a horse, was another source of danger. On the other hand, when the zealous padres sought the infidels during the dry season, they had much difficulty in finding drinking water on the plains between the rivers.

The Indians of this area were more primitive than those of Cumaná and the right bank of the Orinoco. While the latter lived in groups in settled communities, engaging in farming a part of the time, and acknowledging certain of their number as chiefs, the Indians of the Llanos of Caracas were

119

The Indians of the Llanos of Caracas ordinarily depended on hunting and fishing for their food

scattered in family rather than tribal units. They ordinarily depended entirely on hunting and fishing, seldom cultivating the soil. They had no fixed settlements and recognized no chiefs, although they united temporarily in order to oppose the missionaries and other Spaniards.[3] Father Ildefonso de Zaragoza, prefect of the missions of the Llanos of Caracas, described these Indians as follows:

They have no worship false or true; no idea of divinity; and although they have rational souls, they live like irrational beings, without human manners or customs; all nomads, without a house in which to live, without reason to understand or understanding to reason. . . . They walk along paths like cattle, the men entirely naked and the women with a *guayuco* woven of palm or herb.[4]

II

Nevertheless, between the years 1658 and 1758 the Capuchins founded in this region some one hundred missions.[5] Father Pedro de Berja advanced into the Llanos of Caracas in 1661 and 1662 and founded San Francisco del Pao; Father Diego Marchena entered them in 1665, reducing some three hundred Indians; [6] and during the following years the Capuchin missionaries went into the Indian country annually after the floods subsided in order to convert and reduce the natives. Until 1676, they were without the protection of escorts of Spanish soldiers, so that not only were the lives of the missionaries in danger—two of them were killed by the savages during this early period—but the neophytes were constantly on the verge of fleeing into the wilds. In that year the prefect of the missions petitioned the king to found towns of Spaniards to protect the missionaries and prevent the Indians from leaving the reductions. Permission for the establishment of these towns was granted, and a cédula of September 28, 1676, gave the Spanish encomenderos certain privileges in return for aiding and protecting the padres.[7] A royal decree issued on February 22, 1689, however, directed that peaceful means be used in reducing these savages. It read as follows:

My Governor and Captain General of Caracas: I have resolved to command you, as I now do, that the Indians of those plains be reduced solely by means of the religious, with gentleness and persuasion, and in no manner with arms, advising the Indians that if they are thus reduced they will be exempt from tribute for ten years and will not be subjected to personal service, that they are not to be made to labor for Spaniards, and that they will be directly under the protection of the Royal Crown, this being the most fit course of procedure.[8]

Yet, in spite of this benevolent language, permission to employ armed escorts was renewed in 1692; and thereafter they appear to have been used repeatedly. Gil Fortoul cites instances of escorts numbering from more than a hundred up to nearly five hundred going out with the padres and bringing the natives in to the places selected for the reductions.[9] Between 1707 and 1720 more than thirteen hundred soldiers—Spaniards, mulattoes, and native converts—were required to persuade some fifteen hundred wild Indians to settle down and become Christians.[10]

The missionaries of this field were more ill favored in the matter of royal aid than were those of most other mission fields of South America. In other sections they were allowed from 110 to 200 pesos annually; but the missionaries of the Llanos of Caracas received a stipend of only fifty pesos per year, and even this pittance was seldom paid.[11] In 1702 the prefect of these missions complained to the Royal Council that the sínodos had not been remitted in four years, and a cédula of the same year admitted that in founding two Spanish towns and twenty-five Indian villages the crown had been at no expense except that of transporting the Capuchins to the port of La Guaira.[12] Father Pedro de Berja had to ask his provincial to send him some cloth to make his habit. And one padre stated that the Capuchins had founded a hundred towns without any royal aid whatsoever.[13]

The failure of the royal authorities to furnish promised aid to missionaries was not peculiar to the Llanos of Caracas, but was common throughout Spanish America. It was not difficult for the authorities of Church and State to convince themselves that poverty was a virtue of great benefit to the padres. On January 11, 1713, for example, the bishop of Puerto Rico wrote to the Spanish king concerning the Capuchin missionaries of Cumaná: "These Missionaries are those which are the least expensive to Your Royal Treasury, for while others have assigned to them the stipend of a hundred and fifty pesos annually for each religious, these Capuchins live each with only fifty pesos in the abstinence and poverty admirable for their state." [14]

The Indians of the Venezuelan plains disliked farming, particularly when a part of their products went for the support of the mission. They were disposed to flee down the rivers in their canoes; and if they were successful in reaching the Orinoco, it was practically impossible to bring them back to the reductions. The most effective way to check this exodus was to establish Spanish towns downstream from the missions for the purpose of stopping the Indians whenever they tried to pass. A royal cédula granting this permission was issued as early as August 5, 1702. [15]

The activities of the Spaniards on these plains were very likely another important reason for the desire on the part of the natives to leave the missions. The whites were developing ranches and plantations; they needed the services of the reduction Indians, and the Spanish officials here as elsewhere were guilty of corruption. On August 5, 1702, the king ordered the religious of these Capuchin missions to protect the Indians from extortion by the corregidores and to report any ill treatment of the natives by these officials. [16]

Despite these handicaps, however, the padres made considerable progress as the years passed. Many of their more than one hundred establishments were ephemeral, and some soon became the nuclei of civil towns, but after the close of the seventeenth century the Capuchins had constantly from fifteen to almost thirty missions under the care of as many missionaries. In 1702 there were some seventeen missions,

Calabozo and San Antonio de Araure among them; [17] in 1758 there were nineteen under twenty-five religious; [18] in 1770 there were said to be twenty-eight reductions with a population of more than ten thousand, the neophytes on each mission ranging from a thousand down to less than a hundred.[19]

III

From time to time exploring expeditions went out from the missions of the Llanos of Caracas to visit the *tierra adentro* toward the Orinoco and the Meta. In 1727 Father Marcelino de San Vicente penetrated with an escort of soldiers as far as the Orinoco, where he was successful in reducing some Indians who had fled from the older missions.[20] Other entradas were made into this region, and in 1735 the Capuchin padres had two Carib missions near the juncture of the Orinoco and the Apure.[21]

Father Jerónimo de Gibraltar, who was prefect of the Llanos of Caracas in 1761, is given credit for having founded the Capuchin missions between the Apure and Meta rivers. Shortly after his term of office as prefect expired, he went to Spain, and in 1769 returned to these plains with eighteen religious. In that year he was commissioned by both the captain general of Venezuela and the prefect of the missions of the Llanos of Caracas to explore, with the aid of Father Juan de Málaga, the territory between the Apure and the Meta. In December, 1769, he reported the completion of his task and declared that the missionaries might look forward with confidence to the successful reduction of the natives of this area of tropical savannas and forests. He later went to Caracas, where he described to the colonial officials in glowing terms the wonderful opportunities for conversion of the Indians in the land he had visited. With the aid of armed escorts and a few settlements of Spaniards, such as San Carlos del Meta and San Fernando de Apure, the Capuchins founded during the course of the next half century nearly a score of reductions in this new field. A cédula of April 17, 1771, assigned an annual stipend of one hundred and fifty pesos to each missionary in the region between the Apure and the Meta.[22]

Shortly afterward several padres who had come from the upper Orinoco because of illness and persecution were incorporated into the body of Capuchin missionaries in the Llanos of Caracas, but they were not permitted to have a voice in the government of the missions.[23] In the year 1770 there were twenty-eight missionaries in this province, many of them of advanced age with long years in the service, as the following table will reveal: [24]

NAME	AGE	YEARS ON THE MISSION
Antonio de Jaén	68	29
José de Alhama	60	31
Pedro J. de Villanueva	61	28
Isidoro de Sanlúcar	60	28
Pedro de Ubrique	69	22
Cirilo Bautista de Sevilla	63	28
Felipe de Palma	54	22

A report of 1790 indicates that some of the missions of twenty years before had been transferred to other locations, while others had become the sites of civil settlements and still others had been abandoned. Yet twenty-four Capuchin missionaries still occupied a chain of reductions extending southward to the Apure, and even beyond to the Meta, more than thirty establishments in all. But the missions soon began to decline, and during the bloody struggle for independence, which was attended by energetic recruiting in this region, they appear to have been deserted altogether.[25]

THE MISSIONS OF THE LLANOS OF THE META
AND THE CASANARE

I

IGH above the plateau of Cundinamarca, a short distance east of Bogotá, rises the eastern cordillera of the Andes. To the west of these mountains, water finds its way to the sea through the channel of the Magdalena. To the east, the turbulent and crystal clear mountain torrents tumble down toward the plains, receiving as they go additional tributaries until they form such large rivers as the Casanare, the Meta, the Apure, the Guaviare, and finally the broad Orinoco. The distance from Bogotá to the head of canoe navigation on the nearest of the streams that traverse the llanos of Colombia and Venezuela is less than a hundred miles.[1] Once beyond the mountain rampart, the traveler finds at his disposal numerous waterways on which he can visit territories comprising hundreds of thousands of square miles and can go as far afield as distant Brazil.

During the course of the sixteenth century hardy adventurers, German as well as Spanish, explored the Orinoco and its principal western tributaries. Such intrepid leaders as

126

Missions of the Meta and the Casanare

Diego de Ordaz, Alonso de Herrera, George Speyer, Nicholas Federmann, Philip von Hutten, Hernán Pérez de Quesada, Gonzalo Jiménez de Quesada—the great conqueror of the semicivilized Chibchas on the Plateau surrounding Bogotá— and Felipe de Urre traveled for hundreds of miles and confronted almost indescribable hardships in their search for the Gilded Man, the White King, and the mythical kingdoms of Meta and Omagua. They failed to find wealth sufficient to justify their efforts, but they contributed much to the knowledge of this portion of South America.[2]

The search for gold and plunder eventually gave place to the quest for souls, and that section of the great plains which is drained by the Casanare and the Meta rivers was an important field of Jesuit missionary activity during more than a century of the colonial period. In some respects it is a more genial and attractive country than most of the other lowland mission areas of tropical South America. These llanos are not so frequently inundated as the plains along the left bank of the lower Orinoco, while travel across country, particularly in the dry season, is much less difficult than in the tropical rain forest of the Amazon. The landscape on the southeastern plains of Colombia, called in colonial days the Llanos of San Juan, is beautiful to behold during the season when frequent rains give new life to nature's plant children. The broad sweeps of emerald plain are dotted with little groves of moriche, cumaná, and corneto palms. The numerous streams are bordered by dense forests which hide anacondas and bushmasters and give shelter to birds of brilliant plumage.[3] The land is well adapted to farming and grazing, and some of the mission villages flourished under the direction of the Jesuit padres.

The first of the Black Robes reached Colombia in 1590. In that year the captain general of the New Kingdom of

Granada brought with him Fathers Francisco Victoria and Antonio Linero. A short time later Father Antonio Martínez came to Bogotá from Lima, and when Bartolomé Lobo Guerrero was appointed archbishop of Bogotá in 1598, he brought with him to the highland capital two more Jesuits, Alonso de Medrano and Francisco Figueroa, the latter of whom was to achieve fame in the missions of the oriente of Ecuador.[4]

The Society of Jesus was formally established in New Granada by a royal cédula of December 30, 1602, which declared:

. . . It is understood how important it is for the welfare of that Kingdom that the Religious of the Company of Jesus be established in it, in order that with their good teaching they may aid in the conversion and education of the Indians, and that the youth may occupy itself in virtuous and necessary exercises for their good rearing, since there are many young people and creole priests who have need of study and instruction in the Christian faith. . . . And for the present I give permission to the Religious of the Company of Jesus in order that they may be able to establish themselves in the said Nuevo Reino de Granada, notwithstanding any order to the contrary. And I command the President and Oïdores of my said Audiencia, and the Archbishop of the said Kingdom, and other Justices, and ecclesiastical and secular Judges, that they shall not impede it, for this is my will.[5]

II

A short time later Fathers Medrano and Figueroa began teaching in the llanos of Casanare just east of the cordillera, where they built churches at Chita, Tame, and elsewhere, and labored among the natives until they were commanded by the archbishop of Bogotá to return to the capital. This was the beginning of Jesuit missionary activity in the lowlands of eastern New Granada.

For three decades after the recall of Medrano and Figueroa

—between 1629 and 1660—these llanos were virtually deserted by the missionaries of the Society of Jesus. In 1639, however, the provincial of the order sent Padre Francisco Alvarez and Padre Francisco Jimeno to "explore and reconnoitre all that country, with the intention of establishing in this part of the New Kingdom" missions of "infidels." [6] After the completion of their task the padres were to return to Bogotá in order to report on the prospects for the success of new missions in this region.

They found the reductions established by the first missionaries in a sad state of decay, but were well received by the natives. Father Rivero says that they were met at the settlement of Tame by a crowd of Indians of both sexes and all ages who greeted them with the words, "Praised be the Most Holy Sacrament!" The news of the arrival of the Jesuits spread, and the Indians of the region flocked to Tame to see the holy men. Two of the heathen Indians of the Tunebo nation approached the padres and asked to be baptized. Father Jimeno supposed that the older of the two was already a Christian, and proceeded to use him as interpreter to instruct the younger. He soon took the neophyte to the church, which had not yet fallen down, and administered baptism. As he performed the ceremony, he noticed that the elder Tunebo appeared to be very sad. When the padre inquired the reason for his depression, the Indian replied, "How do you expect my heart not to be sad if my brother is to become a Christian and I, who have heard so many good things, am to return to my country as much a heathen as before?" Father Jimeno then baptized him; and the convert, rejoicing as the earth when the sun rises, promised to sin no more. [7]

The padres felt that the Indians of these plains were in desperate need of their apostolic services. Here, as in many other sections of South America, the natives often engaged in bloody tribal feuds, buried their baby girls alive, and were much addicted to intoxicating liquors.[8]

Of all the savage tribes of South America, none was in greater need of the civilizing influence of the missionaries than the Tunebos. While the Cacatios of this part of New Granada were physically handsome, of light color, usually intelligent, and willing to accept the teaching of the padres, the Tunebos were degraded to a disgusting degree. Coarse and filthy, they liked nothing better than to sit in the sun and munch the vermin which they picked from their hair. It was even alleged that they preferred putrid to fresh meat! Many of them were afflicted with a disease called *carate*, which resembled leprosy, for their faces and hands were covered with blue and white spots. Yet the Tunebos so gloried in this infirmity that people who did not have it were scorned by those who did. The girls not afflicted with *carate* had difficulty in finding husbands, and therefore did everything in their power to contract the disease! [9]

Several years after the explorers returned to Bogotá, three missionaries—Fathers Alonso Neira, Ignacio Cano, and Juan Fernández Pedroche—were sent to the llanos (1661) to establish missions. They confirmed previous reports regarding the condition of the old mission villages, which were now not only in disrepair, but almost deserted. The village of Tame, which at the time of the visit of the explorers had contained some four hundred and fifty Indians, now had a population of only sixty or seventy. In the town of Tunebos there were only forty or fifty natives, a church, and a few houses. Impelled by holy zeal, the three padres, with Pauto as their base of operations, explored forests, traversed plains and swamps, and glided along unknown streams in their search for heathen to reduce to the Catholic faith. The good padre Rivero, who knew this country from personal experience, remarks:

Well may be understood the calamities and miseries that the fathers passed through in these beginnings, in unfamiliar countries, waters, and forests, and among such a labyrinth of rivers, lakes, and quagmires—the trail sown with thorns and thistles—encountering at each step ferocious lions and formidable tigers, and stumbling upon vipers and snakes in great multitude and different species, all poisonous and deadly. . . .[10]

In 1662 two French missionaries, Fathers Antonio Monteverde and Dionisio Meland, caused some excitement by reaching the Casanare region by way of the Orinoco, the Meta, and the Casanare rivers and thus opening a possible direct water route between Spain and the Casanare reductions. Two years later the superior of the Jesuit college at Bogotá sent Padre Francisco Ellauri downstream over this same route to the settlement of Santo Tomás on the lower Orinoco. Father Francisco had spent much of his life working among the Indians of the high, cold plateau in the Sogamoso region about a hundred and fifty miles northeast of Bogotá, and he was sixty-two years old at the time. From the personal viewpoint his choice for the journey into the torrid tropical lowlands was highly imprudent. He died the next year, probably largely as the result of the hardships of the hazardous expedition. He had done much for his mission village of Tópaga, and might have lasted another decade. He had built a tile-roofed church, adorning it with images and tapestries, candlesticks, lamps, and silver chandeliers. He had also purchased an organ and other musical instruments, and imported musicians to instruct the Indians, in order that God might be worshiped in a worthy manner even in this far corner of the world.[11]

III

The difficulties encountered by the padres in these plains were increased by the fact that the Spaniards had long mistreated the Indians. The protecting arm of the sovereign of Spain could not reach that far; and the natives were not only oppressed but even killed by ruthless encomenderos. Captain Alonso Jiménez, for example, entered the Meta region in 1606 with a body of infantry for the purpose of capturing natives for service in the mines. Employing a ruse, he persuaded the savages to build a large church. As the edifice neared completion, he had them enter it each day to pray and sing. At the opportune moment he ordered his gallant soldiers to surround the building. Without warning they attacked the worshipers, whom they easily captured and sent to slavery in the mines. Another Spanish captain, who was escorting a number of captive Indians, misunderstood, or pretended to misunderstand, an Indian word meaning wait for an order to kill the Spaniards, whereupon the Spanish soldiers slaughtered the natives without mercy.[12] The cruelties of the early days of the conquest were so impressed upon the minds of the Indians that atrocity stories were handed down from generation to generation.

Another problem confronted by the padres was that of tribal warfare among the Indians of the region. The missions were sometimes attacked by neighboring heathen tribes. The llanos village of Atanarí, occupied by a group of Achagua Indians, was raided on one occasion by a hostile tribe under a chief called Bacacore. During the fight Bacacore directed his personal attack against the missionary, Father Juan Ortiz Payán. The padre had no arms except a cross and a picture showing the death of San Francisco Xavier, which he always carried with him as a defense against dangers of this kind.

The cacique struck the missionary and was about to deliver a second blow when a Spanish soldier rushed up and deprived him of his weapons

The cacique struck the missionary on the shoulder with a heavy wooden weapon known as a *macana*, and was about to deliver a second blow when Father Payán threw his arms about the Indian and called for help. A Spanish soldier and some Achaguas rushed up, took Bacacore prisoner, and deprived him of his weapons. The padre kept the *macana* as a souvenir of the encounter; Bacacore and several other caciques were shot by the Spaniards. Father Payán never recovered the complete use of his arm, but he gloried in this infirmity, since it constantly reminded him of how God had aided him in his hour of need.[13]

Since the mission of Atanarí was constantly in danger of attacks from the wild Indians, the padres decided to move the whole population toward the fortified town of Casanare, where there were sufficient Spaniards to repulse any ordinary onslaughts of the savages. The exodus began with one padre at the head and another at the rear. Indians and missionaries took with them all of their portable possessions, including garments, tools, hammocks, and food for the journey. The mothers transported heavy loads of baggage as well as infants upon their shoulders. The friars, who made part of the journey barefoot, often carried the babies in order to give the mothers a rest, and even helped the men with their loads. After two weeks the food was exhausted, and the party had to live on turtles and such fish as could be caught in the streams which they crossed. Shortly afterward, smallpox broke out among the pilgrims, attacking three or four new members of the group daily. The Indians became frightened and wished to return to their own country. At last they decided to go no farther. They said it was not strange that the padres, who had not been attacked by the dreadful malady, should wish to continue the journey, and they began to apprehend some kind of foul play. Unable to persuade the converts to proceed, the two missionaries retired to their hammocks, where in the darkness of the night they prayed that something might occur to dissuade the Indians from running away. About eleven or twelve o'clock Father Payán awoke with a high fever. He realized that he had smallpox, and looked upon the attack as a visitation from heaven. When morning came, he was able to restore the confidence of the Indians and to persuade them to continue toward Casanare. Although nearly all of the neophytes were suffering from the epidemic, they followed Payán, eating herbs and big worms which they found growing on the palm leaves. After a trek of fifty-five days, the bedraggled company approached their destination. Here, however, they were met by one Sánchez Chamorro with a group of soldiers, and many of the Indians, fearing that they would be forced into slavery, fled in spite of every effort of the padres to restrain them. It was some time before the missionaries were able to reassemble the natives and persuade them to proceed to Casanare.[14]

The Jesuits of the plains of New Granada found enemies not only in the wild Indians, but also in the Spaniards, both lay and ecclesiastical. The Spanish ranchmen and planters opposed the padres because the latter objected to the abuse of the natives. The Spanish traders complained that the Jesuits engaged in commerce with the heretics, raised cattle, sugar cane, and other products with the labor of captured Indians whom they enslaved, and took land away from the Spaniards to enrich their own holdings. So persistent were these complaints against the Jesuits that the archbishop of Bogotá decided to take their missions away from them and give them to other orders. Since there were royal decrees supporting the padres, he dared not do this without an investigation. He therefore sent Don Pedro de Urrutabisqui to Casanare. This judge reported that the Jesuits of the region had no other riches than the souls of their converts, and that the accusations against them were the outgrowth of the corruption of their accusers. He averred:

I, having observed carefully the fact that they do not avoid labors and expenses, nor even spare their own lives, in order to spread the Gospel, can be nothing less than their advocate, having before been their judge; and especially when I see the many infidels reduced by their ministry to our Holy Faith, and so many vassals [brought] to Your Catholic Majesty.[15]

The archbishop declared the depositions of the witnesses in favor of the Jesuits null and void, and even fined Don Pedro for defending the missionaries; but the sons of Loyola appealed to the ecclesiastical tribunal and the audiencia, and in the end were permitted to continue their work on the llanos.

Although the frontier missionaries of the Society of Jesus in New Granada, as elsewhere in South America, were subject to the orders of a superior, yet during the early years of their activity in the eastern plains the padres, who were often hundreds of miles from the nearest superior officer, were allowed a large degree of individual freedom and initiative. After the missions had been well organized, they were occasionally visited by an official called a provincial, who went from reduction to reduction distributing the Black Robes where they were most needed, and exercising a general supervision over the missions.[16] The Indians were permitted to transmit complaints to this official, and the Tunebos, in particular, had a special functionary known as "speaker" whose duty it was to deliver such complaints. Whenever the provincial arrived at one of their villages, the whole town would turn out to hear the speaker harangue him, setting forth at length the alleged outrages perpetrated upon the natives by the white population, and sometimes accusing their padre of beating them. Often the gist of their speech was that they were good Indians and had no need of a missionary. The provincial, however, usually concluded that the complaints were much exaggerated. These traveling officials of the Society of Jesus also performed the service of coördinating the activities of the missionaries over large areas on the frontier.[17]

One of the missionaries of the Meta region was an Indian named Antonio Calaimi, who in the early eighteenth century rendered the Jesuits of the llanos a service by going of his own accord among the wild savages and persuading them to enter the reductions. At one time he brought to the mission of Tame sixteen Indians whom he had persuaded to become Christians. The Jesuits gave these converts houses and farms and made Calaimi their chief.[18]

While some of the missionaries lost their lives within a year or two after entering the lowlands east of the cordillera, others lived many years in the llanos. Father Juan Rivero spent the span of a generation on this frontier, and Father Alonso Neira died in the llanos of Colombia after forty years of service.[19] After 1715 this area was also the scene of the fruitful labors of Joseph Gumilla. On the whole, the task of the Jesuit padres in this field was a thankless one. They were hated by the Spaniards, who did all in their power to make their task more difficult. Few of them were fortunate enough to receive at the end of life's road such honors as were given to Father Jerónimo de Escobar. When he died at Bogotá, all the bells of the city tolled in sign of the grief of the people. The corpse was carried to the church by four prebendaries, and the archbishop himself officiated. The president of New Granada exchanged his hat for that of the deceased padre in order that he might retain it as a relic, and he and others kissed the feet of the saintly corpse. The multitude was so desirous of obtaining souvenirs that the body was stripped almost naked.[20] When another padre named Alonso de Andrade died, the crowd not only took his clothes for relics, but cut off his fingers and ears and pulled out his hair and beard.[21] The average missionary during the early days of the llanos missions might look forward, however, to nothing better than an unhallowed grave at the bottom of a muddy river, in the slimy depths of some swamp, or beneath the floor of a crude little church hundreds of miles from Bogotá and a thousand leagues from his ancestral home in Spain.

Nine Jesuit missions were said to be in existence in the Casanare-Meta region in 1736, and according to a report made by Don Eugenio Alvarado to the Council of the Indies in 1790, the Jesuits had founded since 1618 nine villages on the Casanare, eight on the Meta, and twenty-five on the Orinoco and the Guaviare. At that time there were still in existence six of the missions on the Casanare, four on the Meta, and six on the Orinoco.[22] Shortly before their expulsion the members of the Society had in charge the following missions in the Meta-Casanare region: [23]

MISSIONS ON THE CASANARE

Mission	Population
Pauto	600
San Salvador del Puerto de Casanare	350
Nuestra Señora de la Asunción	1,800
El Pilar de Patute	70
San Javier de Macaguanes	1,000
San Ignacio de Betoyes	1,600

MISSIONS ON THE META

Surimena	400
San Miguel de Macuco	800
Casimena	700
La Quebradita de Jiramena	300

IV

The expulsion of the Jesuits from New Granada occurred in 1767. On July 7 of that year the viceroy, Pedro Messía de la Cerda, received sealed papers written in the hand of the king of Spain containing directions for the destruction of the Society of Jesus in that colony. Messía de la Cerda fixed August 1 as the date on which to communicate the decree of expulsion to the Jesuit fathers at Bogotá. On July 30 he named the judges who should execute the decree. At midnight of July 31 a body of troops was stationed about each of the three Jesuit edifices in the city. The judges, accompanied by scribes and witnesses, knocked on the doors, and all the Jesuits were ordered to come to the first floor, where the royal decree was read to them. It is said that all wore on their breasts the crucifix that they were accustomed to carry on voyages. The Father Provincial took the decree in his hands, and raised it to his lips as a sign of obedience; and all the members of the Society who were present signed the document. They were declared to be prisoners, and the keys of the buildings, archives, library, and private coffers were confiscated.[24] The following poem, written by one of the Jesuits expelled from New Granada, shows the devotion of a son of Loyola to his order:

> From the dagger that has given thee
> That deep wound
> I shall not hide my breast,
> For I regret more thy death than mine.
>
> To remain without thee would be for me
> Greatest misfortune,
> And it is glorious for me to suffer
> In the arms of a tender and pure mother.

Judges, accompanied by scribes and witnesses, communicated the decree of expulsion to the Jesuit fathers at Bogotá

I shall follow thy footsteps
Lovable pilgrim,
Over sea and land,
Along precipices, through brambles, through thorns.

I shall go beneath thy shadow,
I shall go in thy company
To Italy, to Siberia,
To Tartary, to Mongolia, Japan, or China.

I renounce forever
My Country, the Province,
America and Spain,
For without thee I should not desire life.[25]

Missions of the Meta and the Casanare

When the Jesuits of the plains missions were notified of the royal decree of expulsion, their superiors at once surrendered their account books, money, and other valuables to the governor of that region. The fathers quietly left their missions in the dead of night in order that their Indians, who now numbered more than twenty thousand, might not take up arms in their defense. Thus were rewarded these faithful padres who for over a century had labored to build in the llanos a Christian civilization. Most of the mission property was confiscated by the royal treasury without adequate compensation to the Indians who dwelt on the reductions. Farms were sold for a song, and churches were despoiled of their furniture and decorations. Many of the Indians returned to the wild life of the forest and plain, so that the achievements of the padres were largely undone.[26]

The charge that the Jesuit missionaries of the llanos engaged in commerce was undoubtedly true, but that they did so for the purpose of building up private fortunes is doubtful. They organized their missions on a sound economic basis, encouraged their Indians to produce a surplus of marketable commodities, and aided them in finding purchasers. With the profits they bought tools, clothing, ornaments, and other things that were needed on the reductions. Even the secular authorities in time came to realize that the missions, in order to be successful, must be established on a firm economic foundation. The missions were an aid to the Spanish authorities, since they furnished food and other supplies for the garrisons. It should also be remembered that there was nothing in the canon law to prevent the Jesuits from selling commodities which they produced, so long as they refrained from trafficking in articles for profit without adding anything to their value.[27]

V

After the expulsion of the Jesuits from the region, the mission work was taken over by the Franciscans, Dominicans, and Augustinians. In March, 1777, Father Antonio de Miranda, a Franciscan, reported from the province of San Juan de los Llanos that three new reductions had been founded. The members of this order kept careful records of their missions on these plains, and some of the statistics throw light on the marriage customs of the missions as well as the longevity and fecundity of the natives! The following are some unusual matrimonial matches reported among the mission Indians: [28]

> Bautista Catamais, 99 years of age; wife, 26; three children.
> Salvador Mico, 99 years; wife 20.
> Albino Merchán, 90 years; wife, 17.
> Juan Bobo, 27 years; wife, 90.
> Diego Logrero, 93 years; wife, 15.
> Bruno Sufuega, 98 years; wife, 30; two children, 13 and 8.

In 1794 the Franciscans had nine towns in the Llanos of San Juan and the plains of San Martín, in the Guaviare region to the south. Two years later the total population of these places was 1,230.[29] Another report of about the same time stated, however, that there were eight mission towns with a total population of 1,700.[30]

In 1789 the Dominican friars * on the Casanare had five towns, as well as other reductions in the Barinas, Pedraza, Apure, and Guanare regions.[31] In 1793 their five towns in the Casanare area numbered a total population of 5,316.[32] In the

---

* The Dominicans had been occupying a few missions in the lowlands east of the New Granadan cordillera for some time, although their establishments had never been so important as those of the Jesuits. The first Dominicans, twenty in number, had reached New Granada in 1529. An important missionary field of this order was the plains of Apure and Barinas, and most of the missionaries were recruited from Bogotá. (Lodares, *op. cit.*, III, 212, 257-68.)

following year the Augustinians were reported as having in charge eight towns on the Meta, with a total population of 4,309 and herds of cattle estimated at 52,000 head.[33]

After the departure of the Jesuits, the colonial government of New Granada had made some effort to maintain the missions, but the new padres lacked the skill and tact that were necessary to manage the reductions successfully. The viceroy, in his report of 1803, stated that a militia of three to four hundred men was needed in the province of San Juan de los Llanos, a suggestion which indicates that the natives were restive and hostile.[34] Although some of the reductions prospered for a time under the new missionaries, there was a general decline in the missions of this region until the disorders of the war for independence gave the *coup de grâce* to the expiring Indian pueblos.

The mission Indians of the Casanare and Meta regions soon reverted to savagery, assuming once more a seminomadic life and becoming dependent upon the chase for their livelihood.[35] The native tribes seem to have declined in population, and the mission villages disappeared entirely, so that one who journeyed along these rivers a century later could find no trace of them. The names of some of the missions may still be found upon the map, but their sites have long ago been covered with tropical growth. Where once the pealing of joyous bells called the sons and daughters of nature to prayer and song, there now float through the forests or across the grassy plains the silvery notes of the bellbird (*campanero*), as if summoning the chance traveler to worship in some ghostly chapel. Father J. A. Zahm describes the scene:

As we quietly sailed up the broad forest-clad Meta, we could not help harking back to the distant past, when, ever and anon, along its bank were to be seen the smiling homes and villages of happy Indians under the watchful eye and protecting arm of

143

their "father priest," and comparing it with the present desolate and deserted land that for days at a time does not exhibit the slightest trace of a human habitation.[36]

But to this day the Indians along the Meta erect crosses of plaited palm leaves as a protection from the *chubascos*, or squalls.[37]

THE GUIANA MISSIONS

I

PANISH GUIANA, which comprised an area of between sixty and seventy thousand square miles, was bordered by what is now British Guiana, the Atlantic, the Orinoco, and Brazil, although on the west and south its boundaries were rather indefinite, as boundaries usually were in colonial days. It is an area of tropical forests, luxuriant in the northeast and lighter, with occasional savannas, in the rest of the country. Except for a section along the seacoast in the northeast and a strip along the right bank of the Orinoco, the region consists mainly of highlands.

Its occupation during the colonial period was a slow and difficult process, for it was an outpost of empire menaced by the Caribs and the Dutch, and to some extent by the English. As early as 1595 there was a Franciscan "convent" at the settlement of Santo Tomás de Guayana on the lower Orinoco. Very likely the building was no more than a crude wooden hut thatched with palm leaves; but its walls may have been constructed of mud reinforced with poles and vines.

The establishment was burned by the Dutch in 1637, and the religious went to Cumaná.[1]

The French Jesuits, Fathers Antonio Monteverde and Dionisio Meland, as already noted, passed through Guiana in 1663 on their way to the Casanare River. Monteverde wrote to the Superior of the Society of Jesus at Bogotá advising the establishment of a mission in Guiana to facilitate the passage of the padres between the Casanare reductions and the Island of Trinidad and Europe; and in 1664, as likewise pointed out in another connection, that dignitary sent Father Francisco Ellauri (or Llauri) down the Casanare to the lower Orinoco, where the aged missionary died the following year.[2]

Soon afterward, in September, 1668, Fathers Ignacio Cano and Julián Vergara left the mission and presidio of Puerto de Casanare with the intention of proceeding to the settlement of Santo Tomás de Guayana. They started out in several canoes rowed by Indians under the command of a Spaniard whose overbearing conduct so antagonized the rowers that they overturned three of the boats, lost the padres' supply of biscuits, and then fled. The two missionaries nevertheless continued downstream, and reached Guiana in October. They found no settlement at the former site of Santo Tomás, for the Spaniards had retired some distance from the river in quest of security from the raids of the Caribs, the Dutch, and the English. When the padres eventually discovered the garrison they found it in a miserable state of disease and poverty, while an Indian village previously established in the vicinity was now occupied by only forty people, the rest having fled largely to escape the Spaniards who were accustomed to force them into service as rowers on their long journeys to Trinidad and Cumaná. In spite of discouragements, however, the missionaries persisted in their work,

146

In spite of discouragements, the missionaries persisted in their work, Father Ignacio ministering to the soldiers

Father Ignacio looking after the soldiers and Father Julián ministering to the Indians and teaching them the Christian doctrine. Dwelling in a straw hut in which they could scarcely stand erect, the two padres continued their labors in Guiana until 1670, when the Carib danger forced their retirement to the plains of Casanare.³

In June, 1681, the Jesuits gave up their claims to Guiana, leaving the field to the Capuchins of Catalonia.⁴ In April of the following year the audiencia of Bogotá authorized the governor of Trinidad, who was at that time also the chief executive of Guiana, to have Capuchin missionaries sent to the latter region, and Padres Angel Mataró and Pablo de Blanes soon set out for the banks of the Caroní. Each of them was assigned the stipend of one hundred and thirty-two pesos annually. They began their labors among the Indians at once, but an untoward fate awaited them. Father Angel died before the end of the year; Father Pablo decided to return to Spain in order to report on the state of the mission, but died in Cuba before accomplishing his purpose.[5]

In 1687 the mission of the Island of Trinidad and Guiana was declared independent of Cumaná, and shortly afterward additional missionaries left Spain for Trinidad. Three of the first arrivals—Tomás Lupián, Basilio de Barcelona, and Raimundo Figuerola—went from that island to Santo Tomás in 1687, proceeding by water. On the voyage they experienced remarkable evidence of divine favor. When their provisions were exhausted, they began to pray for succor, whereupon a great bird appeared, disgorged a large fresh fish, and then tamely submitted itself to be eaten! [6]

The Capuchins remained in Guiana from 1687 to 1702, and managed to found four or five reductions during this period; but between the latter date and 1724 this region was virtually without missionaries.[7] In 1715 the Council of the Indies ordered the Capuchin provincial of Catalonia to collect friars to send to the area for the purpose of reorganizing the missions, and commanded the governor of the Canary Islands to enlist thirty families to accompany the padres. The friars left Cádiz in 1717, and proceeded to Guiana via Puerto Rico and Trinidad; the agriculturalists also arrived safely in the colony; and it now appeared that the mission was on the point of being established on a firm basis. It turned out, however, that the missionaries and lay settlers were unable to obtain either armed protection against the hostile Caribs or aid from the royal treasury, and were therefore obliged to return to Trinidad.[8] Nor was a group of Spaniards and friars who went from the Llanos of Caracas to the Orinoco in 1720 any more successful. Two of the religious continued down the river to the port of Guiana, arriving there in 1721,[9] but in 1723 the mission field of Guiana was without padres or means to support any if they should arrive. At that time. however, the missionaries of the Píritu region contributed one hundred head of cattle for the maintenance of the work in Guiana, and this small beginning served as the nucleus from which developed the large herds that later contributed so richly to the economic prosperity of the reductions in this area.[10]

II

The year 1724 may be considered the date of the permanent foundation of the Capuchin missions in Spanish Guiana. In that year Philip V ordered the Capuchins of the province of Catalonia to send thirty padres to this field, and on April 10, 1724, the missionaries reached the colony.[11] Since at that period the fierce Caribs were fighting the Cabre Indians on the Cuchivero River far to the west, there was temporarily little danger from these savages.[12] During the next half century the Capuchins established some forty villages mainly in the valleys of the Caroní and the Cuyuní rivers, while the Observant Franciscans who crossed the Orinoco and entered the valley of the Caura in 1755 founded fourteen during the next two decades.[13]

It would be extremely difficult to make a map showing accurately the location of the colonial missions in Guiana, or for that matter in the other frontier regions of South America. The maps drawn by the padres were frequently grossly inaccurate, for missionaries usually lacked training in civil engineering; and the surveying and astronomical instruments that they used were crude. The missions were often moved and not infrequently destroyed. Furthermore each mission usually had two names: one that of the stream on which it was located and the other that of its patron saint. Since some of these names were long, the reduction might popularly be known by only a part of its name. The mission of Divina Pastora de Guarimna or Santa Rosa de Cura commonly went by the name of either Divina Pastora or Cura. The mission of Santa María was originally named Nuestra Señora de los Angeles de Amaruca.[14]

The French in what is now French Guiana were also interested in the establishment of missions, and Jesuits from Cayenne were successful in reducing some Caribs.[15] That the Spaniards did not intend to permit any interference by French ecclesiastics in the affairs of the Spanish missions is shown, however, by the severe treatment of Nicolás Hervasio, a French bishop who entered Guiana. While he was not the first Frenchman to visit the region, his case was unique because he actually defied the secular authorities and attempted to establish missions within Spanish territory. The governor of Trinidad, who was sent to investigate the activities of the clergyman, reported on May 18, 1729, that the bishop was in the region without credentials showing the assent of the Spanish monarch; that he was visiting the towns already reduced by the Capuchin fathers; and that "at times he went to the shores of the Orinoco with the object of having vessels from foreign lands come with provisions for their maintenance."[16]

The Spanish governor placed the French ecclesiastic on a Spanish boat, which took him to the Dutch colony of Essequibo; and the king of Spain subsequently approved this action. The bishop of Puerto Rico, in whose diocese the Guiana missions lay, also supported the action of Governor Arredondo. On November 16, 1729, he wrote to the king:

In view of the foregoing, and pending my visit to said Province, which I expect to visit soon, I informed said Governor that he had fulfilled his duty, and I also charged him not to desist in his resolution, as it was part of his duties to preserve intact Your Majesty's Domains and rights in his Province, and that, should it be necessary, he should lend his aid to the Vicar of Trinidad and the Capuchin Missions of Guiana to oppose his entrance into those lands and to detain him until my arrival in said province, where I could decide what was most convenient to Your Majesty's service.[17]

The French bishop wrote to the commissary of the Capuchins in the province of Guiana complaining that on the voyage to Essequibo he had been deprived of food and dealt with so violently that his life had been in danger, and asking that the commissary excommunicate the governor and the subordinate officers who had participated in ejecting him. He soon returned to Guiana, claiming that he had orders direct from the pope, and that the "Holy See could not divest itself of such a great privilege as the one granted to . . . [the king of Spain], thus doing injury to the successors of the tiara." [18]

The embarrassing situation was relieved when the Frenchman and his companions were murdered by Caribs. Don Agustín Arredondo reported that friendly Indians had buried the bishop on the banks of the River Aguire and had brought parts of his garments as a proof that he had been murdered. Although Arredondo may have advised the rough treatment which the bishop had received at the hands of his guards while going to Essequibo, he now proposed (in a letter of April 26, 1730) to "seize the perpetrators of such sacrilegious murders and to punish them as they deserve, and to ascertain with certainty the spot where the bodies are interred, to have them taken to Guayana in due time where the obsequies and funeral rites corresponding to the dignity of said Most Illustrious Bishop shall be performed." [19] Following this episode the king of Spain gave specific instructions to the governor of Trinidad to seize any other clergyman who should enter Guiana without a license from the Spanish sovereign.[20]

The bishop had been acting, however, not as a French subject representing the French government or church, but in the capacity of a representative of the pope. There appears to have been little real danger of interference on the part of France in the internal affairs of the missions of Guiana. Their greatest peril would come from other quarters; it was the peril of Carib, Dutch, and English attacks. In 1740 the English sacked and burned two Spanish missions in this area. Others were destroyed by the Caribs and the Dutch—menaces which will be discussed at some length in a subsequent chapter—or even by the mission Indians themselves, so that it was necessary repeatedly to make new beginnings.[21]

It may be noted in passing that although the Hollanders began to found permanent establishments along the coast of Demerara and Essequibo soon after the opening of the seventeenth century, it was not until the middle of the eighteenth century that Dutch reports to their West India Company began to voice complaints regarding the Spanish settlements in the vicinity of the Orinoco. Governor Storm van's Gravesande wrote on July 20, 1746, to the Dutch West India Company concerning a report that the Spaniards had established a mission on the Cuyuní, where they had erected a small fort, and that they were engaged in manufacturing bricks with which they intended to construct another fort and mission some distance nearer the Essequibo.[22] In 1750 Governor van's Gravesande went to Holland, where he complained to the West India Company that the neighboring Spaniards were fortifying themselves everywhere under the pretext of establishing missions.[23] The Spaniards, he said, admitted that at least one of these reductions was established on Dutch territory and withdrew after van's Gravesande had written to the governor of Cumaná "requesting that he would cause that mission to remove from there, and adding that I should otherwise be compelled, though unwillingly, to use means which would certainly be disagreeable to him."[24]

III

José Diguja, governor of Cumaná, after visiting Guiana in 1761, made a report to the king on the condition of the province. He stated that the only Spanish settlement in Guiana was the fortified town of Santo Tomás de Guayana, although unsuccessful attempts had been made to establish the towns of Real Corona and Ciudad Real. There were, stated Diguja, sixteen missions under the Catalonian Capuchins, four under the Jesuits, and three under the direction of the Franciscans of Píritu.[25] In the same year Fray Fidel de Santo, prefect of the Catalonian Capuchins of Guiana, made a report tracing the development of these missions since 1724. According to him, there were in 1761 sixteen Capuchin missions having a population of 4,406. Since 1724 there had been 7,388 baptisms and 1,195 marriages according to the rites of the Catholic church. A total of 3,384 had died "in the communion of the Faithful." Eight missions had been destroyed, while 1,686 Indians had returned to the forest. The missions had experienced epidemics of smallpox in 1728 and 1742, and of measles in 1744. These misfortunes, together with a Carib invasion in 1735 and the English attack in 1740, had caused the death of 917 mission Indians.[26] Of the Capuchin missions Diguja wrote:

These Missions are most of them situated in very fertile lands, fresh, salubrious, abounding in water and well provided with all the necessary products fit for the maintenance of the Indians, except those of Suay, Arepuco, Caroní, and Piacoa, that are not salubrious nor abundant in eatables on account of their proximity to the Orinoco river and sandy ground. The houses of all the settlements are built with symmetry in extension and sufficiently convenient for the Indians. The three churches, although poor, are very clean and capacious, the same as the house of the pastor close to the church.[27] *

* The English translations in this source are awkward, but they have been quoted literally. The Spanish originals have not been available.

153

Diguja advised the king to assign to these missions enough money to support twenty-five to thirty missionaries and to provide them with bells and ornaments for the churches and an armed escort of thirty soldiers.[28] He pointed out that the missions were not only performing a great service to God by evangelizing the natives, but that they constituted a bulwark against the Dutch.[29]

According to a report of Manuel Centurión, there were in 1771 in the province of Guiana thirty-two towns of Indians and Spaniards with a population of over eight thousand. This seems a very small population for so large an area, but the figures do not include the wild Indians, whose numbers could not be accurately determined.[30] Diguja's figures reveal that the average population of the towns was only two hundred and fifty, but the statistics kept by the Capuchins indicate that they were larger than this. The following figures show the size of the reduction villages of the Catalonian Capuchins in this region: [31]

Caroní	393	Carapo	507
Alta-gracia	519	Miamo	512
Cupapuy	461	Palmar	407
San Antonio	316	Caruachi	78
Santa María	333	Murucure	338
Divina Pastora	315	Monte Calvario	406
Ayma	397	Tupuquén	369
Guasipati	440	Cumamu	290

The Capuchin padres in Guiana kept detailed statistics relative to their converts. The figures showing the sex and marital status of the reduction Indians are especially interesting. They indicate a large percentage of married people. The Spanish missionaries usually encouraged early marriage. The number of widowers was less than the number of widows, which may indicate that the death rate among married men was higher than among married women. This is a reasonable conjecture, since the men engaged in the rather hazardous activities of hunting, fishing, and traveling through regions infested with snakes and other dangerous animals. It is more probable, however, that the widowers married sooner than the widows, thus again entering the married class. It is noticeable that in the majority of missions the number of boys exceeded the number of girls. While this may indicate a higher death rate among girls, suggesting that infanticide of girl babies may not have been entirely suppressed, it is more likely that the padres began to classify "girls" as "single women" at an earlier age than they classified "boys" as "single men."

The following are statistics for the populations of four of the Guiana missions in 1799: [32]

MISSION OF PURÍSIMA CONCEPCIÓN DE CARONÍ

Married men	160
Married women	160
Widowers	8
Widows	15
Single men	96
Single women	90
Boys	70
Girls	60
Total population	659

MISSION OF NUESTRA SEÑORA DE LOS ANGELES DE YACUARIO

Married men	134
Married women	134
Widowers	4
Widows	24
Single men	38
Single women	34
Boys	96
Girls	76
Total population	540

MISSION OF SAN JOSÉ DE CUPAPUY

Married men	210
Married women	210
Widowers	4
Widows	30
Single men	25
Single women	24
Boys	193
Girls	180
Total population	876

MISSION OF SAN FRANCISCO DE ALTA-GRACIA

Married men	207
Married women	207
Widowers	10
Widows	13
Single men	50
Single women	56
Boys	200
Girls	203
Total population	946

IV

Theoretically the land, buildings, and herds on the Guiana missions belonged to the Indians,[33] and in practice the natives did have the use of the products of the lands, but the farms and ranches were entirely under the control of the missionaries. It would be more nearly correct to say that the Capuchins owned the material property, which they employed, like benevolent despots, for the benefit of the natives. The cultivated land was divided into three types of farms: those for the common benefit, those for the special benefit of the padres, and those for the particular use of the Indians or of other non-ecclesiastical inhabitants of the reduction.[34] Since the royal appropriation of one hundred and fifty pesos annually was not regularly paid, the padres were mainly dependent on income from the farms and ranches. They regularly sold some of the produce of the missions (there was a good market for mules), and with the receipts they purchased from the distant ports of Cumaná and La Guaira such articles as linen, flour to make the host for Mass, axes, machetes, and trinkets. They had to import directly from Europe, or from one of the ports of entry in America, such commodities as wine, olive oil, adornments for the churches, cloth for their habits, books, and cocoa. Large shipments of salt, used mainly in preserving meat, were imported from Trinidad.[35]

The mission Indians were required to work on the common lands three days a week from six o'clock until ten o'clock in the morning. The rest of the time they might employ in cultivating their own land. This arrangement hardly implies that the padres enslaved the Indians, as they have been accused of doing. The natives received wages for their work on the common lands, and the income from these farms, after the Indians had been paid, was used for the support of the mission. Each family of natives was permitted to have personal property and to sell products of its own manufacture, such as turtle oil, wax, hammocks, and a fever medicine called "Angostura Bitters" (*Amargo de Angostura*). The Indians also cured hides, made shoes and harness, and manufactured soap, bricks, and tiles.[36] The Indian women on the Guiana reductions were required to spin and weave as well as to make candles and hammocks.[37] In order that there might be a local supply of raw material, the missionaries taught the Indians to cultivate cotton.[38] The neophytes were obliged to construct not only their own houses, but the church, the padre's dwelling,* and the "royal house," which was used for the reception of travelers.[39]

---

* The cattle and horse ranches of the Capuchins of Guiana are discussed in Chapter XIX.

The Capuchin missionaries of Guiana were not strict in their observance of fasts, penance, and other mortifications commonly practiced by members of their order in Europe. They were not particular about refraining from eating meat on Fridays. They wore the same habit that was used in Europe except that it was made of light cloth, frequently uncolored. Their legs were bare, and on their feet they wore slippers instead of the customary sandals. When traveling, they usually rode horseback, since much of this country was fairly open, and they went armed with pistols and sabres [40]— a pretty picture for a man of God, reminding one of the stories of frontier preachers in the United States who were said to place a pair of "six-shooters" on the altar before beginning their exhortations. By the middle of the eighteenth century the missionaries in Guiana had learned through hard experience that heaven best protects the padre who goes armed with baser weapons than crucifixes.

An advocate of the Capuchin friars of this region was Don Eugenio Alvarado, a member of the commission that went to the upper Orinoco about 1756 to determine, together with a Portuguese commission, the boundary between the Spanish and Portuguese possessions. He spent several months in 1755 on the Guiana missions, and praised the practical hard-headedness of the padres, who knew how to combine business acumen with sincere apostolic zeal:

Thus, had they not accumulated gains for their maintenance, they would not have been able to subsist from want of the necessaries of life, nor to help their churches, as was the case before the coming of said Fathers, in 1724. There is no doubt that the good management of these men, especially the late Fray Thomas de Santa Engracia, and the present Prefect, Fray Benito de Moya, has won many souls for Heaven, and to a certain extent fertilized the Province of Guayana. I shall not inquire whether their vows of poverty have been legitimately

suspended by the Apostolic Bulls, thus permitting the law of nature to prevail over that of God. But politically speaking, and having in mind their beautiful maxims of government, I find them deserving the renown of the most illustrious worthies, in the same manner as their religion in Catalonia has merited, among others [i.e., other characterizations] that of holy.[41]

Some of these padres must have been effective preachers and sincere followers of Christ as well as men skilled in worldly affairs. It was not unusual to see their converts in the Guiana churches touching their faces to the floor or beating their chests, an indication that they were profoundly moved—unless they hoped by this procedure to influence the missionaries to give them preferential treatment.[42] Fray José de Carabantes told how an Indian woman about a hundred and fifty years old was carried over fifty miles on the shoulders of natives in order to receive baptism before she died.[43] At least one of these padres observed a practice that expressed a humility by no means common even among Spanish frontier missionaries. Fray Joachim María de Martorel wrote to his superior April 16, 1770: "Greeting in the Lord. I spent three days of Holy Week in Hupata, where I went on Wednesday afternoon, after having washed the feet of 12 Indians and fed them in this (town) of Cupapuy." The answer came back: "Greeting. It has been hinted to me that Your Reverence has washed the feet of the *Cimarrones* (savage Indians). It is something that has never been put in practice in these Missions." [44]

V

The control of the missions was so complicated that it is not surprising that the missionaries and the lay officials at times had disputes. During the early years of a frontier mission, the friars were ordinarily dominant on the reductions. Nevertheless, the governors of provinces and the bishops had the right to visit the missions when they wished and to intervene in important matters. As a consequence, the missionaries might be given orders by either of these officials. In addition to these two dignitaries, the padres of Guiana owed allegiance to a prefect of missions, whom they elected every third year, after praying for the assistance of the Holy Ghost, at the reduction of Suay.[45] The friars had beneath them Indian officers to assist in the supervision of the missions. With the aid of these native officials the padres closely supervised the lives of their wards, even requiring them to marry within their reductions.[46] The Indian officials were not permitted to have an independent voice in the government. They carried out the directions of the missionaries or gave advice and aid when requested to do so. They preserved order and saw to it that the neophytes punctually performed their tasks. Their titles were captain, lieutenant, justice of the peace, sergeant, adjutant, fiscal, and constable.[47]

In 1771 the Capuchins became embroiled in a bitter quarrel with Don Manuel Centurión, the commandant-general of Guiana. Centurión claimed that the missionaries were unruly and that they insisted on controlling the civil and financial, as well as the religious, affairs of the missions. On July 29, 1771, he wrote:

What is quite certain is that these Fathers proceed in all without obedience and humility, for they always oppose the orders of the Governor-General of this Province. They will not even submit to those of the Diocesan Ordinary, not even when they reside here as parish priests and chaplains. . . . No official has the courage to oppose them; and thus they consider themselves masters not only of all the villages which they instruct, for there are some that were founded in the last century, and even these they do not wish to see taken over, nor hand them over to the Ordinary, unless on the understanding that, as constituting an ecclesiastical administration, they are allowed to

161

manage and freely apply to their own use the produce of the plantations and the Indian communities without the knowledge of the Government, nor giving any account to anybody of these properties.[48]

Centurión further claimed that the soldiers of the escort were the ones who really converted the Indians and built the missions, supervising the construction of the church and other buildings while the missionaries did nothing. When the new village was completed and the Indians comfortably settled, the friars would boast of how they had founded the reduction. The commandant-general accused the Capuchins of exploiting the Indians like slaves while making it appear that they were defenders of the natives, and of vilifying him if he so much as asked for information for the purpose of correcting abuses.

The Capuchins naturally claimed that Centurión was distorting the facts. The procurator of the Capuchin missions wrote from Spain to the provincial of the Catalonian Capuchins concerning the affair (August 8, 1771):

It is not possible to give Your Reverence in writing an exact idea of these persecutions, whereof we are every day the victims, of this Minister, and there is yet more than a year to run of the five in which they usually remain in the Government. Add to this that he now wields absolute power, with no subordination to that of Caracas; what will he not do? And all this under the pretext of its being the best service of the King; his sole object is to get great credit for himself at our cost and to our detriment.[49]

The dispute dragged on for several years. The commandant-general wished to place civil officers (corregidores) in the missions to govern them. A cédula of July 6, 1774, stated that Centurión had gone too far in imputing to the Capuchins excesses which they had not committed.[50] That official subsequently made a complaint to the viceroy at Bogotá, accusing the Capuchins of insubordination. The viceroy ordered that the missions on the Caroní should pay to the government a tenth of their harvests, and that civil administrators should be appointed to oversee the collection. When the commandant-general proceeded to place these officers on the missions, the Capuchins sent Father Jaime de Puigcerdá to Madrid to place their views before the Council of the Indies.[51] The king, by a decree of November 10, 1774, ordered Centurión to withdraw the corregidores, leave unchanged the internal administration of the missions, and refrain from persecuting the missionaries.[52]

VI

In 1773 Centurión made a report on the missions in Guiana. According to his statistics there were in all the region thirteen towns of Spaniards and mixbloods with a population of 4,386; eleven towns under the Observant Franciscans with a population of 1,718; thirty towns belonging to the Andalusian Capuchins with a population of 2,990; twenty towns belonging to the Catalonian Capuchins with a population of 6,832; five missions that had been taken away from the Jesuits with a population of 1,492. He stated that forty-three of these towns had been established during the years 1766 to 1773 with a consequent addition of 8,558 persons to the mission population.[53] These statistics do not harmonize with the view of the viceroy of New Granada, Pedro Messía de la Cerda, who reported in 1772 that the missions of New Granada had not done well for a century.[54]

Miguel Marmión, the governor of Guiana, in his report to the secretary of state for the Department of the Indies on July 10, 1778, gave a pessimistic view of the Capuchin missions:

The missions conducted by the Catalonian Capuchin Fathers, comprising thirteen thousand Indians of different nations, situated in the most important, best cared for, and most fertile part of this continent, notwithstanding their antiquity, are still to be classed among the newly subjugated, and with very remote chances of their reaching the state of civilization which is desired, however much the pious Fathers may exert themselves in bringing to their knowledge (so important to them) a social and Christian life. For, not having any individual landed property and contenting themselves with cultivation on a small scale of corn, *casabe*, and some roots for their necessary sustenance, they look upon everything else with repugnance, and as a subjugation from which they flee as well as they can to give themselves up to idleness and to licentiousness. . . .[55]

Francisco de Saavedra, intendant-general of Caracas, reported on February 21, 1785, that the province of Guiana was no longer able to bear the burden of the ten or twelve thousand pesos required to pay the armed escorts on the missions in that province. He proposed that each town should plant corn, rice, and manioc every year for the purpose of securing funds to pay the soldiers, and that later cacao plantations should be established for this purpose.[56]

In the 1790's it was still difficult to keep the converts firmly settled on the missions. In 1792 eight hundred Indians fled from the village of Cura and from the neighboring reductions. Only twenty natives were left at Cura. Some of the fugitives returned, reporting that they had fled because the infidel savages in the forest had threatened to kill them. In the opinion of Don Pedro de Lerena, an official of the royal treasury, the best way to solve this difficulty was to persuade European families to immigrate and settle in the villages so as to exert a moderating influence on the converts.[57] At this time many of the mission Indians were inveterate drunkards. Men and women often refused to wear clothes, preferring to flee rather than be burdened with more raiment than the guayuco. Some had not confessed or received the sacrament at Easter for ten years.[58]

164

The Guiana Missions

On September 7, 1797, the intendant of Caracas, Don Esteban Fernández de León, reported to the king that the natives on the missions were still as rude and as ignorant of religion and industry as they had been on first being reduced. He charged that the missionaries of Guiana would not permit their Indians to speak the Spanish language. The prefect of the Capuchin missions in Guiana countered with the statement that the mission Indians were more advanced than the Indians in the capital of the province, that they spoke Spanish more frequently than their native languages, and that there were among them skilled shoemakers, carpenters, weavers, blacksmiths, tile-makers, and tanners.[59]

Humboldt gives, on the whole, a favorable picture of the missions of Guiana and the upper Orinoco, stating that the reductions of the Catalonian Capuchins at the time of his visit (about 1800) had a population of 17,000, while the missions of the Observant Franciscans were inhabited by 7,300 souls. According to him all the missions from the lower Orinoco to the Río Negro were practically closed to white people who were not members of the religious orders, so that the natives called every white man, "Padre." [60]

The wars for independence sounded the death knell for these missions. In 1816 the Capuchins had twenty-nine reductions and 21,142 neophytes in Guiana.[61] The patriot officer, General Piar, forced the mission Indians into the revolutionary army. In order to escape military service, many of the Indians fled from the reductions; and in a short time most of the country reverted to a state similar to that of two centuries earlier.[62] One of the worst blots on the record of the South American revolutionaries was the execution of the Guiana missionaries. When General Piar invaded the Caroní reductions on February 2, 1817, he captured thirty-four padres and carried them to the settlement of Caruache. Fourteen of them died in prison of smallpox and other natural causes. The other twenty were massacred on May 7, 1817; their bodies were burned, and the ashes thrown into a river. Five missionaries and two nurses (*enfermeros*) had managed to escape. Thus were "destroyed in a moment the building that had cost them so many years of labors and so many lives of Missionaries cut down while in flower, the churches, the houses and haciendas sacked, the herds decimated, the towns incited to revolt. . . ." [63]

The missions of Guiana were divided into five districts in 1820 by a decree of the Congress of Angostura, but by this time they had almost ceased to exist. [64] In 1821 the Republic of Colombia promulgated decrees entirely suppressing all Venezuelan missions. [65] Later, Simón Bolívar tried to reverse this action by publishing decrees on July 10, 1826, and September 10 and 18, 1828, ordering that steps be taken to restore them; but by this time the majority of friars had either died or returned to Spain. [66]

The fate of the mission village of Santa María de Yacuario was that of many others. Its rise and fall are shown by the following figures: [67]

1730	founded	
1788	481	inhabitants
1791	512	"
1803	570	"
1816	661	"
1820	256	"
1833	37	"
1846	35	"
1849	0	"

At present there are at the site of this mission only some shelters that serve as resting places for carriers. Natives in the vicinity have made excavations in search of buried treasure, but have been able to find little except a crucifix of yellow metal. At the town of Divina Pastora,[68] which had 145,000 head of cattle during the days of the Capuchin padres, one will now find only a few huts and a small chapel.*

* Mary W. Waters, in her *History of the Church of Venezuela* (Chapel Hill, 1933), pp. 4-31, presents an excellent brief discussion of the Catholic missions in Venezuela during the colonial period.

THE MISSIONS OF THE UPPER ORINOCO

I

ESUIT Fathers Antonio Castán and Antonio Monteverde, about the year 1670, established missions among the Salivas on the Orinoco above the mouth of the Meta, but these reductions were ordered to be abandoned in 1675 because of the danger of Carib attacks. Four years later Fathers Ignacio Fiol and Felipe Gómez went down the Casanare and the Meta rivers to the Orinoco, and after visiting certain Indian villages near the debouchure of the Meta, rowed for several days up the Orinoco, discovering a multitude of savages, all of whom spoke similar dialects. They then returned to the Llanos of San Juan, where Gómez remained, while Fiol went up to Bogotá to inform the superiors of the Society of Jesus of their discoveries and to make reports to the audiencia and the archbishop.

A decision to send missionaries to the upper Orinoco was soon reached, and a request was sent to Spain for additional Black Robes to carry the Gospel to this remote region. Some missionaries designated for this field left Cádiz on January 28, 1681, and arrived at the port of Cartagena on April 2 of the same year. Arriving at Bogotá after a tedious trip up the Magdalena, they remained for a while in the capital to recuperate, although Father Ignacio's account of the Orinoco country "resounded in their ears like war trumpets when they call to arms."

The Jesuits sent to the Orinoco at this time were Ignacio Fiol, Cristóbal Radiel, Gaspar Bek, Agustín Campos, and Julián Vergara. On reaching their ultimate destination these five padres were cordially received by the Indians, who were so docile that within a short period the missionaries were able to found five villages. They not only catechized and baptized the natives, but built churches and houses, planted maize and yucca, and a short time later introduced the raising of cattle. In 1683 Father Ignacio Teobast, who had recently arrived from Flanders, went down from the New Granadan capital to take the place of Campos, who returned to the missions of the llanos.

But the time for the harvest had not yet arrived. The year 1684 was a tragic one for this field. Radiel was drowned; Fiol, Teobast, and Bek were killed when a band of almost two hundred Caribs attacked the missions; and the reductions were temporarily abandoned.[1]

Between that date and 1691 the superiors of the Society of Jesus refused to send missionaries to the upper Orinoco region. In November, 1691, however, Fathers Alonso de Neira, José Cavarte, Vicente Loberzo, and José de Silva were dispatched to this area with an escort of twelve soldiers. Since the archbishop of Bogotá was an enemy of the Jesuits, he influenced the governor of the Llanos of San Juan to suspend the pay of the escort. The result was that all the soldiers except Captain Tiburcio deserted the padres. Nevertheless, the missionaries and the captain proceeded to their destination, and found that the Indians were loath to settle again, since there were no white soldiers to protect them from Carib raids. The suffering of one of these padres is described in a letter written by Father Vicente Loberzo to the provincial of the Jesuit order, in which he says:

In one of these incursions necessity reached such an extreme that I had by great fortune and largess to maintain myself by eating worms, mice, ants, and lizards, there being added to these labors the whisperings among the Indians who guided me that the Caribs were near; the guides hid among the lakes and morasses to escape their ferocity, and from this it followed that they became sick, and some died because of the infectious and fetid nature of the water, and the same would have happened to me if I had permitted their advice to direct me.[2]

Captain Tiburcio and Father Vicente were soon murdered by the Caribs, but Fathers Neira and Silva managed to escape by hiding in the forest. In danger of starvation, they started for the missions of Casanare. After walking for a number of days, they reached the Meta, where they began to construct a canoe. While they were engaged in this task, a party of Spaniards bound for Casanare came along and rescued them. Arriving at the Puerto de San Salvador de Casanare, they told of the peril in which they had left Father José Cavarte; and six soldiers were sent forthwith to bring him to safety. The Caribs were on the point of attacking the padre's mission when the soldiers reached it, and the seven Spaniards returned at once to the older missions. Thus, in 1695, ended the second attempt to found permanent reductions on the upper Orinoco, ended "without the attainment of any more fruit by this entrada than that the enemies remained more obstinate in their hostilities and insolence."[3]

II

In 1733 the Jesuits proceeded once more from the Meta-Casanare region to the Carib-infested Orinoco, and within a short time founded five or six reductions. The most active of these Jesuit missionaries were Padre Manuel Román and the famous Gumilla.

In 1734 an agreement was made dividing the Orinoco Valley between the Jesuits, the Capuchins, and the Observant Franciscans. The pact was the work of the orders themselves, and was not imposed upon them by the secular authorities. The jurisdictions of these orders were to be separated by meridians running through Angostura—the location of the modern town of Ciudad Bolívar—and the mouth of the Cuchivero River. The country east of Angostura was apportioned to the Capuchins, that between the Angostura and Cuchivero meridians to the Observant Franciscans, and that to the west of the Cuchivero meridian to the Jesuits. The territories of these three orders were to reach from the Orinoco southward to the Amazon, for the missionaries ignored the Portuguese claims to territory north of the mighty river. This agreement was fully approved and ratified by a royal cédula of September 16, 1736,[4] and Governor Gregorio Espinosa de los Monteros of Guiana stated in 1743 that according to its terms each order had a monopoly of the conversion of natives within its jurisdiction. Once a group of Indians had been reduced by members of one religious order, they were not to migrate to the territory under the jurisdiction of another, and each order bound itself to return any Indians that might come to its missions from the reductions of the other.[5]

The provisions of this agreement were not closely observed. Since the boundaries were not actually surveyed, the padres encroached on each other's territory and boundary changes were made from time to time by local arrangement. More-over, the pact did not mention the Dominican order, which founded missions along the tributaries of the Apure, and the missionaries could hardly extend their activities far southward toward territory claimed by the Portuguese without coming into conflict with the representatives of that country, especially with the slavers from Pará.

By 1749 the Jesuits had on the Orinoco above the mouth of the Cuchivero thirteen flourishing reductions guarded by an escort of only fifty soldiers,[6] and shortly before their expulsion the Society had in charge the following missions in the region: [7]

MISSION	POPULATION
Carichana	400
San Borja	330
Cabruta	400
Uriana [Urbana?]	600
El Raudal [de Maipures]	300
La Encaramada	290

Territorial disputes with Portugal and the survey of the boundary between Spanish America and Brazil led to renewed emphasis upon the work of the missionaries in the upper Orinoco region. The Spanish commissioners who had charge of the survey in the north founded four civil settlements along the headwaters of the Orinoco and the Negro, and urgently requested the aid of the padres. In 1764 the Capuchin fathers were designated for the new field, and José Antonio Jerez, who had led an expedition of three Capuchins up the river as far as the southernmost Jesuit outpost three years before, became the moving spirit of the undertaking. In February, 1766, he arrived with five companions at Maipures. None of them except Jerez was accustomed to the extremely hot and unhealthful climate of the region, but they set about their task

*The undaunted Father Jerez continued his apostolic labors,
journeying down the Orinoco*

with great courage and persistence and founded six missions
within the next three years. Two of the friars soon died,
however, and the three others, almost exhausted by privations
and sufferings, returned to the Llanos of Caracas. The region
seemed to defy their redemptive talents.

Father Jerez, undaunted by the departure of his brothers,
continued his apostolic labors in company with the little group
of Spaniards who were surveying the boundary. He
journeyed down the Orinoco to the Casiquiare, followed the
latter to the Río Negro, and descended the Negro for some
distance in order to reconnoitre the Portuguese fortifications.
At Fort San José de los Maribitanos he was courteously received by the commander, who gave him information regarding Portuguese activities in the region. He was now almost
two thousand miles from Caracas—a journey of two months
or more by land and water. He also ascended the Negro for

several leagues and discovered a new route between that point and the junction of the Orinoco and the Guaviare.

III

The departure of the Jesuits in 1767 cleared the field for further activities in this region on the part of the Franciscans. Father José asked repeatedly for more Capuchin missionaries to take charge of the six reductions left by the Black Robes and to continue the work of conversion among the Indians of the distant southern selvas. According to his report, the Caribs and Dutch were molesting some of the natives of the upper Orinoco, who were now begging to be reduced and protected from the slavers. While exploring the Orinoco above its junction with the Casiquiari, he had observed a large number of cacao trees, which he hoped would become the foundation for a prosperous economic life in the missions which he intended to establish. He suggested that with the reduction of the natives and the introduction of Spanish settlers, a thriving commerce could be developed. In this manner, he insisted, the civilization of the natives and "the greater service of God" would be promoted. Utilitarian considerations would move His Majesty's vassals to introduce themselves with merchandise, and "mutual convenience" would "unite the savages to the Spaniards." [8]

In June, 1769, an expedition of nineteen Capuchin missionaries left Seville for the missions of the Llanos of Caracas, where they were to become acclimated before proceeding to the Upper Orinoco. In October of the following year seventeen of these set out from the Venezuelan capital, crossed the plains to the Orinoco, proceeded up that river, and met Padre Jerez at the mission of Maipures. The villages recently taken away from the Jesuits were to be placed under the care of some of these friars, while the rest were to aid Father José in extending the boundaries of his field.

But they were soon to suffer severe vexations. Don Manuel Centurión of Guiana, whose civil authority extended also into the region of the upper Orinoco, wished to secularize the former Jesuit missions. He accordingly refused to turn the reductions over to the Capuchins, prevented their collection of the stipend allotted to them, and declined to permit them to have Indian servants even when they were ill. Father Andrés Cádiz, who was elected prefect of this field in 1771, complained bitterly of the conduct of Centurión, declaring that the padres had suffered more from the oppression of this official than from all their privations and all the afflictions of the torrid and unhealthful climate. He said that Centurión had usurped the powers of the prefect, and referred to Don Manuel as "this second tyrant Aguirre,* who has us dying of hunger, without succor of any kind or liberty to seek it." "It is possible," added Father Andrés, "that this man wishes to make us appear solely responsible for all these disasters, but there is a God who sees all." [9]

In 1771 two of the Capuchin missionaries returned to the Llanos of Caracas to report to the prefect of this field regarding the hardships through which they had passed. They went on to the city of Caracas, where they laid their complaints before the bishop and the captain general. Since they were weak and ill, they were allowed to remain for some time in the capital. The outcome of the dispute was the removal of the Capuchin padres from the upper Orinoco and the suppression of this prefecture by the Council of the Indies, apparently

---

* The reference is to the notorious Lope de Aguirre, who had started with an expedition under Pedro de Ursúa down the Amazon, had killed his leader, and, after finding his way to the Atlantic, had attempted in 1561 to make himself master of the Northern coast of Venezuela (Henao and Arrubla, *op. cit.*, pp. 176-78).

with the approval of the high Capuchin authorities themselves. Of the seventeen missionaries who left Caracas for the Alto Orinoco in 1769, five died on the missions, four returned to Spain, one went by way of the Amazon to Puerto Rico, and seven were transferred to other missions. The upper Orinoco reductions which had been in charge of the Jesuits prior to 1767 were soon given to the Observant Franciscans of the College of Píritu. According to Centurión's report to the king in 1773, there were at this time in the area thirty-six small villages scattered along the Alto Orinoco, the Ventuari, the Casiquiare, the Negro, and other rivers. Perhaps half of them had been founded by the Observant Franciscans.[10] *

During the few years in which the Capuchins were in charge of the region they founded several settlements whose inhabitants gathered cacao for shipment down the river to Guiana, and some of the commodity eventually reached Germany, Spain, Italy, and France. Other products sold by these missions were beeswax, honey, and turtle lard.[11]

When Humboldt visited the upper Orinoco about 1800, the Capuchins were again established on these missions, and the noted scientist was favorably impressed by the friars. At San Fernando, San Baltazar, and Javita, he observed that the padres lived in well-constructed houses covered with vines and surrounded by gardens.[12] The missionaries were friendly, tolerant, and unusually broad-minded, although Humboldt's host at one of the villages argued insistently in favor of the slave trade and slavery, maintaining that Negroes were inherently wicked and that in a state of slavery they were in the best position to profit by contact with Christians. The

* Lodares says that all these missions were established by the Capuchins, but this seems to be an error. Some nineteen reductions listed in the map at the end of his third volume, namely those stretching southward from the upper valley of the Ventuari, are clearly in the area allotted to the Observant Franciscans by the pact of 1734.

padres exhibited a keen interest in what was happening in the outside world, particularly "on the other side of the pool" (Europe).[13] Humboldt thought that the prospects of future success in these reductions were bright, but he was unable to foresee the revolution.

Father J. A. Zahm, comparing the status of these missions in the twentieth century with their condition during Humboldt's visit, says:

Now all this is changed. If he could return to the scene of his famous exploration he would not be able to locate even the site of many of the missions where he was so kindly entertained and of whose hospitality he writes in terms of such unstinted praise. From Ciudad Bolívar to San Carlos on the Río Negro—a distance of nearly a thousand miles—he would not find more than one or two at most.[14]

THE DUTCH AND CARIB MENACE

I

ADRES of Spain on the Dutch and Portuguese frontiers had to contend with the opposition of the nationals of these powers and their native allies, as well as with the numerous other difficulties universally encountered among savage Indians in inhospitable regions. In the lower Orinoco valley the combination of Dutch slavers and Carib warriors presented a constant menace to the missions of the Spanish friars. In their relations with the Portuguese the padres possessed several advantages: the two Iberian languages were sufficiently similar for the rivals to understand each other fairly well; the vast majority of the Portuguese were Roman Catholics; the Jesuits operating under the two flags were subject to the orders of one general, and, if they were "professed of the Four Vows," they acknowledged allegiance directly to the pope. In fact, some attempts were made on the part of the higher officers of the Society of Jesus to coördinate the activities of the Portuguese and Spanish Jesuits in South America according to a continental plan. In the relations between Spaniards and Hollanders, however, none of these ameliorat-

ing circumstances existed. Besides the great difference in language, the political rivalry, and the commercial competition, there was the religious hatred which during the Spanish colonial period in South America existed between Catholics and Protestants.

With the possible exception of the Araucanians and the Chiriguanos, the Caribs were the most ferocious natives on the continent. In addition to hunting, fishing, and engaging in a little crude farming, they regularly raided the territory of the neighboring Indians. They robbed, enslaved, and killed. Commonly believed to be cannibals, the Caribs were hated and feared by the other tribes. They were accustomed to assert that they alone were human beings, while the other Indians were born for slavery. As to the origin of the Caribs, the Salivas said that the great god Puru had sent his son from heaven to kill a horrible snake that was accustomed to murder and devour the people of the Orinoco valley. This son conquered and killed the serpent to the great joy of all the tribes; but what was their horror to perceive that as the reptile putrified, hideous worms were formed in it, each of which gave birth to a Carib warrior and his wife! The Achaguas believed that the Caribs were descendants of jaguars.[1] A Carib was said to have come to Father Joseph de Gumilla to ask permission to go out on a man-killing expedition, and when the padre objected, the savage was reported to have replied: "My Father, I have to slay men; for that are we born. I am valiant, and I like meat, and thus with great humility do I ask permission. You must give it to me, because you perceive certainly that I am to kill people and eat their flesh." The missionary was unable to persuade him that such conduct was a crime.[2] Despite their fierce cruelty and appetite for human flesh, however, the Caribs were a people who possessed more promising qualities than the average tropical Indian. They were brave, resourceful, aggressive, and intelligent, and they made long speeches that were seldom obscure or confused. Humboldt expressed the view that they were capable of a high degree of civilization.[3]

II

These fiendish savages became tools in the hands of the Dutch settlers in Guiana. The Hollanders employed them as catchers of slaves for their plantations in the vicinity of the Essequibo; and the Caribs carried on a very profitable business raiding the settlements of the Indians of the interior, including the Spanish missions. At one time, when the demand for slaves was evidently brisk, the Caribs received for each able-bodied male slave a box containing ten knives, ten machetes, ten axes, ten bundles of glass beads, a piece of French linen, a mirror, and some scissors. In addition to this, they received some brandy, a gun with powder and balls, and supplies of pins and fishhooks. They frequently managed to buy slaves in the interior for a small part of what they received from the Dutch, possibly a healthy adult for a machete, an axe, or a few trinkets. They procured the majority of their slaves, however, by force instead of by purchase.[4] Often these Indian slavers went on their expeditions alone, but occasionally they were accompanied by Hollanders, who sometimes went disguised as Indians. The Dutch commonly made their incursions during the dry season. According to Father Caulín there was a brisk demand for Indian women:

The men they sell as slaves to the Hollanders of Essequibo, where they are condemned to perpetual slavery of soul and body, living and dying without the light of faith, as blind as their masters. The women they use for the service of their persons and as pabulum for their uncontrolled passions, robbing them of the best jewel of the soul, and the precious treasure of purity. . . .[5]

While the Dutch and Caribs engaged in a profitable commerce in humanity, the Jews of Surinam were the most skillful slave traders of them all. The Caribs were almost constantly in debt to these Semitic bargainers, so that they were obliged to engage in manhunts even when they preferred to be idle. When Father Gumilla wrote to the governor of Essequibo in 1733 complaining of the damages that the missions had suffered at the hands of the slavers, the Dutch officer courteously replied that he was unable to remedy the situation, claiming that all blame should be placed on the Surinam Jews, who secretly supplied the Caribs with arms.[6]

The Dutch were not ignorant of the advantages of a peaceful commerce with the Spaniards. As early as 1682 some trade was being carried on between the rival colonies, the principal items of commerce being axes, knives, and sky-blue beads, which were in great demand among the Spanish settlers.[7] Indians as far away as the Marañón were able to obtain firearms from the Dutch with which to resist the Portuguese.[8]

Nor was Dutch commerce with the Indians altogether unethical. Besides encouraging them to capture slaves, the Hollanders pointed out to the natives certain products of the forest which possessed economic value: gums, oils, resins, medicinal plants, valuable woods, and fruits.[9] Some Hollanders even hoped to persuade the Caribs to raise cotton, indigo, sugar, ginger, hops, and dyestuffs, and to engage in the mining of gold and silver. And there were Dutchmen who doubtless thought sincerely that they were doing a service not only to themselves, but to the Indians and to civilization in general, by encroaching upon the monopoly which the Spaniards were trying to maintain in Venezuela. William Usselinx, the merchant prince of Antwerp, spoke thus of the possibility of Protestant evangelization in America: "Besides the worldly blessings, it was to be hoped also that such a trade would conduce to the honor and praise of God, inasmuch as the saving faith and the gospel of our Lord Jesus Christ could thus in the course of time be transplanted thither. . . ."[10] It was the opinion of the French traveler, Depons, that Dutch popularity with the Caribs was due mainly to the fact that they refrained from bothering the savages with religion and embarrassing questions of morality, allowing them to retain their barbarous customs without interference and apologizing for, instead of criticizing, their habits and manners.[11]

In their encouragement of the slave trade, the Dutch encountered the opposition of the Spanish friars. The frontier padres, who were such staunch defenders of the Indians against exploitation by Spanish encomenderos, could hardly have been expected to look upon the Dutch commerce in Indians with indifference. They were implacable enemies of the transplanted burghers of the Low Countries. The basis of their enmity was more than a matter of sentiment or the ancient hatred of Catholics for Protestants. It was absolutely necessary that the missionaries defend their wards if they were to preserve their missions; for otherwise the reduction Indians would flee to safety along the upper reaches of the Casanare and the Meta. Since the best way to protect their neophytes was to close the rivers which were the only convenient routes between coast and reductions, the missionaries advocated the construction of fortifications along the streams.[12]

III

The Dutch, both because of opposition by the padres to what they considered a legitimate commerce and because of the political and religious rivalry of Holland and Spain, encouraged their Carib allies to attack the Spanish missions.

In the lower Orinoco basin Spanish Capuchin missionaries were established, as we have observed, not only on the banks of the Orinoco, but also in neighboring regions on the Corentyn, the Barima, the Wainy, the Marocco, the Pumaron, the Essequibo, the Cayenne, the Caroní, the Cuyuní, and the Massaruni. In all these sections the missions were a threat to Dutch commerce and territorial claims.[13] The Caribs who made the attacks on the missions were of two kinds: first, wild savages who in their search for human prey found the missions a barrier; second, Caribs who had once been reduced but who, finding the restricted life on the reductions too dull for their fierce character, had returned to the forests, often leaving behind them mutilated padres and burning villages.[14] The Caribs especially hated mission Indians because the converts refused to coöperate with them by capturing members of weak tribes for sale to the slavers. Sometimes Dutch adventurers participated in the attacks of the Carib slavers on the missions. According to José Joaquín Borda,

The Hollanders established in Guiana, enemies at once of Catholicism and of the Spanish name, not only waged war directly on the new towns, but made an alliance with the Caribs, from whom they bought oils and drugs as well as slaves, giving them in exchange trifles and firearms, in the use of which they instructed them. These nomadic and fierce Indians disturbed the reductions for a long time, coming against them in squadrons of canoes and many times led by Dutchmen disguised as Indians, that is to say, naked and painted like them.[15]

The towns established by the Jesuits on the Orinoco were first attacked by the Caribs in 1684, when several padres were killed and the converts fled to the forest. In 1693 they again raided the missions, so that the reductions were temporarily abandoned. In 1723 a fort which the king of Spain had ordered to be constructed on the Orinoco for the defense of the missions was still unbuilt.[16] Between 1730 and 1775

Carib attacks on the Spanish missions occurred with a frequency that indicated that the Spanish lay authorities were either not sufficiently interested in the lower Orinoco and Guiana reductions to give them adequate protection or that the treasury was so nearly empty as to make impossible payment of salaries to much needed troops.

In 1735 the Caribs attacked the settlement of San Miguel de Richado, killing and capturing a large number of Christian Indians. In the same year they also attacked the mission of Miamo and killed the padre, two soldiers, and most of the native converts. Having shot Father Andrés López through the body, they struck him on the mouth with a wooden weapon and then hanged him. A few days later they attacked the colony of San Joseph de Otomacos, burned it, and forced the missionary and his neophytes to flee. After seeing the ruin of missions whose foundation had been accompanied by so much mental anguish and physical hardship, Father Joseph de Gumilla wrote to the king of Spain asking for aid against these attacks:

Though here set forth in a few words, these are bitter afflictions which have caused, and still cause, the missionary Fathers many tears; but their grief is no sooner . . . [abated] than they seek places of greater security, gather together the dispersed Indians, and form new Colonies, with the grievous obstacle of fierce and repeated assaults from the Caribs on the small guard which assists them; but with the evident protection of God and the firm hope that Your Majesty's pious zeal will put an end to these evils, the Jesuits, Franciscans, and Capuchins still stand firm on the Orinoco; and though they know the boldness of the Caribs will be daily increased by the encouragement they receive from the Dutch, the knowledge is so far from inspiring them with terror that many others at sight of their glorious labours desire to bear them company.[17]

The Spanish missions were a refuge for slaves who managed to escape from the Dutch plantations. It was positively against the policy of the padres to return any of these fugitives. In 1734 the governor of Essequibo wrote to the Dutch West India Company asking that it petition the States General to make representations to the king of Spain relative to the Orinoco missionaries' practice of giving asylum to slaves from the Dutch plantations. It was the governor's opinion that, since the success of some slaves in reaching the missions disrupted the morale of the rest and caused all to seek a chance to flee, it would be better for the Dutch to pay fifty guilders each for their return than to permit the fugitives to remain on the missions. He saw no reason why the Spanish authorities should object to their return, "since the Spaniards derive no other benefit from them, save that the priests teach them a little mumbling, and highly pride themselves on having made Christians of them." [18] There was another side, however, to the story of fugitive Indians. When the Spaniards on the Cuyuní River gave evidence of intending to move down the stream, and were making brick for the purpose of building a fort and mission below their older settlements, the wild Indians fled toward the Dutch settlements, asking the Hollanders for protection.[19]

The demand for slaves increased near the middle of the eighteenth century because of the entry of an increasing number of planters of different nationalities into the Dutch colony. When the Swedes also attempted to establish a settlement on the Venezuelan coast, the king of Spain ordered the governor of Cumaná to enlist the Capuchin missions in checking the movement.[20] By 1746 the demand for slaves was so great that the Dutch governor reported the Caribs were making their livelihood entirely by the slave trade.[21] The governor of Essequibo now found it to his interest to restrain these warlike savages. When the Spaniards founded a mission and a little fort on the Cuyuní, the Caribs feared that their slave trade would be interfered with and proposed to destroy the settlement. Governor Storm van's Gravesande held them in check, however, even though he was of the opinion that the mission was in Dutch territory, for he feared that the Spaniards would think the Hollanders had engineered the attack and would make reprisals. Nevertheless, he wrote: "It is very perilous for this colony to have such neighbors so close by, who in time of war would come and visit us overland; and, above all, the making of fortifications upon our land is in breach of all custom." [22] It was Gravesande's opinion that "It is urgently necessary that the limits of the Company's territory be known, in order successfully to oppose the continual approach of the neighboring Spaniards. . . . And, because the limits are unknown, we dare not openly oppose them as might very easily be done, by means of the Carib nation, their sworn enemies." [23]

By 1750 several missions had been established by the Spanish padres among the Caribs, who proved for some time to be unruly neophytes. In that very year the Caribs on the five missions of Cunuri, Miamo, Tupuquén, Curumo, and Mutanambo revolted, killing four soldiers who were garrisoning them and eight other Spaniards. The next year some of the Caribs returned and told the missionary that they had acted under the leadership of a group of Hollanders. The special grievance that had caused this attack was the location of the Curumo mission, which the Dutch considered to be either on or dangerously near their territory. In January, 1751, the Caribs raided three Spanish missions and killed four or five missionaries, and on August 4, 1752, Governor van's Gravesande reported that these savages had recently murdered the total population of two Spanish missions. A Hollander on the Orinoco wrote on August 19, 1754, to the Essequibo colony warning the settlers that the Spaniards were planning an attack on the Dutch as reprisal for these Carib outrages.[24] And on October 12, 1754, van's Gravesande reported to the West India Company:

All the Caribs have also been warned to keep themselves ready and armed, but I find this warning in no instance necessary, since I have learned from one of their Headmen who came to me last week the nation is furious with the Spaniards because they have located a Mission in Cayuní between them and the nation of the Panacays, and hereby try to hinder their communication with that nation, and entirely to prevent their whole Slave Trade. . . .[25]

The Caribs and Panacays made an alliance, surprised the mission, burned the buildings, and killed the padre and a dozen other Spaniards.

The Dutch postholder at Marocco in 1755 brought to Gravesande a letter which he had received from a Spanish missionary. The padre threatened that if the postholder did not return to him some Chiama Indians who had been living at the post for ten years, he would lead against him a force sufficient to take the Indians away.[26]

Fray Benito de la Garriga estimated in 1758 that the Caribs annually captured three hundred young Indians as slaves, while they killed each year over four hundred who were too old to be of value in the Dutch market. Of the former, some frequently managed to escape to the missions, and the fugitives might be recognized by the brand burned on their skin, "as the Essequibo Company orders that all the Indian slaves be iron-branded, under penalty of forfeiture." [27]

In retaliation for the attacks of Caribs and Dutch upon the missions, the Spaniards attempted to persuade the Negroes, who had escaped from slavery on the Dutch plantations to the safety of the interior, to attack their former masters.[28] And the Spanish padres sometimes went so far as to invade the Dutch posts. The postholder at Marocco reported in 1769 that this place had been visited by two padres accompanied by twelve soldiers:

[Approaching] the Post with a burning piece of wood, the Fathers came on shore with their black corporal, who immediately asked where were the Indians whom they had seen, and where my wife was. I replied that the Indians were at their house, and that my wife had fled in terror. But they said, "Your wife is in the forest with the Indians," and that it was our fault that they had found no people; . . . but if I would say where my wife was, that they would leave my wife one maid; but they seized immediately one maid caught under the gallery. . . . They have taken my two female slaves, . . . and two free maids. . . . My wife, who luckily came from their path without being seen, is at the Post half dead with fright. . . . They have removed property of mine, worth quite 100 guilders, that they found outside; but in the house they touched nothing.[29]

The Dutch postholder at Maykouny reported in 1769 that the Caribs in that vicinity were wearing clothes and that some of them had on garments and ornaments ordinarily worn by Spanish missionaries, the presumption being that they had robbed some mission in the interior. Governor van's Gravesande denied that the Dutch had instigated such an attack, but feared that the Spaniards would place the blame on them.[30]

Finally, on June 23, 1791, there was signed a "Convention between Spain and Holland for Restoring to each other the Deserters and Runaways from their respective Colonies in America." This arrangement must have lessened to some degree the causes for conflict between the two powers in South America. The convention permitted Dutch runaways who had been converted to Catholicism in the Spanish missions to retain their religion on returning to the Dutch settlements.[31]

Humboldt estimated that in 1800 there were about forty thousand Caribs in the Orinoco region. By this time a considerable number of them had been persuaded to live peaceably on the Spanish reductions. The independent Caribs were no longer the menace that they had been during most of the eighteenth century, but they were still mistrusted and hated by both the Spanish secular authorities and the missionaries. Whereas formerly they had resorted to the most horrible atrocities in order to collect slaves and to destroy the missions that stood in their way, they now limited their activities to smuggling, stealing cattle, and persuading the recently converted Indians who lived "within sound of the bell" to return to their former haunts. According to Humboldt,

The missionaries of the Carony and the Orinoco attribute all the evils they suffer from the independent Caribs to the hatred of their neighbors, the Calvinist preachers of the Essequibo. Their works are therefore filled with complaints of the *secta diabólica de Calvino y de Lutero*, and against the heretics of Dutch Guiana, who also think fit sometimes to go on missions, and spread the germs of social life among the savages.[32]

THE MAYNAS MISSIONS

I

EDEMPTION of the Indians of Peru fell into two distinct epochs. The first was that in which the semicivilized inhabitants of the former Inca empire were subjected to Christian doctrine and discipline. Although attended with numerous difficulties, the Christianization of the Aymarás and Quechuas, the principal racial groups of the Inca empire, was for several reasons carried on with great rapidity. In the first place, these Indians, being agriculturists, were living a settled life before the Spaniards came. Since they dwelt in fairly dense communities, and since access to them from the coast was comparatively easy, it was possible for a few padres to convert, or at least to baptize, large numbers. In the second place, the inhabitants of the Inca area had long been accustomed to the domination of the priests. Thus the missionaries, who substituted themselves for the heathen priests, found Indians disposed to accept what was taught them and ready speedily to change their religious practices, if not their fundamental religious beliefs, so as to harmonize

them with the teachings of the Catholic Church. In the third place, the Incas already had a highly developed religion, with a god called Pachacamac, who was considered a divine creator similar to the Christian God. And finally, the climate of the Peruvian coast and highland was healthful for people of European birth. Accordingly, by 1600 the natives of the coast lands and the cordillera of both Peru and Ecuador had been rather thoroughly evangelized, and the religious orders had begun to look about for new fields in which to exercise their religious powers. They soon entered upon the second great epoch of missionary activity in Peru and Ecuador, an epoch during which the padres carried the gospel into the *Montaña Real*, a vast region stretching from the eastern slopes of the Andes down through the valleys of the Marañón, the Huallaga, the Ucayali, the Pastaza, the Napo, and the Putumayo, and into the selvas of western Brazil.[1]

From the very beginning of the conquest of Peru missionaries had accompanied the conquistadores of the sword. Padre Reginaldo de Pedraza, a Dominican who had founded the convent of Panama in 1519, sailed with Francisco Pizarro on his first voyage to Peru. Returning to Spain with the courageous swineherd of Estremadura, he persuaded seven other friars to accompany him to the New World. These religious were with Pizarro when he invaded the land of the sun god;[2] and it was one of them, Vicente de Valverde, who, after the Inca had thrown the Bible in the dust at Cajamarca, gave the signal to the Spaniards to massacre the heathen, guaranteeing eternal salvation to all Christians who should fall in the fray.[3] And Friar Marcos de Niza was present with six companions of the Franciscan order in 1532 when the Inca Atahualpa was strangled. Five of these padres went to the Río de la Plata in 1537, and were the first to carry the gospel into that region.[4] The Franciscans were soon followed into

Peru and Ecuador by the Mercedarians and the Dominicans, and in June, 1551, twelve friars of the Augustinian order reached Lima.[5]

In the meantime the newly organized Society of Jesus was not only gaining strength and prestige in Europe, but was expanding its field of endeavor into Africa and the Orient; and America was soon to present them other opportunities to achieve eternal glory in the service of the Most High and the Roman pontiff. Although late in reaching the ancient kingdom of the Incas, the sons of Loyola were destined to become the most successful agents for the evangelization of the natives of the region.

On their arrival in Peru, the conquest had progressed far. The discords which prevailed among the conquerors concluded, the conversion of the natives was being seriously considered, for which object there had been brought religious of the Dominican, Franciscan, and Augustinian orders. With the coming of the Jesuits, the missions received greater impulse, and . . . their labors were of great utility, not only for the moral advancement, but also for the intellectual progress of the country.[6]

On May 3, 1566, Philip II had written to Francisco de Borja, general of the Society of Jesus, requesting him to send to the Indies twenty-four Jesuits, "learned persons of good life and example." Early in November of the following year eight members of the order left the port of Sanlúcar for Peru. The voyage was an eventful one, accompanied by signs and portents which indicated that the padres were proceeding under the shadow of God's wing. When the enraged Lucifer brought on a terrific storm which made the vessel sway until its very sails touched the water, Father Jerónimo Portillo, the leader of the group, began to pray. The ship immediately assumed an even keel and proceeded to Panama, where the Black Robes were received like apostles. While two of the company remained on the isthmus, the other six

The enraged Lucifer brought on a terrific storm which made the vessel sway until its very sails touched the water

continued the journey southward, reaching Callao on Sunday, March 28, 1568. Most of the inhabitants of Peru had never seen a Jesuit, and a great crowd was at the port to meet them. They landed in the shadows of a sun in eclipse—no doubt a sign that the end of the demon sun god of the Incas was at hand, a most auspicious omen. Entering Lima on April 1, the padres began "to seek souls to win for God." The newcomers were well received by the secular clergy of Lima, and Father Jerónimo was asked to preach a sermon. He had scarcely spoken the first word from the pulpit of the cathedral when the earth trembled so violently that all the people fled for fear that the roof would crash down upon them. But the Jesuit remained in the pulpit undaunted, realizing that God was with him. In a short time the tremors ceased, and the congregation returned, confident that this was a holy man.

The people of Lima helped the Jesuits build their church, some paying for the lot while others furnished lime, brick, stone, adobe, wood, and other supplies. The padres visited the hospitals to console and serve the sick, and went to the prisons to receive the confessions of the criminals. Three additional Jesuits reached Lima in April, 1573; and in June, 1575, Father Diego de Bracamonte, who had gone to Rome specifically to ask the pope for reinforcements, arrived with fourteen companions, including an Italian painter, Bernardo Billi, who was to decorate the churches of the capital.[7]

Jesuits from the college of Lima reached Quito in 1585.[8] The first foundations for a Jesuit college were laid there during the following year, and in 1594 the seminary of San Luis was founded in connection with it.[9] Besides educating the young men of Ecuador and New Granada, this college and seminary trained missionaries for work among the savage tribes of the eastern frontier. From the seminary of San Luis came most of the Jesuit missionaries who established reductions on the upper Amazon and its numerous tributaries.[10] On November 30, 1595, a royal decree was published to the effect that the Jesuit college at Quito should devote itself to preaching the gospel and teaching the Indians "for the universal wellbeing of the Republic and for the ornament and ennoblement thereof." [11] Father Manuel Rodríguez wrote of the establishment:

There, then, is that college, the hospitium of the Indians of the missions, the infirmary of the missionaries who come out loaded with ailments, the drugstore from which are sent medicines for others. There is a warehouse, with a proctor appointed from the missions, who continually arranges the things necessary for the shipments, whether ornaments, clothes for the padres, or something that they may give to the Indians.[12]

In this warehouse were also tools, fishhooks, and cheap jewelry to attract the wily Indian to the mild yoke of Christ.

During the first half of the seventeenth century other Jesuit colleges were founded at Popayán and Cuenca.[13]

The principal point of departure for missionaries proceeding to the vast country east of the Ecuadorian and Peruvian Andes was Quito, a city far removed from Spain and quite difficult of access during colonial times. Two routes were commonly followed by travelers going to this inland settlement located on a plateau between two great mountain ranges at an altitude of more than nine thousand feet above sea level. The easier route from Spain to Quito was by the Isthmus of Panama, the Pacific, and the Gulf of Guayaquil; but some of the padres disembarked at Cartagena, where the heat "makes the missionaries understand that they are going to the Indies to labor and sweat." From Cartagena they journeyed up the Magdalena to the head of navigation and on overland to Quito, a distance of over five hundred leagues.[14]

II

The oriente of Ecuador and Peru may be divided into two geographical areas: the eastern slopes of the Andes, and the tropical lowlands beyond. Much of the eastern slope is a delightful country where springtime reigns perpetually. Even at the higher altitudes there are beautiful forests or open meadows containing luxuriant grasses and a variety of wild flowers, and up to a height of ten thousand feet the temperature is pleasant during most of the year for persons sufficiently clothed and accustomed to a cool climate. In short, it is an area that will grow plants of both temperate and tropical origin, a land of tumultuous beauty, of majestic color, where the green of virgin forests, the browns and yellows of bare cliffs, and the kaleidoscopic hues of an ever changing sky combine to make a scene beyond the ability of mortal artist to depict. Father Zahm calls it a "Peruvian Paradise," [15]

The missionaries were most profoundly impressed by the dizzy chasms that must be crossed

and the padres were very successful in introducing a variety of European crops. In the early colonial days it was a wild country, and the missionaries were most profoundly impressed by the dangerous streams that must be forded, by the precipitous acclivities which must be climbed, by the dizzy chasms that must be crossed, and by the swift rapids that must be run in frail canoes.

Eastward from the Andean foothills stretches the vast plain of the Amazon basin. Broken by few undulations, this country is covered with giant forests, in which are found mahogany and other hardwoods, as well as trees which produce rubber, quinine, vanilla, and cinnamon.[16] The region possesses majesty; but for the traveler who journeys on foot along the trails of the rainforest, it is a gloomy majesty. Above him reach to great heights trees whose branches are entwined with serpentine lianas. The leafy canopy shuts out the sunshine so that even at high noon the forest floor is shaded; and night closes in upon the wanderer before sunset. It is a land of almost constant heat, of dangerous beasts and reptiles, of vampire bats, of sticky humidity and insect pests and miasmatic fevers, where strength seems to be drawn from one's body, and activity becomes a matter of will instead of a spontaneous and joyous expression of inward vitality. In short, it is a "Green Hell."

Into these gorgeous foothills as well as to this uninviting lowland came the padres in search of those who had been held for centuries in thralldom by the Serpent. In this montaña lived numerous tribes of Indians speaking many languages and having a variety of social customs and religious beliefs, but sunk all alike in the depths of savagery. Some of the many tribes among whom the padres labored during a period of two centuries were: Paeces, Chunchos, Cofanes, Jíbaros, Jeberos, Maynas, Pilcozones, Roamaynas, Coronados, Cocamas, Cocamillas, Omaguas, Icaguates, Abijiras, and Jurimaguas.[17]

The mission field usually referred to as the Maynas was a large area covering an irregular section of the upper Amazon valley. The authorities at Bogotá, Quito, and Lima had repeated disputes as to the limits of their jurisdictions in this region, and in colonial days the boundaries of Maynas were not definitely determined. The location of the area was, however, approximately as follows: The northeastern boundary was the water divide between the Putumayo and the Napo. To the east, it reached to a point on the Amazon between the Putumayo and the Yavari. The southeastern boundary was the Yavari from its mouth to the head of navigation; and from this point a line running due west to the Huallaga formed the southern boundary. From the intersection of this line with the Huallaga another line ran in an irregular direction toward the northwest and formed the western boundary.[18]

This transmontane region was always most difficult of access. In the course of time three routes were opened from Quito to the Maynas district: one through the provinces of Loja and Jaén, another by way of the Pastaza, and the third to the upper Napo, down the Napo to the Marañón, and up the Marañón to the Maynas missions.[19] From Quito through Jaén to Borja—the religious and administrative center of the Maynas area, a town located on the Pongo de Manseriche, or Canal de Pongo, which was a narrow and dangerous part of the Marañón where the river curves to the east and breaks through the easternmost range of the Andes—was, according to Father Figueroa, two hundred and sixty leagues by land, in addition to sixty leagues by water. In the middle of the seventeenth century three months were considered a short time in which to make the journey between the two cities; and not infrequently three years would pass before a padre in the Maynas country could receive a reply to a letter he had written to Quito.[20] The third route to the Maynas region was not so dangerous as that by Jaén and the Canal de Pongo, but it was nevertheless long and tedious, and it passed through a country inhabited by warlike tribes. After reaching the mouth of the Napo it was necessary to go up the Marañón for sixteen days before arriving at Borja.[21] The great difficulty in reaching the oriente may be indicated by the fact that in recent times, but before the use of the airplane, Peruvian officials going from Lima to the Amazon port of Iquitos went first to England, either by way of Panama or the Strait of Magellan, and then returned to Iquitos by way of the Amazon.

In early colonial days it was practically impossible to make the trip across the mountains on horseback. Usually the padres went overland on foot, but occasionally they were carried on the shoulders of Indians who, with the solace of a quid of coca leaves, could carry a load of two hundred pounds for hours in succession without apparent fatigue. The picture of an able-bodied missionary riding on the back of a convert is not a pleasant one. Father Manuel Rodríguez says that while an Indian is able to carry a man easily enough for great distances, this mode of transportation is uncomfortable because the native perspires freely, and the heat of his body is transmitted to the rider. Rodríguez preferred to walk.[22] Besides the ordinary discomforts of traveling through a wild and broken country, there was danger of mountain sickness, which Father Acosta graphically describes:

Being then alone with one Indian, whom I entreated to keep me on my beast, I was surprised with such pangs of straining and casting as I thought to cast up my soul too; for having cast up meate, fleugme, and choller, both yellow and greene, in the end I cast up blood, with the straining of my stomacke. To conclude, if this had continued, I should undoubtedly have died; but this lasted not above three or four houres, [until] we were come into a more convenient and natural temperature. . . .[23]

III

Father Juan Ramírez, a Franciscan, is said to have been the first missionary to enter the Peruvian montaña (1560).

In 1595 two Jesuits, Juan Font and Nicolás Durán Maestrillo, went to the country of the Chunchos and Pilcozones, who were located just east of the principal ranges of the Peruvian Andes;[24] and the Jesuit father, Rafael Ferrer, is credited with having been the first padre to begin missionary work east of the Ecuadorian Andes.

It was in 1599 that Father Ferrer entered the montaña for the first time. Three years later he advanced into the country of the Cofanes some sixty or seventy leagues east of Quito, an almost inaccessible region traversed by numerous streams and covered with dense forests. He subsisted largely on Indian corn, slept in his blankets on the ground, and kept a record of his experiences on scraps of old letters. For companionship and solace in the loneliness of the wilderness he had his breviary and his Bible. "His words were all of Heaven, his letters cast beams of God's love, and his zeal was that of an angel."[25] For protection he carried a crucifix. The Indians of this region, while not acquainted with the missionaries, knew enough of the Spaniards to fear and hate them. Nevertheless, Father Rafael was able to overcome their hostility and reduce some of them to village life. Returning to Quito, he persuaded a French Jesuit, Father Anton Martin, to accompany him back to the montaña in 1605; and later he went again to Quito and induced an Italian, Father Fernando Arnulfini, to aid him in the new mission field. For several years these padres worked among the Coronados, Omaguas, Icaguates, and Abijiras, who lived near the rivers Aguarico and Napo.[26] Between 1605 and 1608 Father Ferrer voyaged down the Napo to the Marañón.[27] He was killed in 1611 by the savages.[28]

In 1618 General Diego Vaca de Vega asked permission of the viceroy of Peru, Don Francisco de Borja, to conquer the Maynas Indians who lived on the banks of the Marañón.

This permission having been granted, Vaca de Vega entered the Maynas country with sixty-eight soldiers, a secular priest, and two missionaries.[29] A year later he founded the town of San Francisco de Borja, the location and subsequent importance of which have already been described. The garrison of this town was destined to give much assistance in the spiritual conquest of the natives of the Maynas region.[30]

The Jesuit and Franciscan orders were the most active in the vast area east of the cordillera. In 1632 religious of the Observant Franciscans asked leave to preach to and convert the natives of the territory along the Marañón,[31] and in September of that year the first Franciscans reached that river.[32] The principal scene of their labors in the montaña during the next century and a half, however, was in the valleys of the Huallaga and the Ucayali.[33] Franciscans and Jesuits first explored large areas of the upper Amazon basin and then began to gather the natives into numerous reductions. As often occurred elsewhere on the South American frontier, religious of the two orders, and sometimes even those within the same order, had disputes regarding the territory in which they were to work.[34]

In the years 1635 to 1637 Franciscan missionaries, accompanied by soldiers, were sent out from Quito with instructions to explore the country as far as the Amazon. All of the friars soon returned to Quito except Domingo de Brieba and Andrés Toledo, who embarked with six soldiers in canoes on the Marañón and proceeded downstream until they eventually reached Pará. From there they went to the city of San Luis de Maranham, where they made a report to the Portuguese governor, the kingdoms of Portugal and Spain being at that time united. The governor fitted out an expedition under Pedro Teixeira to accompany the two padres back to Quito. The return expedition left Pará on October 28, 1637, with forty-seven canoes, seventy Portuguese soldiers, and twelve hundred male Indians, besides native boys and women. The journey upstream and over the Andes lasted more than a year. Finally, however, Teixeira and a few followers, the rest having been left in camp east of the Andes, reached Quito, where they were well received.[35]

On the trip back to Pará, which lasted from February 16 to December 12, 1639,[36] Teixeira was accompanied by two Jesuits, Father Cristóbal de Acuña and Father Andrés de Artieda. From Pará the two padres went to Spain, where Acuña published a book entitled *A New Discovery of the Great River of the Amazons*, containing an account of their journey and a description of the country which they had explored. Acuña memorialized the king to command that the upper Amazon region be settled and fortified.[37] Both of these padres returned to Quito, and Acuña proceeded from there to Lima, while Artieda went to Maynas in company with Father Lucás de la Cueva and an armed escort of Spanish soldiers.[38]

Already the Black Robes had received a special call to this region. A number of Indians had risen in rebellion in 1637, and the governor, despairing of subjugating them by force of arms, had asked that Jesuit missionaries be sent to reduce them to a settled and peaceful mode of life. In answer to this invitation, Fathers Lucas de la Cueva and Gaspar de Cujía had gone that same year from Quito to the oriente,[39] where they founded among the Jebero Indians the first Jesuit mission in the Maynas field.[40] When Father Lucas asked a Jebero cacique how many nations there were in the forests, the Indian took up a handful of sand and, scattering it in the air, replied: "Countless as the grains of sand are the nations of this land; for there is neither lake nor river, hill nor valley, plain nor forest, which is not full of inhabitants."[41]

IV

The establishment of this Jebero mission, under the protection of Our Lady of the Immaculate Conception, was the beginning of a period of Jesuit activity in Maynas that was to last with few interruptions for a hundred and thirty years. According to one estimate, one hundred and fifty-seven Jesuit padres penetrated the region during this epoch, carrying the gospel to over five hundred thousand natives.[42] Some of the missionaries were creoles, while others were natives of Spain and still others were foreigners. They came from such widely separated places as Guayaquil, Panama, Quito, Madrid, Mallorca, Toledo, Valencia, Andalusia, La Mancha, Cartagena, and various parts of Portugal and Germany.[43] During the first years of their expatriation, the padres from Europe may have felt sharp pangs of nostalgia, although Father Acosta remarks: "And this point serveth often against many Spaniards, who beeing here, sigh for Spaine, having no discourse with us, imagining that we have forgotten and make small accompt of our native soyle. To whom we answer, that the desire to returne into Spaine doth nothing trouble us, beeing as neare unto Heaven at Peru, as in Spaine."[44]

During his career among the Jeberos, Father Lucas de la Cueva exhibited not only much evangelical ability, but also remarkable courage. It required great boldness even to go among such Indians, and greater to remain there as he did for years. On one occasion, when he proceeded, as was customary, to give Spanish Christian names to a number of reduced Indians, the Jeberos thought the padre was making a list for their more convenient distribution among the Spaniards as personal servants and slaves. Father Lucas knew nothing of their suspicions until one night about twelve o'clock almost the whole population of the village began to flee in all directions as if attacked by an army, leaving most of their possessions behind them. The padre was abandoned in the reduction with only a few old people and a servant boy. After several days had passed, he went into the forest to try to persuade the Indians to return, and while he was away a number of them came to his house to kill him. Unable to induce the natives to resume their residence in the village, he sent two old Indians to the nearest Spanish settlement for aid. These emissaries soon encountered a group of Spanish soldiers who returned with them to the town. By this time the fugitive Indians were tired of hunger and the torment of mosquitoes; and they finally came back to the reduction after they had been threatened with capture and shipment to Borja as slaves of the Spaniards in case they refused to settle down. Father Francisco de Figueroa attributed this occurrence to the machinations of the devil, who was enraged because Father Lucas had constructed a beautiful church and baptized two hundred and fifty Indians within the short period of one week, and was teaching the savages to attend the class in doctrine, to hear Mass, to have only one wife, and to refrain from their barbarous practice of eating the livers and hearts of their victims.[45]

As the years passed, according to Figueroa, the Jeberos were thoroughly reformed. No longer did they engage in drunken festivals, imbibing intoxicants from the skulls of slain enemies. They became so humble that they even asked the padre's permission before going hunting or fishing, or gathering fruit in the forest. In the words of the good padre:

All know how to pray, except the very old. They hear Mass on Sundays and on festival days, and many of them every day, because of their devotion. They pray in the courtyards of their houses every night in a loud voice, and it is a great consolation to hear so many and such good choirs at the time that the evening bells ring.

The children and youths pray with great punctuality in the church every day; in the morning in the Inca language, and in the afternoon in their maternal tongue, in which the catechism is also recited. On Wednesdays, Fridays, and Sundays there is a general *doctrina* for all. On Sundays, in the afternoon, there is no lesson in the doctrine, and this serves as a vacation for the children. For the learners there are teachers, men for the men, and women for women, divided into classes, in which after having prayed in the doctrina, they teach some of them the Paternoster, others the Ave Maria, and others the Credo.[46]

The Jeberos were such enthusiastic Christians that they aided the padres in converting other natives of the region. They would take new converts into their huts and care for them until their crops were ready to be harvested.[47]

About 1640 some of the lay Spaniards in Maynas began to cause trouble for the missionaries, because the padres wished to keep their Indians on the missions as long as possible, while the encomenderos wanted the natives to work for them. At this date such interference was not a new experience for missionary friars, for they had to endure the hostility of grasping lay Spaniards during the whole epoch of colonial missionary activity.[48]

There arrived at Borja from Quito in 1641 two more Jesuits, Father Bartolomé Pérez and Father Francisco de Figueroa,[49] the latter to become one of the greatest figures in the history of the reductions of the montaña of Ecuador. Already an experienced missionary, he spent the period of a generation in the Marañón country, finally suffering a martyr's death. He tried to make the conversion process more thorough, asserting that before his arrival it had been a common occurrence to baptize the Indians merely by throwing water on whole groups of them at a time, after which the savages were deemed to be Christians.[50]

In 1644 a group of twenty-five soldiers and thirty Indians,

accompanied by a priest, reached the country of the Cocama Indians on the Ucayali. In order to make the natives understand what an important person a priest was, the Spaniards permitted him to paddle them on the hand with a rod, even the captain of the Spanish soldiers submitting to this chastisement. The whites also used a combination of gifts and gunpowder to persuade the savages to listen to reason. Some of the Cocamas were said to have died merely at sight of the Spaniards, who they thought were devils.[51]

Father Alonso Caballero also reached the banks of the Ucayali River in 1651, where he remained for several years laboring among the savages, and where he finally lost his life at the hands of the people whom he was trying to serve.[52] In 1658 Francisco de Figueroa and Domingo Fernández went down the Marañón and up the Ucayali. Father Domingo attributed a storm, which came on just as they entered the Ucayali, to the devils of this region, who were angry because the padres were coming to rob them of their victims.[53] It was at this time that the mission of Santa María de Huallaga was established on the Huallaga River.

The Indians along the Ucayali were called Cocamas, while those along the Huallaga were called Cocamillas.[54] The country between the two rivers was known as the *Pampa del Sacramento*. Both Franciscans and Jesuits founded missions in the area drained by the Huallaga and the Ucayali.[55] But the Cocamas revolted in 1660; a number of missionaries lost their lives; and their efforts to evangelize the Indians of this particular section during the latter half of the seventeenth century were largely fruitless. Shortly after 1700 most of the missions of the Pampa were abandoned.[56]

Missions were established on the Napo River about 1660,[57] and the Mamoré was first visited by a Jesuit named Cypriano Baraza in 1674.[58] Father Raimundo de Santa Cruz explored a route to the Maynas by way of the Pastaza and Bohono rivers and was drowned in the latter in 1662.[59]

The first twenty years of missionary activity in Maynas were on the whole quite successful. Father Figueroa estimated that there were in 1663 some seven thousand baptized Indians in the missions on the Marañón, the Huallaga, the Ucayali, and the Pastaza.[60] He complained, however, that the death rate among the natives was high because of the diseases which the converts contracted from the Spaniards.[61]

The padres sometimes went out alone in search of savages to convert, sometimes with Indian interpreters and helpers, and sometimes with the aid of Spanish soldiers. Raynal describes them as spending months climbing trees to see if they could discover in the distance some hut or wisp of smoke indicating a settlement.[62] Father Manuel Rodríguez tells most interestingly of their entry into the forest: "Some indeed alone, and others with the aid of interpreters, penetrated the land, followed the rivers, often drenched by rains and from wading lakes, with feet wounded by roots of trees and clothes torn by the branches and thorns of the narrow paths." [63]

After persuading a group of savages to give up their nomadic life, the padres often helped them clear land for their villages. Sometimes the missionaries furnished their converts with axes, machetes, and other tools purchased with their own meagre stipends or with alms collected in Quito and Lima. After completing the huts, padres and Indians cooperated in building the first church of wood, clay, and palm leaves.[64] The friars then taught the Indians to farm, so that Maynas soon produced corn, rice, beans, yucca, coffee, cacao, quinine, cinnamon, wax, tobacco, sugar cane, indigo, resins, woods, and oils.[65] Father Rodríguez stated in 1684 that until that time it had been impossible to raise cattle satisfactorily on the Maynas missions because of lack of pasturage and salt and because of the multitude of insects. One bull and two cows had been placed on a Jebero mission, but they had failed to thrive on the diet of banana peels that had been fed them.[66] The Indians were naturally lazy; and since they had not developed a taste for the white man's goods, the padres found difficulty in persuading them to work on the farms and to gather sarsaparilla, cacao, and vanilla to export to Quito in exchange for the commodities needed by the mission.[67] The natives were also taught to smooth beams, saw lumber, build houses, manufacture furniture, and make clothes. "Always did the padres participate in their labors, being companions in their cares, in their sowing, harvesting, fishing, and hunting. They were mediators in their disputes, and in all things solicitous of their well-being." [68]

V

The padres usually asserted that the natives, once having heard the word of God, were eager to embrace Christianity, and that they were devoted to the missionaries. One padre wrote from the country of the Roamaynas: "In general all desire baptism and ask for it, and the disposition they exhibit to become Christians is the best I have seen among savages. I have told them that in time of need they should invoke the names of Jesus and Mary. They do so carefully." [69] Father Figueroa declares that when a missionary was transferred from one reduction to another, the converts whom he was leaving would sometimes raise loud cries and mourn as though a close relative had died. In one instance they "came to the house of the Father and stopped to look at him and to cry, the tears serving as words that signified their sorrow and affliction; so that the Father, unable to contain himself, retired into a corner also to give way to tears, regretting greatly to leave these poor people, as if they were his own children." [70]

On the other hand, the royal inspectors (*visitadores*), Jorge Juan and Antonio de Ulloa, averred that the Indians of the Peruvian oriente did not willingly receive missionaries. Natives who were located nearest Spanish towns objected strenuously to being reduced. The most difficult Indians to reduce were those who, having once been settled on a mission, had revolted and fled to the wilds, for they feared that they would be punished, particularly if they had killed any Spaniards. Renegade Indians further made things difficult for the padres by telling unconverted tribes into whose country they fled horrible tales of cruelties perpetrated by the Spaniards.[71]

Undoubtedly the Indians sometimes developed a sincere affection for those missionaries who were capable of inspiring love. Father J. A. Zahm, who has visited Indians in their own huts in the depths of the Amazonian wilds, says that even the Jíbaro is capable of love for his family and deep affection for those who show him kindness. The Páez Indians, however, far from exhibiting this love and regard for their padres, paid no attention to their religious teaching except to laugh at and mock the missionary. Among these savages the ambassadors of God, remembering the admonition in regard to pearls and swine, concentrated their attention upon the children, with whom they had considerable success.[72]

Moreover, the missionaries found the fierce Jíbaros, who roamed over the forested area between the Santiago and the Pastaza rivers, beyond the reach of their redemptive powers. Gold was thought to exist in the streams of the region, and the Spaniards, as always, were eager for the yellow metal; but neither soldiers nor padres, nor both combined, were able to subdue any very large number of these savages. Vain efforts were made in 1654 and in 1692, and a third attempt in 1766 was only a little more successful, although Chantre y Herrera asserts that the Jíbaros were on the point of being

Christianized when the Jesuits were expelled. He lists Corazón de Jesús de Xívaros, on the Pastaza, among the Jesuit
missions in existence in 1767, and says that the reduction contained two hundred souls.[73]

They were perhaps the most independent and savage of all
the many Indian tribes of the Ecuadorian and Peruvian oriente.
The most hideously repulsive of their many barbarous practices was the ceremony of head shrinking. It was the custom
of the Jíbaros to decapitate their slain enemies. But since,
according to the belief of these Indians, the soul remained in
the head even after decapitation, and was capable of perpe-
trating injury upon the killer, an elaborate process was required to drive out the soul. The back of the head was cut
from the top downward and the skull was carefully stripped
from back to front. The skin, with a small amount of flesh,
was also peeled from the face, and the detached surface of
both the face and the head, with its thick mass of long black
hair, was immersed in a pot of boiling water, where it was
allowed to remain for a few minutes and then taken out to
cool. A small hot rock was next inserted in the mask and
rolled around so as to burn the flesh, after which the seared
tissue was scraped off. Hot sand was then poured in and
allowed to remain for a time before being poured out. Afterward the burnt flesh was again scraped. This searing process
was repeated until the soul of the dead Indian was forced to
flee. In the meantime the heat dried and shrank the skin, and
the savage sculptor molded the mask into a shape approximat-
ing that of the original head and face, although the finished
product was perhaps no more than a fourth of its former
size.[74] One of the perilous duties of the missionary was to
persuade these benighted heathen that head shrinking was
an infamous practice, without becoming a victim of the
ceremony.

The Indians participated wholeheartedly in pageants and processions

Most of the numerous tribes of the Maynas region, however, gradually embraced the practices of the Roman Catholic Church. The Indians of Nuestra Señora de Loreto de Paranapuras observed the fast days of the church so strictly during Lent that they laid aside their blowguns and poisoned arrows and abstained from meat, eating fish, herbs, and fruits instead.[75] But Father Baraza was not so successful in his attempt to persuade some natives not to eat seven captive Indians whom they were saving for a feast. The savages promised to grant the request; but when he visited their village some time later, he saw the bones of four victims who had already been consumed.[76] The Indians participated wholeheartedly in pageants and processions, for these took the place of their primitive dances and appealed to their love of ostentation. Even before the construction of the town of Loreto de Paranapuras was completed, the natives asked permission to have a procession. They cleared a road from the banks of the river through the forest to the site of the proposed village, and placed an altar at the end of this roadway, along which the procession marched, all of the Indians carrying torches. Some played their native musical instruments while others did penance, probably by beating themselves or crawling upon the ground; and the procession ended in a great dance. Such celebrations as these were common on the missions, especially on Christmas, Easter, and Corpus Christi.[77]

A number of the Indians of the Maynas region revolted again in 1666; and Father Francisco Figueroa was murdered. Yet Father Manuel Rodríguez called this year a happy one in the annals of the Maynas reductions since Figueroa's martyrdom was a jewel in the crown of the Society of Jesus. The revolt was suppressed, and within a year new nations were being brought into the fold of Mother Church.[78] In 1667, however, the Avigiras killed Father Suárez.[79]

The Maynas Missions

Since the natives of the montaña were constantly on the verge of breaking away from their missions, the padres repeatedly sent memorials to the viceroy begging for more soldiers or more money. His viceregal highness was but little interested, however, in these distant settlements. In 1689 the Duke of Palata, then viceroy of Peru, complained of the numerous solicitations of the friars in the viceroyalty.[80]

VI

The period from 1672 to 1685 was one of stagnation in the Maynas missions; but during the latter year new missionaries arrived, including the Bohemian Jesuit, Father Samuel Fritz, to give a new impetus to the apostolic labors in this territory. Father Samuel was one of a number of padres of German and other nationalities who worked among the Indians on this Spanish frontier. Others were Father Adam Widman; Father Heinrich Frantzen, who wrote his memoirs after having lived forty years on the Marañón; Father Carlos Brentano, who wrote an extensive history of the missions; and Father Martín Iriarte, who had the reputation of knowing perfectly the languages of the Incas, Omaguas, Encabellados, Yameos, and Mayorumas.[81]

In 1681 the Omaguas, who lived some distance down the Marañón from San Francisco de Borja, had asked Father Lorenzo Lucero, who was the prefect of the missions on the Huallaga and was living at the town of Laguna, to send missionaries to them. He had been unable to do so until the arrival of these new recruits from Quito; and he now sent Father Samuel Fritz.[82] Fritz did not, however, limit his missionary activities to the Omaguas. He worked among the Jurimaguas and Aysuares and extended the Spanish mission field far down the Amazon.

The Bohemian padre gained an astounding reputation

among these savages, some of them even thinking that he
was immortal. An Aysuare chieftain once said to him: "You
do not have to die, because, if you should die, who would
be our Father, Lover, and Protector?" They looked upon
him as the cause of earthquakes and eclipses.[83] During his
ministry in the Amazon country Father Fritz reduced Indians
inhabiting vast areas of country between the Napo and the
Río Negro,[84] and his influence was felt as far away as the
Orinoco. The Jurimaguas told Fritz, before he had received
the news by way of Quito, that they had heard of the murder
of some Jesuit missionaries on the Orinoco. According to
the Jurimaguas, the Orinoco Indians, hearing of the great
Father Samuel from some native traders, had now decided to
heed his teachings.[85]

Having to cope with the hostility of the Portuguese as well
as of Indian tribes, receiving little support from Lima or
Quito, and operating over a territory so enormous that it was
impossible for one man to baptize all the Indians, much less
teach them Christianity, Father Fritz could hardly have exerted a permanent influence upon the natives. But his ministry does exhibit the heroism, the devotion, and the untiring
energy of the best of the frontier missionaries.

While in a village among the Jurimaguas, Father Fritz became ill with dropsy and decided to go down the Amazon to
the Portuguese settlement of Pará to seek a remedy for his
illness. His journey downstream occurred during the year
1689. So great was his fame that even in Pará tales were told
of him as strange as those believed by the Indians of the
Marañón. Said Father Samuel:

It should be observed that in this voyage of mine a great stir
arose about me, not only among the surrounding natives, but it
made its way as far as Pará and San Luis de Marañón. Some
said that I was a saint and a son of God, others a Devil; some,

because I carried a cross, said that a Patriarch or Prophet had come; others an envoy from Persia, even the negroes of Pará said that their liberator had come from the way of Angola to free them; others from fear retreated, saying that I carried fire with me and came along burning as many settlements and people as I met.[86]

At Pará Father Samuel happily survived the remedies which were applied to him, although the physicians proved almost as dangerous to human life as the savages of the forest. Fritz was detained a prisoner at the Jesuit college in Pará by order of the Portuguese governor until word could be had from Lisbon as to what to do with him. After a period of eighteen months an order was received directing that he should be freed and returned to his mission at the expense of the Portuguese royal treasury. Some time passed, however, before an expedition for this purpose could be fitted out, and in all Fritz remained in Pará almost two years.

On July 6, 1691, he finally began his voyage upstream to the Spanish settlement of Pueblo de Laguna, on the Huallaga, accompanied by a Portuguese officer, six soldiers, a surgeon, and thirty-five Indian rowers. From the Maynas missions he continued his journey to Lima with the purpose of obtaining financial and military support for his reductions. In the City of the Kings he appeared dressed in a short cassock made of palm fibre, wearing hemp shoes, and carrying a wooden cross. Tall, thin, and bearded, he gave the impression of some anchorite come to accuse the people of Lima of their sins. He was well received at the viceregal capital. The Jesuits there gave him clean new clothes, and the authorities were courteous enough to him, but he was unsuccessful in securing substantial material aid for the reductions on the distant Amazon. Fritz returned, however, to the scene of his labors, where he continued his ministry until his death in 1725.[87]

VII

It is difficult to determine accurately the growth of the Maynas missions, or, for that matter, of the missions on other Spanish frontiers in South America. The population figures may indicate all the Indians in the mission area, the baptized natives, or only those who were settled in villages. On new reductions, where the population had not been definitely determined, there was a tendency to exaggerate the numbers of the natives. Between 1683 and 1727 thirty-four tribes in the territory of Maynas were reduced and seventy-five towns founded. Between 1727 and 1768 thirty-six tribes were reduced.[88] The total population of the Jesuit missions in Maynas in 1727 was 5,456.[89] Juan and Ulloa reported that in 1745 the Jesuit missions in Maynas and Quijos had forty towns and a population of 12,853, of whom 9,858 were baptized. At that time the capital of Maynas, San Francisco de Borja, had a population of only 143 Indians and 66 Spaniards.[90] The largest mission on the Marañón was the village of Jeberos, which contained a population of 1,216. Nuestra Señora de Loreto de Paranapuras had a population of 150; San Antonio, 120; Santa María Mayor de los Jurimaguas y Aicuares, 300; San Xavier de Chamicuros y Tibilos, 200.[91] In addition to the Jesuit missions there were in the Marañón country in 1738 at least one village of the Mercedarians and one of the Capuchins.[92]

Chantre y Herrera says that between 1638 and the date of their expulsion the Jesuits founded more than eighty reductions in the Maynas mission field. He lists by name thirty-three reductions with a total population of approximately fifteen thousand which were in existence at the end of this period. Among the most important of these were Laguna, Xeveros (Jeberos), Omaguas, and Iquitos, settlements which are still in existence. He also enumerates six other reductions of the Yamea nation without giving the number of neophytes residing in them.[93] Another writer says there were some thirty-six villages with ten thousand inhabitants in 1766. A number of these reductions were within two days' journey of each other, while the distance between others could be covered only by a tedious voyage of three weeks.[94] At that time the Franciscan college of Santa Rosa de Ocopa had twelve towns on the Ucayali. In 1766 another Indian revolt occurred on these missions, and sixteen Franciscan friars were killed.[95] But the Franciscans of Santa Rosa, undaunted by this terrible blow, immediately began to restore the ruined reductions.

The expulsion of the Jesuits in 1767 marks the beginning of the decline of the Maynas missions. After the expulsion, secular priests were at first placed in charge of a number of reductions, but it soon became evident that they were unsatisfactory shepherds for the flocks of the montaña. They were accused of neglecting their charges, of having illicit relations with Indian women, of drunkenness, of appropriating for their own use payments made by the Indians for ecclesiastical purposes, and of robbing the altars of gold and silver articles to sell to the Portuguese. Whether these accusations were true or not, the secular priests knew little or nothing about the management of reductions; nor did they possess the zeal for evangelization which was so characteristic of the Jesuits.[96]

Most of the missions were soon transferred to the care of the Franciscans of Santa Rosa de Ocopa.[97] In 1768 thirty-two Franciscan religious and four lay brothers reached Peru from Spain, their intention being to enter the missions of the oriente. In 1780 there were thirty-two missions of Maynas in charge of ten or twelve padres,[98] and in the same year the Observant Franciscans of the college of Popayán in New Granada had seven mission towns and fourteen religious on the Caquetá and Putumayo rivers.[99] By the end of the century the population of the Maynas missions had decreased fifty per cent, and there were not enough missionaries to care for the few reductions that existed. Some of the padres on the missions were said to be so ignorant that they could not say Mass, while others were but little interested in their work.[100]

The meager success of the Franciscans in Maynas was probably mainly attributable to lack of the support from the royal authorities. Some of the padres were able men. A Franciscan, Padre Sobreviela, aided by Padre Girbal y Barceló, produced the best map of the montaña of Peru that was made prior to the twentieth century (published in 1791).[101] Father Alvarez Villanueva, writing in 1792, exhibited an interest in the material improvement of the Maynas missions. His list of the products of the region at this time includes Peruvian bark; quinine; cinnamon; cocoa (including white cocoa); almonds; coca; tobacco; balsam; sugar cane; white, yellow, and black wax; ulmeche, a fruit used for making candles; incense; sarsaparilla; "dragon-tree blood;" piñons; indigo; rice; maize; fish; white, black, and red salt; animals of different kinds; gold; and diamonds.[102] The statement made by the viceroy of Peru in 1796 that until that time the missionaries had acquired only some vague ideas of the vast interior of the Montaña Real may have applied to the padres who were then working east of the Andes; but he must have forgotten the dozens of courageous friars who had voyaged along thousands of miles of interior waterways during the preceding century and a half.[103]

The decline of the missions of the Peruvian montaña was certainly not due to a lack of religious in the viceroyalty. A census taken in 1793 of the religious orders in Lima alone showed that there were in the capital not only Dominicans,

Franciscans, Augustinians, and Mercedarians, but Benedictines, Agonizantes, Mínimos de San Francisco de Paula, brothers of the Congregación del Oratorio de San Felipe Neri, members of the order of San Juan de Díos, and the Belemitas.[104]

With the coming of the wars for independence, the Maynas missions lost the support of Spain, and the Indians reverted to savagery. There is a difference of opinion as to whether any of the civilizing influences of the missionaries remained with them. Father J. A. Zahm speaks of the physical beauty of the Indians of the montaña and refers to them as gentlemen of the forest, while Clark Wissler tells of cannibalism, coca chewing, snuffing of mimosa seeds, phallic decorations, necklaces of human teeth, mutilation of the body for purpose of decoration, belief in evil spirits, and whipping of boys in puberty ceremonials.[105] Occasionally one may still observe in the market-places the shrunken heads of the Jíbaro victims.

Father Zahm, who made a journey through this region a few years ago, remarks:

Everywhere along the Paranapura, the Huallaga, and the Amazon, there exist the same evidences of ruin and abandonment as I observed along the great waterways of Venezuela and Colombia. Where, during the heyday of missionary activity, there were flourishing towns and villages, there are now but a few rickety huts tenanted by a few wretched Indians, or a riot of tropic growth, which conceals every trace of former human habitations.[106]

THE MISSIONS OF THE CHARCAS FRONTIER

I

ORE inaccessible even than the Maynas country was the land of the Mojos, Chiquitos, and Chiriguanos in the eastern part of the Audiencia of Charcas (at present the republic of Bolivia). The Mojos inhabited the eastern slopes of the Andes and the lowlands along the upper reaches of the Mamoré and Beni rivers. The Chiquitos lived to the east and southeast of the Mojos in the country between the headwaters of the Mamoré and the Paraguay. The Chiriguanos dwelt to the south of the Mojos between the Río Grande and the Pilcomayo, on the northern fringe of the Gran Chaco. Much of this region was more easily approached from Paraguay than from Lima, or even La Paz; and as a consequence, much of the missionary work among its inhabitants was done by Jesuits from Paraguay, who found it advisable to pacify and reduce the savages to the north of their Paraguay reductions as a safeguard against attack from that direction. It is a land of thorny, clammy, intertwined woods and gigantic swollen rivers, where men agonize under festering stings and

scorching fevers, where rains lie for weeks in pools among the palm trees, and the goldenrod of the savannas clashes with orchids among the mahoganies.

II

A Jesuit missionary to the Mojos described the location of this area as follows:

It is situated beneath the Torrid Zone, between the Equator and the Tropic of Capricorn, on the slopes of the chain of mountains that surrounds Peru: It extends, from the South to the North, from the twentieth parallel to the eleventh. . . . To the East it contains the Nations of the Chiriguanos, Chiquitos, Toromonas, and many other Barbarians, who inhabit the immense lands extending toward the famous River Marañón. All the Country is cut up by many Rivers; the two principal ones are the Mamoré and the Beni, that run from the South to the North, and having received the waters of many others, enter the Amazon River.[1]

The Mojos had been attached in a very loose fashion to the Inca empire, Inca armies having at times been sent among them; but they had absorbed little of the more advanced culture of the Indians of the highlands.[2] There were in reality among the Indians commonly referred to as Mojos no less than twenty-nine tribes speaking thirteen distinct languages besides a number of dialects.[3]

The land inhabited by the Mojo savages was characterized by a hot, humid climate; and, like the rest of the lowlands east of the Andes, it produced multitudes of insects and snakes, many of which were poisonous. The Indians, partly because of the nature of the climate and partly because of their own backwardness, were not agriculturists. After missions were established, it proved to be impossible to grow such temperate zone crops as grapes and wheat. Sheep did not thrive, although cattle got along satisfactorily. The Indians were mainly hunters and fishermen.[4]

In 1605 the Bishopric of Santa Cruz was erected in the eastern part of Charcas. It consisted of four provinces: Santa Cruz, Mizique, Mojos, and Chiquitos. The bishopric had within its borders the Chiquitos, Mojos, Chiriguanos, and Chanáes. Its capital was San Lorenzo el Real de la Frontera.[5]

While Father Jerónimo Andión had worked among the Mojo savages prior to 1668, not until Father Julián de Aller began in that year to preach to them were the missions definitely established.[6] In 1674 Padre Cypriano Baraza, a Jesuit from Lima, made a twelve days' voyage down the Río Grande, a tributary of the Mamoré, to the Mojo country. He carried a supply of needles, beads, fishing hooks, and other cheap gifts to attract the Indians to the Faith. Father Cypriano remained among these savages four years, during which he succeeded in reducing some two thousand of them.[7] Returning to Santa Cruz de la Sierra because of an attack of quartan ague, he was transferred to the Chiriguanos; but some time later he spent another five years among the Mojos.[8]

Father Cypriano taught these Indians to be farmers, weavers, carpenters, and other artisans. He administered the sacrament to the sick of soul and cared for the sick of body as well. He directed the natives in building a church. He introduced cattle into the missions, driving a herd of two hundred all the way from Santa Cruz, the journey requiring fifty-four days.[9] He spent three years opening a new route between Peru and the Mojo country.[10] So herculean were the many tasks that he was called upon to perform that he organized a body of Indian officers to serve under him. "For this he chose among them those who had the most fame as being prudent and valorous: some he made Captains, others family chiefs: these Consuls and those Ministers of Justice, in order that they should govern the People." [11]   Among the Mojos Father Cypriano suffered the usual difficulties of the frontier missionary in the Amazon basin: frequent rains, floods, insects, great distances between missions, and the ever present danger of being murdered by the untamed savages.[12]

The early entradas in this region were made without the aid of soldiers.   Father Stanislaus Arlet, writing from Mojos on September 1, 1698, told how he and a group of Indian guides entered the Mojo country on horseback and converted over twelve hundred Indians.   The savages were so greatly frightened at seeing mounted men—they thought that man and horse were one animal—that they dropped their bows and arrows.   If we are to believe this good padre, the Mojos were peculiarly amenable to the Christian teachings:

'Tis almost incredible that, in the Space of but one Year, a Savage Race of Men, who had scarce any Thing human about them but the Name and Shape, should yet have imbib'd Sentiments of Good nature and Piety in so very short a Time. We already perceive a Kind of Dawn, as it were, of Politeness and Civility breaking forth among them. They salute one another whenever they meet; and make us, whom they consider as their Masters, low Bows; striking their Knees against the Ground, and kissing their Hands before they come up to us. They invite such Indian Strangers as travel through their Settlements, to take a Lodging with them; and exercise in the Midst of their Poverty, a Kind of liberal Hospitality, beseeching these Travellers to love them as Brethren, and to give them Proofs upon every occasion, that they consider them as such.[13]

Two Indian youths in particular seem to have been profoundly impressed by the teachings of the padres.   When one of them proposed improper relations with a girl of the same tribe, he was made very much ashamed of himself by her declaration that she was a Christian.   Another youth confessed that he had thought of sinning with a certain woman; but when he remembered that she was a heathen, he left her,

Some neophytes became painters and sculptors, making ornaments for the church

horror-stricken at the thought of defiling himself in such a manner.[14]

In 1705 Father A. J. X. Nyel wrote from Lima to the rector of the College of Strassburg that there were in the Mojo missions at that time about thirty Jesuits, fifteen or sixteen towns, and between twenty-five and thirty thousand reduced Indians. The reduction villages were built on the same plan as those of Paraguay, having houses of uniform construction and straight streets of equal breadth. Each family had allotted to it a bit of ground, which it was obliged to cultivate. The plan of the padres was to see that each family had enough to live on, but not enough to feel superior to its neighbors. Besides the individual holdings, there were common lands for support of the church and hospital.[15] Indians of one mission were not allowed to occupy lands, cut wood, or take balsam and oil from other reductions.[16] Some neophytes became painters and sculptors, making decorations for the churches. Crops that the padres encouraged were maize, rice, manioc, plantains, cotton, cacao, vanilla, copayba, and cinnamon.[17]

Statistics regarding the number of converts in the Mojo region are a bit puzzling, probably because the various writers differ in the number of tribes included. Padre Diego Altamirano, who visited Santa Cruz de la Sierra in 1700 and tried to establish schools among the Mojos, says that there were twenty reductions in 1708, with about two thousand Indians in each.[18] Diego de Eguiluz says that between 1674 and 1696 nearly twenty thousand persons were pacified and reduced, of whom more than ten thousand were baptized, not counting the "numberless thousands of little angels that by means of baptism have gone happily to heaven."[19] Maúrtua lists by name sixteen missions which were in existence among the Mojos in 1715.[20]

When the Jesuits were expelled from the Mojo region, they left there fifteen towns, with a population of approximately thirty thousand, which were soon placed in charge of the Franciscan order. In 1773 the population of the missions was estimated at 17,185,[21] thus revealing a rapid decline since 1767. In 1780 the Franciscans of the province of Cuzco were said to have ten missions and twenty religious in Apolabamba and among the Mojos and the Chiquitos. The plantations had ceased to produce abundantly, and the herds of cattle were killed. In 1788, however, eleven reductions were still in existence among the Mojos, having a population of some twenty thousand, a decrease of over thirty per cent in twenty years.[22]

III

The Chiquitos occupied a region just north of the tropic of Capricorn in what is now eastern Bolivia and western Brazil. Father Charlevoix described their location in the following manner:

Under the name of Chiquites, it is usual to comprehend several small nations scattered over that tract of land, which is bounded to the north by a chain of mountains, to the south by Chaco, and to the east by the Moxes and Baures; its bounds to the west are not yet ascertained. It has scarce any breadth at its southern extremity, but grows wider as it stretches to the north. Longways it extends from the 14th degree of south latitude to the 21st. The eastern part of it is watered by some rivers; and has, besides, a great number of marshes and lakes. . . . This country is everywhere covered with mountains and thick forests. . . .[23]

The Indians known as Chiquitos included about thirty tribes. While they were all of the same stock, they spoke four different dialects: the Tao, the Piñoco, the Manaci, and the Peñoqui.[24] The principal location of these tribes was the eastern slope of the Andes between seventeen degrees and eighteen degrees, thirty minutes south latitude; but other family and tribal groups were scattered through the lowlands, each group being named after its chief or perhaps after some geographical feature of the locality. The area occupied by the Chiquitos was about two hundred by one hundred leagues in size.[25] The Spaniards called these Indians Chiquitos, or "Little Ones," because the doors of their houses were very low. The adult Indians themselves were quite large.[26]

Because of their relative inaccessibility and their savage nature, the conversion of the Chiquitos was not carried on with any marked degree of success until 1692, although as early as 1586 two padres from Santa Cruz de la Sierra had entered the Chiquito country. In January, 1692, Padre José de Arce began the conversion of these Indians.[27]

Between 1705 and 1721 a number of entradas of religious and soldiers penetrated the land of the Chiquitos. Those Indians who accepted Christianity and Spanish domination freely were reduced on the same basis as the Guaranís of Paraguay; that is, their tribute was less than the average, and the caciques were given military titles. Among the Chiquito tribes reduced at this time were the Great Lulles, Little Lulles, Manacicas, Malbalas, Chunipis, Ojatas, Moratocos, Quies, Zamucos, and Maciturocas.[28]

In 1732 the Jesuits had seven towns averaging about six hundred families each in this region.[29] The Jesuits of Paraguay were particularly interested in the conversion of these savages since they sometimes invaded the Paraguay reductions. The padres not only succeeded in persuading the Indians to settle down in their own land to a sedentary and peaceful manner of living, but they influenced some of them to move to the older missions in Paraguay.[30] The statement of J. Patricio Fernández that the Chiquitos asked that preachers of the gospel be sent to them is hardly in accord with the warlike character of these savages.[31]

In 1766 there were among the Chiquitos ten Jesuit missions: San Javier, La Inmaculada Concepción, San Rafael, San Miguel, San José, San Juan, Santiago, Santa Ana, el Sagrado Corazón de Jesús, and San Ignacio.[32] The population was 5,173 families consisting of 23,788 persons. Since the death rate was far in excess of the birth rate, it was necessary constantly to recruit new converts from the forest.[33]

In August, 1767, eighty cavalrymen were sent to these reductions to expel the Jesuits.[34] The padres, who could very easily have resisted with the aid of the thousands of Indian warriors in their charge, humbly submitted, but begged that the soldiers refrain from entering the villages because of the danger of causing an Indian revolt. Thirteen Jesuits were expelled on November 2, six more on December 28, and the rest on April 2, 1768. Some of them returned to Europe by way of Buenos Aires, while others went by way of the Pacific coast. Several missionaries, worn out by years of devoted service in the unhealthful montaña, were in no physical condition for such a long and arduous journey. Father Pallozzi, who departed by way of Arica and Panama, died at Panama on December 21, 1768. Father Messner was also taken toward the west coast, but he died in the saddle between Oruro and Tacna.[35]

IV

The country of the Chiriguano Indians covered an area of about sixty thousand square miles on the northwestern edge of the Gran Chaco between the parallels of 22° 31′ and 16° 31′ south latitude.[36] This region had been invaded prior to the Spanish conquest of Peru by armies of the Inca, but its inhabitants remained even more savage than the Chiquitos and Mojos.[37] The Chiriguanos were accused of cannibalism, and were said to have killed two hundred and fifty thousand Indians of neighboring tribes during a period of two centuries.[38] According to tradition, evidently erroneous, they numbered about four thousand when Catholic missionaries first went among them.[39] They spoke a Guaraní dialect and were supposed to have migrated from the banks of the Paraná and Paraguay rivers.[40]

In 1592 Father Gaspar de Monroy entered the land of the Chiriguanos.[41] In 1607 Padres Samaniego, Oliva, Ortega, and Villanão explored this region, and tried unsuccessfully to reduce the Indians. Some two years later Fathers Agustín Sabio and Francisco González visited the Chiriguano villages of Tambavera and Tayaguasu, where they were well received. The padres built a church and began the difficult task of converting the savages to Christianity. But the Chiriguanos soon reversed their friendly attitude, revolted, and sacked the church and the houses of the missionaries. In 1631 three Franciscans (Gregorio Bolívar, Juan Sánchez, and Luis de Jesús) entered the Chiriguano country, never to be heard from again. In 1679 Father Cypriano Baraza attempted the spiritual conquest of these Indians, but failed to accomplish his purpose. Father José Arce, in 1691, founded the mission of San Ignacio, but three years later it was abandoned. During the early part of the eighteenth century, however, Dominicans and Augustinians established several reductions among the Chiriguanos.[42] The attitude of these savages toward the teachings of the padres was well expressed by one of them who, upon being threatened with hell fire, replied that he would find a way to extinguish it.[43]

In the early eighteenth century the number of Chiriguano warriors was estimated at between twenty-five and thirty-five thousand.[44] When women and children were added, the total number must have been about one hundred thousand. By this time the Jesuits of Peru and Paraguay had tried at least ten times to reduce these savages, not to mention the evangelistic efforts of Franciscans, Dominicans, and Augustinians. In 1731 the cabildo of Tarija, in a report to the viceroy concerning killings perpetrated by the Chiriguanos, suggested that Jesuit missions be established to restrain them. The viceroy then ordered that Jesuits be sent to this field,[45] and in 1732 three of them (Julián de Lizardi, Ignacio Chomé, and José Pons) entered the territory of the Chiriguanos from the Paraguay reductions. This attempt was also unsuccessful, and Father Lizardi was murdered in 1735. Later, Franciscan padres established ten reductions, six of which were destroyed in 1799. In 1801 an army of two thousand men under Captain General Viedma enabled the Franciscans to restore their missions. The Chiriguanos again destroyed them in 1804, but they were rebuilt the following year. In 1810 Father Antonio Tomajuncosa, prefect of these missions, wrote that the Jesuits had been able to baptize only 324 Chiriguanos during a period of seventy-seven years, while the Franciscans, during a subsequent period of fifty-five years, had founded twenty-two missions and made 16,425 converts.[46] Perhaps the report was somewhat prejudiced.

Father Antonio complained that "only an entirely apostolic spirit" could "live among these unfortunate savages and perform among them" the various offices required: father, master, judge, and administrator. The Chiriguano were perhaps the least successful of all the important missions on the Spanish frontier.

The same padre describes the routine to which the converts were obliged to conform:

To make Christians of them, morning and evening are dedicated to teaching them our Catholic religion. At sunrise, they are called to the church and there they recite the Christian doctrine and commend themselves to God, one day in Spanish and the next in their own tongue. Mass follows, and then they retire to their houses. At sunset, they reunite, recite the doctrine and holy rosary, and again commend themselves to God, and having sung something devout they go to rest.

In the new missions, all the prayers are said by the priests, and when, after several years, the young men are well instructed, the priest causes prayer to be recited by one of them in his presence. Sundays, and on the principal feast days, some point of the Christian doctrine is explained to them. Every year, during Lent, they are examined in it. . . .[47]

Julian Duguid, who crossed eastern Bolivia in the second decade of the twentieth century, says that the Indians still "confuse Christianity with their own barbarous customs." He visited the ruins of the Chiquito mission of Santo (Sagrado) Corazón. "A gigantic crucifix stretching its arms against the dark blue sky seemed to mourn the glory that had departed. A stale aroma of decay, an atmosphere of futility that perhaps came more from . . . [his] heightened sensibility than from anything tangible, hung about" him as he made his way "in silence towards the deserted school." In the old mission of San José he found the cathedral built by the Jesuits in 1748 still standing:

A series of round, white-washed pillars bounded the main aisle on either hand. At the foot of each were small rough-hewn, bodiless cherubim. . . . They were made from *quebracho* wood, and the insects of the country had eaten round holes in the back, though the faces were perfect. Near the altar, on the left-hand side, sat St. Peter, a smooth-faced, black-bearded, noncommittal old man, a bunch of wooden keys dangling from a stiff wrist. He was dressed in fine brocade, purple and scarlet and white, and a long skirt fell straight to his ankles, while on his head was a cotton cap like a chef's. Two curious winged figures, obviously of native workmanship, faced one another across the aisle. . . . In the vestry were images on wheels like gigantic nursery toys, designed to be dragged through the streets on feastdays. A large tableau of the flight to Egypt, pathetically crude, showed the Virgin on a solemn wooden donkey and St. Joseph standing resignedly by. Other and lesser saints languished in corners.[48]

THE PORTUGUESE MENACE

I

S the Spanish missionaries, with the aid of friendly Indians and military escorts, were doggedly pushing the boundary of Spanish civilization farther and farther into the interior of South America, the Portuguese, contemptuous of the Line of Demarcation established in 1494 by the Treaty of Tordesillas, advanced up the Amazon and its tributaries or marched overland into the Matto Grosso or toward the Spanish settlements on the tributaries of the Río de la Plata. In the three-century struggle for control of the far-flung stretches of forest and plain reaching from the Guiana Highlands to Paraguay and from the mouths of the Amazon to the eastern ramparts of the Andes, the Portuguese had a decided geographical advantage. From Pará there extends into the interior the unparalleled Amazon river system, draining an area of almost two million square miles, with its twenty-five thousand miles of navigable streams.[1] By way of the Amazon, the Río Negro, and the Casiquiare, the

Portuguese could reach the Spanish missions on the Orinoco. By way of the Amazon, the Putumayo, the Napo, the Marañón (upper Amazon), and the Huallaga it was possible to approach the Andes of New Granada and Peru. By proceeding up the Madeira and the Mamoré they could reach the audiencia of Los Charcas; and by way of the Tapajos they could approach within a few leagues of the headwaters of the Paraguay. Thus there existed for the Portuguese a complete water highway (broken, however, by rapids) inviting them to venture forth from their settlements near the Atlantic to dispute with their Iberian rivals the possession of the hinterland. On the other hand, there were for the Spaniards the mighty barrier of the Andean cordillera and, to the east of this gigantic wall, foothills in which streams were foaming torrents that threatened to dash the canoe of the intrepid voyager upon some jagged rock and to swallow him in their swirling whirlpools.

When the first governor-general of Brazil, Thomé de Souza, sailed for the Portuguese colony in 1549, six Jesuits accompanied the officials and the three hundred convict colonists. They were: Fathers Manoel de Nobrega, Juan de Aspilcueta, Antonio Pires, and Leonardo Nunes, and the lay brothers, Vicente Rodríguez and Diego Jacome.[2] These Jesuits, who were the first to reach Brazil, were the nucleus from which grew a huge organization, whose members in their search for souls explored practically every river in what is today Brazil. The six were very successful in their work among the natives, learning their languages, teaching and converting them, and often abolishing such practices as polygamy and cannibalism. Like the Spanish padres, they became the champions of the native races. The Society of Jesus soon had colleges and houses in São Salvador, Rio de Janeiro, and Pernambuco, which served as bases for missionary activity in the interior.[3]   A second group of Jesuits led by José de Anchieta arrived in Brazil in 1553.

In 1551 Pope Julius III granted the royal patronage to the Portuguese monarchs, so that henceforth they had complete ecclesiastical as well as temporal jurisdiction in Brazil. This jurisdiction was automatically transferred to the Spanish crown during the period (1580-1640) when Portugal was under the control of Spain. Under the provisions of the royal patronage the kings of Portugal nominated bishops, heard cases appealed from ecclesiastical courts, collected tithes, and dispensed revenues for alms, religious feasts, and the maintenance of churches.[4] Portuguese missionaries, like the Spanish, could be used as instruments of state in royal schemes of expansion. When Portuguese and Spanish padres encountered each other on the muddy banks of some equatorial stream or in some narrow pathway amid the dimness of huge trees, they met not only as men of God seeking the salvation of the children of the forest, but as agents of rival powers. And when each was accompanied by several hundred Indian warriors and a white convoy, they must have wondered whether to embrace with brotherly affection or to greet each other with cutlass and bullet. Spanish frontier missionaries, coming frequently into contact with both lay and secular Portuguese, found themselves forced to assume a position not unlike that of the counts of the marches in Charlemagne's empire. The Spanish padres were expected to restrain the inroads of their rivals; but they were unable to do so because of inadequate support by the secular authorities.

During the years 1580-1640 the religious orders of the two Iberian powers coöperated in some degree. About 1586 Francisco Victoria, Bishop of Tucumán, who was a Dominican, invited the Jesuit provincial of Brazil to send some missionaries to that province. Anchieta, who was provincial of

Brazil at that time, complied by sending five Jesuits: Leonardo Arminio, Juan Salonio, Thomas Filds, Estevam de Grão, and Manoel de Ortega. Arminio was an Italian and Filds a Scotchman. Arminio and Grao soon returned to Brazil, but the other three remained in Spanish territory.[5]

The sixty years during which Spain and Portugal were united were utilized by both lay and ecclesiastical Portuguese to extend their influence farther westward. In their claims to religious authority on the upper Amazon and Paraguay the Spaniards had the better case. Fray Gaspar de Carvajal was thought to have accompanied the Spaniard, Francisco de Orellana, who explored the Amazon in 1542,[6] and the Spanish Jesuits were the first to explore the headwaters of the Paraguay.[7] The journey of Pedro Teixeira from Pará to Quito served, however, as a basis for the claims of Portugal to much of the upper Amazon basin. The Spanish authorities, suspicious of the motives of the Portuguese explorer, requested him to return to Pará;[8] and a short time later (September 16, 1639) the king of Spain published a cédula declaring that no Portuguese should cross the Line of Demarcation for the purpose of reducing or taking out Indians, on penalty of loss of life and confiscation of goods.[9] Concerning slave-hunting friars of Brazil the cédula stated that

if, in any of these expeditions or entradas or purchases or sales of Indians, . . . there may be found, or may be participant, any religious or friar of any order, regular or monastical, or any priest or ecclesiastical person, I pray and charge his prelate that he immediately proceed against him and punish him exemplarily, and without accepting any excuse, eject him from all the state of Brazil; for the same cause, such a friar or monk or ecclesiastical person of the two crowns loses the citizenship that he had, and is held as a foreigner of the two crowns of Portugal and Castile.[10]

In the vigorous westward movement of southern Brazil the missionaries played little part, for the whites and mixbloods would permit no humanitarian interference in behalf of the natives. The padres were lucky if they were allowed to remain in the region at all. In the north, however, they contributed in a large way to the frontier advance. The Portuguese and mixed races moved rapidly for twelve hundred miles along the north coast from Natal to Pará, which was founded in 1616. The frontier of settlement then advanced up the Amazon and reached Tabatinga at the mouth of the Javary by 1780.

As early as 1607 two Portuguese Jesuits were sent from Pernambuco to establish missions near the boundary of the present republic of Ecuador; but this attempt to found permanent reductions in the region failed.[11] In 1653 Antonio Vieira, a famous member of the Society of Jesus, arrived on the scene and soon persuaded the king of Portugal to place the Indians of North Brazil under the guardianship of the Jesuits. The courageous padres set out at once into the wilderness in search of souls. Wherever the Black Robes appeared, the Indians "by the thousands exchanged their liberty for the gentle sway of the Jesuits. . . . Even the redoubtable cannibals . . . began to assemble . . . and submit to work in the fields."[12] The members of the Company did not fail to encounter difficult and turbulent days. As in Spanish America, they confronted the bitter and determined opposition of Brazilians who wished to subject the converts to forced labor. In 1685 they lost their monopoly of the field, and the Capuchins, Mercedarians, and Carmelites were permitted to share the work with them.

In spite of every handicap, however, the efforts of the missionaries of all orders achieved considerable success. A contemporary map of the Spanish-Portuguese frontier represents the Portuguese Jesuits as having, about 1749, numerous establishments upon the upper right bank of the Madeira and all along the southern basin of the Amazon from the mouth of the Madeira to that of the Tapajos, while the Carmelites are shown to occupy the western bank of the Negro as well as the southern basin of the Amazon between the junction of the Purus and that of the Javari. In 1755 the Jesuits had twenty-eight missions in Brazil, the Capuchins fifteen, the Carmelites twelve, and the Mercedarians five—a total of sixty mission establishments located mostly in the steaming tropical jungle and grasslands.[13]

II

Portuguese and Spanish padres were often bitter rivals on the international frontier, but the inhabitants of Brazil who caused the greatest injury to the Spanish reductions were the Mamelukes of São Paulo, fierce and lawless men who repeatedly made incursions into the country inhabited by wild Indians and even into the Spanish mission villages, capturing natives and carrying them to the coast for sale. Mainly mestizos who seem to have inherited some of the worst traits of their ancestors on both sides, they were practically independent of the Brazilian colonial government during much of the period. São Paulo became a slave market to which thousands of unfortunate wretches gathered from the borderlands of the Uruguay, the Paraguay, and the Paraná, were brought, and from which they were shipped to serve out miserable lives on plantations as far away as Bahía and Pará.[14] According to one Spanish friar, the intention of the Mamelukes was "to take possession of all these lands, and to open a road to Peru, taking little account of the ruin of Christianity so long as they can satiate their ambition and greed." [15]

The Mamelukes were not averse to resorting to the basest deception in order to ensnare their victims. One of their ruses was to go disguised as Jesuits into the territory of Indians

Fierce Mamelukes made incursions into the country, capturing natives and carrying them to the coast for sale

whom they knew the sons of Loyola had already visited as a preliminary step to reducing them. Here the slave-catchers erected crosses, distributed presents, administered medicine to the sick, and after the manner of missionaries, harangued the natives, explaining the principles of the Catholic religion and exhorting them to accept the Faith. Since many Mamelukes were well versed in the Guaraní language, they often were successful in persuading the unsuspecting natives to abandon their camps for the purpose of settling on a reduction where, as they were assured, they would lead lives of ease and pleasure. In course of time the gullible Indians found themselves not on a mission, but in the slave market of São Paulo. Such practices caused the savages to fear and hate the real Jesuits,

whom they thought to be authors of these crimes.[16]   Don
Pedro Estevan Dávila reported about 1640 that he had seen
Indians being sold as slaves even in the markets of Rio de
Janeiro.   He estimated that between 1628 and 1630 Mamelukes had captured sixty thousand Indians, many of them
from Paraguay.[17]   Spanish friars, when they had the opportunity, interceded in favor of the captives, but their prayers
had little influence on the Paulistas.   When Father Mola,
whose mission had been destroyed and whose converts were
being carried away into slavery, told the Mamelukes that
after the perpetration of such atrocities there was little hope
of their salvation, they replied that they had been baptized
and they would fight their way into heaven if God should
oppose their entrance! [18]

In order to resist the inroads of the Paulistas, the Jesuits
organized their Indians into armies consisting of both infantry
and   cavalry, and so became self-appointed generals as well
as ministers of the gospel.   By 1642 the Paraguay reductions
were enjoying a period of peace; the mission forces were
sufficiently strong to beat off the slave hunters, and the
Mamelukes were constrained to limit their activities to attacks
on unconverted natives or to the seizure of unwary neophytes
who wandered from their reductions.[19]   In 1649 Philip IV
declared the Paraguay Indians to be the barrier of Paraguay
against the Portuguese, called them his most faithful vassals,
made them responsible directly to him or to officers whom he
should specifically designate, and partially exempted them
from payment of tribute.[20]   During the eighteenth century
these missions were stronger than ever, but the Portuguese
likewise increased their strength by supplying arms to wild
Indians on the borders of the reductions.[21]   Nevertheless, the
Paraguay missions, as long as they retained the moral support
of the Spanish crown, were a more effective rampart against

Portuguese expansion than were the reductions on any other Spanish frontier in South America.[22]

III

Portuguese encroachments extended even farther than Paraguay into territory claimed by Spain. An Augustinian friar, Domingo Teixeira, referred to Buenos Aires as the southernmost city within Portuguese territory. A map published in Lisbon in 1668 placed the boundary of Brazil as far west as Tucumán, while other maps located Potosí within the possessions of Portugal.[23]

Mamelukes attacked both the Mojo and the Chiquito missions.[24] In 1723 a Portuguese expedition was reported to have ascended the Madeira River to the Mojo reductions,[25] and it is certain that Manoel Felix de Lima visited the Mojos in 1742. The Jesuits staged a military review for his edification, and casually remarked that the missions could place forty thousand archers in the field. After the padres had entertained Manoel Felix with proper kindness, they courteously informed him that Portuguese were expected not to prolong their visits in the region.[26] In 1749 a group of Portuguese desperadoes who had fled from Matto Grosso settled on a long island in the Guaporé River within territory claimed by Spaniards. The Spanish Jesuits attempted to make friends of them with the view of employing them in possible contests with other Portuguese, but the exiles retained their national feeling to the extent at first of refusing to let a Spanish padre, Raimundo Laines, celebrate Mass in their settlement for fear that this act would impair the territorial claims of Portugal. They finally permitted him to perform his priestly duty, but took down a cross that he erected and requested him not to visit their island again. At this time two other Portuguese were employed by the Spanish mis-

*For the edification of the Portuguese officer, the Jesuits staged a
military review and casually remarked that the missions
could place forty thousand archers in the field*

sionaries to help them seek escaped converts.[27]   During the
1740's another Portuguese force established itself on the borders of Mojos, and when the superior of the Society of
Jesus in this region informed the Portuguese commander that
his remaining there would be a violation of treaties between
Spain and Portugal, the officer replied that such violation
had always been very far from his mind; but he made no
move to withdraw.   Some Spanish soldiers were then sent to
drive the interlopers away, and the Portuguese withdrew, but
returned in 1751 and built a fort.   After the expulsion of the
Jesuits in 1767 the Portuguese established themselves in Mojos
more firmly than ever.[28]

In 1695 a band of Mamelukes invaded the Chiquito missions, where they were ambushed by the mission Indians
and forced to retreat after suffering severe losses.[29]   About

1740 a group of Portuguese under Antonio Pinheiro de Faria again reached these missions, but did not make any permanent settlements.[30]

IV

Spanish reductions in the Peruvian montaña were continually being threatened by bands of adventurous Brazilians. Sometimes these expeditions were sent out by the Portuguese authorities, but more often they were privately organized parties of slave hunters. Father Juan Lorenzo Lucero, writing from the mission of Laguna in the oriente of Peru on June 3, 1681, stated that some Indians had fled to his reduction in fear of the Portuguese, who they said were coming up from Pará in search of slaves. These natives reported that three thousand other Indians were also on their way to the mission for protection.[31] A Spanish padre among the Omaguas was said to have had in 1684 seven thousand Indian warriors to resist any Portuguese or Dutch who might come in search of slaves.[32]

Father Samuel Fritz, the Bohemian Jesuit engaged in Spanish mission work, frequently came into contact with Portuguese on the Marañón. When he went to Pará in 1689 for medical treatment, he was kept prisoner, as previously noted, for almost two years because the Portuguese considered him a powerful opponent of Portuguese expansion along the upper Amazon. The military escort which accompanied him up the river on his return carried orders to reconnoitre the reductions founded by missionaries from Quito and send to the royal authorities at Lisbon a report as to their location and condition. Father Fritz wished to send a message to the viceroy of Peru asking him to forestall Portuguese attempts to spy on his missions, but he was unable to do so.[33]

After Fritz had returned to his reductions, the king of

Portugal issued an order prohibiting incursions of armed troops into territory inhabited by wild Indians for the purpose of capturing slaves. Only those Indians might be legally enslaved who had killed Portuguese without provocation. In order that Brazilian plantations might not be without a labor supply, importation of Negroes from Africa was permitted. It is doubtful, however, whether this order had much influence on the Portuguese Indian slavers, for the Spanish missions continued to have trouble with slaving expeditions. Fritz did meet a Portuguese, Francisco Sosa, who assured the Spanish padre that he was not after slaves, but was visiting the Spanish reductions merely for the purpose of buying cacao;[34] but Fritz also reported the arrival in his missions of other Brazilians who were not so peaceably inclined. An Indian cacique told him that a Portuguese Carmelite friar had seized all the women and children of his district and taken them to the slave market at Pará. Father Samuel was further informed of the arrival at the settlement of Nuestra Señora de las Nieves of another friar who carried a set of stocks and a large number of handcuffs.[35]

Father Fritz tried as best he could to protect his Indian wards from the slavers. His opinion of Portuguese he expressed in no uncertain terms: "May God free us from such a set of rascals. . . . If God sends no speedy remedy the whole Mission very shortly will be destroyed. . . . Gracious God! Is it to this that Portuguese Christianity has arrived, to oppress and carry away by violence our toil and labor of so many years for Christ . . . ?"[36] The Jurimagua Indians, who attributed to Fritz superhuman powers, quite naturally appealed to the padre whenever in danger from the slavers; and when the Portuguese tried to persuade them that they were rightly under the jurisdiction of Portugal, the reply was: "We have neither master nor protection, but our Father, whose love for us is far greater than your love, since with you there is no Father like ours with knowledge of everything." [37]

During his entire career of thirty-seven years among the natives of the upper Amazon and its tributaries Fritz was in continual dispute with the Portuguese regarding the boundary between the possessions of the crowns of Spain and Portugal. Pedro Teixeira, on his return from Quito to Pará in 1639, had taken possession, with permission of the Spanish authorities, of a village somewhere in the upper Amazon basin, marking the position with the trunk of a tree. As the years passed the tree decayed and disappeared. The Portuguese claimed that this marker had been placed at the mouth of the Aguarico, a tributary of the Napo. Father Samuel maintained that it had been located on the main stream of the Amazon farther down, in the direction of the Río Negro. He argued further that even if the marker were still in existence at the place claimed by Portugal, he would be justified in ignoring it, since Teixeira's act of possession had not been confirmed by the Spanish monarch, Philip IV, who then ruled both countries. Fritz wrote both to the Spanish ambassador in Lisbon and to the procurator-general of the Indies justifying his activity in the region. It was impossible for the two powers to reach a definite and satisfactory agreement in regard to limits in this heavily wooded and frequently inundated territory, which possessed no natural boundaries running in a north and south direction and which had never been surveyed. [38] Fritz also addressed a letter to the viceroy of Peru asking for additional missionaries, money, and other gifts, as well as ten or twelve armed men. His twofold purpose in requesting soldiers was that they might "assist" him "among those barbarians in the propagation of the Holy Faith" and aid in "the extension of the Empire of His Catholic Majesty." The viceroy granted Fritz one thousand pesos for the purchase of bells, decorations, and furnishings for his mission churches, and added to this subsidy personal gifts of wine and silver to the value of another thousand pesos; but he refused to furnish armed forces.[39]

On July 20, 1697, the governor of the Brazilian state of Maranham wrote to the king of Portugal reporting that Father Samuel was continually visiting Indians on the Amazon within Portuguese territory and claiming that Spanish jurisdiction reached as far as the Río Negro. The governor had sent a Carmelite friar and some soldiers up the river to take possession of the Spanish missions and to warn Fritz "as to the manner in which he must conduct himself in those parts." Fritz had temporarily withdrawn from his Amazon missions nearest Pará, but the Portuguese official, in his letter to the king, continued:

I hope also that it will please your Majesty to send me orders as to how I am to deal with the said Father Samuel, if he or others of that Government resist the presence of our Missionaries, so that I may be able to carry out my duties in all that concerns the service of your Majesty and the conservation of your dominions.[40]

A short time after the letter quoted above was written, two Jesuits from Quito, Samuel Fernández and João Baptista Sanna, were reported to have invaded Portuguese territory with a force of eighty men, captured a Portuguese Carmelite missionary and five other Portuguese subjects, and burned a church as well as a number of houses. The governor of Maranham sent a force of one hundred and fifty men to arrest the Spanish padres who were guilty of this attack, and any other Spanish missionaries who might be found within Portuguese territory.[41]

When the Portuguese began distributing gifts among the Omaguas occupying lands claimed by Spain, in order to encourage them to capture other savages for sale as slaves, Fritz persuaded the natives to return the presents, and protested that the Portuguese were acting contrary to law. Fritz also asked some Brazilians who came up to the Amazon in 1702 with Father Antonio de Andrade to refrain from further advances until the boundary should be definitely determined by the crowns of Spain and Portugal. Although the Portuguese friar agreed to this, he and the soldiers who accompanied him soon attacked some Indians who were with Fritz and captured a cacique. Andrade later returned the Indian to Fritz, but he threatened to take Father Samuel in chains to Pará if he did not get out of the country.[42] In 1706 Fritz went to Quito after more missionaries, returning the next year with ten padres.[43]

In 1709 the Spanish missionaries were informed by the Omaguas that an armada of Portuguese under the command of Ignacio Correa de Oliveira was coming up the Amazon. A message soon arrived from Correa to the effect that if the Spaniards did not retire westward to a point designated by the Portuguese authorities, all of them would be carried prisoners to Pará and shipped to Portugal. Fritz wrote to Correa:

Señor, I am surprised and distressed at the coming of this Portuguese troop and at the manner in which it has come to these our Missions with disturbance and armed violence. . . . Here there has been neither cause nor motive of any kind to come with armed violence against the Fathers of Jesus Christ, for . . . their Company has gained these Missions with His Holy Gospel, teaching them and having maintained them in peaceful possession without any controversy or injury to the Portuguese dominion.[44]

Correa received notice that a body of two hundred Spaniards, besides Indian allies, would be sent against him; but the Portuguese, ignoring the warning, proceeded to occupy a number of Jesuit missions, the padres retiring upstream. A

short time later the Spaniards retaliated by capturing Correa
and burning several villages which Portuguese Carmelite friars
had established on the Amazon.[45]

In 1710 the governor of Pará sent an expedition of fifteen
hundred Portuguese and four thousand Indians up the Amazon to the mouth of the Napo. They took possession of
forty Spanish mission villages, imprisoned the Indians who
did not hide in the forest, and constructed several forts. Fritz
appealed to Quito and Lima without results.[46] The Jesuit
provincial at Quito wrote to Father Samuel on April 1, 1711,
that although he had informed the royal audiencia of the in-
vasions, there were slight prospects that definite action would
be taken to aid the missionaries in holding the disputed territory. He gave as reasons the great cost, the depletion of the
treasury, and the difficulty of sending troops such a long
distance over mountains and through tropical forests.[47] The
viceroy at Lima informed Fritz that soldiers could not be
spared to defend the distant jungles of the Amazon, particularly since that region was not a source of profit to the crown
of Spain.[48]

In 1712 three hundred Portuguese and three Carmelite
friars captured the Spanish missionary with a Portuguese name,
João Baptista Sanna, on the Napo, dispersed the Indians of
the Omagua reductions, and carried off the doors, altar-
pieces, portraits, and bells of five Spanish missions.[49]

In 1735 "squadrons of Portuguese and thieves" came once
more up the river from Pará and attacked the Spanish missions on the Marañón, destroying houses and churches and
robbing the latter of their ornaments. They forced the Spanish padres to retire, and carried what Indians they could seize
away to Pará. The captured towns were turned over to the
Portuguese Carmelite fathers. "Thus has been executed the
piety of the Portuguese of Pará against the new plantations of

247

the Marañón; and such insults occur even today, supplications, protests, and tears amounting to nothing." [50] A report from Quito published in 1735 claimed, however, that, notwithstanding these setbacks, the work of conversion was going on and that some reductions were steadily growing in size.[51]

Shortly afterward, Father Andrés de Zárate, visitor general and vice-provincial of the Company of Jesus in the Province of Quito, wrote to the Portuguese vice-governor at Pará calling his attention to the existence of the Line of Demarcation. He stated that while it had so far been the policy of the Spanish authorities to maintain no armed forces on the Portuguese frontier, it would be necessary to alter this hitherto peaceful policy if the Portuguese authorities did not take steps to prevent further incursions into the Spanish missions. He said that he had already memorialized the viceroy of Peru to instruct the governor of Maynas to organize and train an army of mission Indians for defense of the reductions. He called the attention of the governor to the fact that in 1734 the latter had promised to withdraw all Portuguese from the provinces of Solimanes and Campebas, and then added:

It is now time that your highness fulfill this just and binding promise, and that you effectively oblige the Reverend Carmelite Fathers that they leave and disembarrass the towns that they unjustly occupy, and that the said Fathers and other subjects of your highness leave my subjects free to preach the Holy Gospel in all the other territories which in this great river Marañón belong to the Crown of Castile.[52]

By 1740 the Portuguese had established numerous missions along the Río Negro and on the right bank of the Amazon above the mouth of the Negro. The Amazon missions belonged to the Carmelites, while the Río Negro reductions were under the care of Portuguese Jesuits.[53] The Portuguese missions were far more prosperous than the Spanish, largely because the markets of Pará were accessible to them. Their churches and the houses of their missionaries were made of stone, and even the Indian women wore cloth imported from Europe.[54]

When the Jesuits were expelled from the Spanish dominions, the members of the Society who were in the Marañón region went down the Amazon to Pará and from there to Lisbon. On this journey they met Portuguese soldiers and engineers who were going upstream to establish settlements and forts at the mouths of the Aguarico and the Napo.[55] In 1775 the Spanish and Portuguese settlements nearest to each other on the Amazon were respectively St. Ignacio de Pevas and St. Paul; they were a week's journey apart.[56]

V

Portuguese from the Amazon region invaded the Spanish missions on the Orinoco as early as 1737, reaching them by way of the Río Negro and the Casiquiare. Portuguese were also in this region in 1738 and 1739, and Father Joseph de Gumilla feared that they would destroy the missions of Spanish Jesuits there. He wrote:

> I say that just as the said Portuguese seriously molest the Missions and the Missionaries of the Company of Jesus in the Province of Quito with great injury to them and hindrance to the conversion of the Heathens of the upper part of the Marañón, in the same way they will harm (as it is seen they harm today) and make impossible the Missions . . . in my Province of the New Kingdom. . . . It is clear that these incursions, and those of the Marañón . . . have not reached the attention of the Most Serene King of Portugal, whose pious and Christian zeal is so notable, that, on learning of them, he would have remedied them with greater promptitude.[57]

The fact that João Ferreira, rector of the college of Jesuits in Pará, made a map showing that the Orinoco and Amazon river systems were connected indicates that the Portuguese were acquainted with this route. In 1744, indeed, a group of Portuguese went up the Río Negro to the Spanish missions on the Orinoco and returned, making the entire trip by water.[58]

Slavers who plied their trade on this northern frontier of Brazil seem to have resorted to wiles similar to those employed by the Mamelukes of São Paulo. One of them was said to have founded a reduction of Indians and while the deluded natives were having a great religious festival, to have made them all prisoners and then shipped them to the slave market at Pará. Borda estimated that five thousand Indian slaves reached this port annually. In the eighteenth century Portuguese law permitted enslavement of Indians captured in a war in which the aborigines were the aggressors. At Pará was a house of trade to which the bewildered and sometimes wounded captives were taken from the tributaries of the Amazon and from the Orinoco. A Jesuit was appointed to inspect these Indians with the understanding that he would declare that all of them had been captured in a just war.[59]

The viceroy of New Granada reported to the king on November 15, 1786, that the Portuguese were making inroads into the Franciscan missions among the Andaquíes on the Putumayo and the Caquetá rivers, enslaving them and robbing them of their possessions.[60]

There seems to have been little serious objection about the middle of the eighteenth century to Portuguese trading expeditions into Spanish territory provided it was clear that the Portuguese were not after slaves and had no intention of establishing settlements. Each year, for instance, Portuguese merchants went from Brazil to Cuyabá near the source of the Paraguay River with a fleet of canoes loaded with goods which they exchanged for gold and diamonds. These fleets sometimes contained sixty or seventy canoes, including a great war canoe fitted with a cabin and carrying a small bronze cannon.[61]

VI

While Spanish frontier missionaries considered themselves to be defenders of the colonial empire of His Most Catholic Majesty against Portuguese expansion, they might, if circumstances made such action advisable, turn upon the Spanish authorities as well. Opposition of padres to individual Spaniards and to local temporal authorities is proverbial. The most famous case of antagonism between the missionaries and the highest Spanish authorities occurred on the Paraguayan frontier. On January 13, 1750, Spain and Portugal signed the Treaty of Madrid. While Portugal recognized Spanish claims in the Philippine Islands, Spain transferred to Portugal seven Indian missions to the east of the Uruguay River, and recognized many Portuguese claims to territory in the Paraná and Amazon basins west of the original boundary as determined in the Treaty of Tordesillas. A joint commission was to be selected to survey the new boundaries.[62] The thirty thousand Indians on these missions were given the option of leaving or staying. In either case they lost their houses, fields, and immovable goods, but could keep their personal belongings such as furniture and tools. As compensation for their losses they were to receive a total of twenty-eight thousand pesos, less than one peso per capita.

Gomes Freyre de Andrada, governor of Rio de Janeiro, and Don Gaspar Munive of the Council of the Indies, were appointed commissioners to execute the terms of the treaty. With Munive went Luis Lope Altamirano, a Jesuit representing the general of the Society, who was to attempt to conciliate and soothe the infuriated missionaries and Indians. The superior of the missions ordered the padres to make no opposition to the transfer of the reductions. Arriving at these establishments on September 9, 1753, Altamirano advised the missionaries to tell the Indians that the transfer of territory and their migration were commanded by Jesus Christ himself and that, like good sheep, they should obey the command of their Master. The Jesuit padres did as instructed, holding up a crucifix as the symbol of divine authority. But it is quite likely that they secretly put very different notions into the heads of their wards, for the Indians claimed that Altamirano was not a Jesuit at all, but a Portuguese in disguise. Refusing to move, they threatened to throw Altamirano into the river. That dignitary was so frightened that he returned to Buenos Aires. The Portuguese thereupon began gathering an army in Rio Grande do Sul, while the Spaniards collected another at Buenos Aires. In the meanwhile the Jesuits sent a representation to the Court of Madrid which claimed that the newly baptized Indians in Paraguay had conceived such an aversion to the Brazilians that they would flee to the interior rather than become subjects of Portugal. They argued that Spain would lose thirty or forty thousand active subjects without receiving adequate compensation, that Portugal would be enriched at the expense of Spain, and that the Portuguese would use the Paraguay forests to build ships to attack the other Spanish colonies. At the same time they sent a document to Lisbon maintaining that Portugal would lose by the exchange, and they used their confessorial influence at both courts in an effort to effect the abrogation of the Treaty of Madrid.[63]

In 1754 the governor of Buenos Aires took the field and destroyed a great many cattle belonging to the Indians of Yapeyú, who were entirely outside the boundaries of the seven missions in question, whereupon these Indians took up arms, imprisoned their padres, and robbed their storehouses, charging that their missionaries had been plotting with the Spaniards. A force of three hundred Indians met the twenty-five hundred Spaniards who came against them, but all of the Indians were either killed or captured. While the Spanish forces were thus engaged, the Portuguese general left Rio Grande do Sul, crossed the Rio Pardo, and moved toward the missions. The Portuguese and Spanish armies united on January 16, 1756, and were met a few weeks later by a force of two thousand Indians. After killing some twelve hundred of these and dispersing the rest, the allies captured the seven villages of the Tapes, and the transfer took place.[64] Not until 1759, however, was resistance completely broken.[65]

VII

On February 12, 1761, a convention was signed by Spain and Portugal completely annulling the Treaty of Madrid; and on October 1, 1777, the Treaty of San Ildefonso was negotiated whereby Portugal recognized the Spanish claim to the Tape missions on the left bank of the Uruguay River. Territory sparsely settled by Portuguese Jesuits and pioneers from São Paulo was declared to be the property of Portugal. This treaty, however, did not stop Brazilian expansion toward the west.[66]

The expulsion of the Jesuits from Spanish South America was tantamount to razing a defensive wall. After their missions had been either abandoned or turned over to less aggressive orders, the Portuguese pushed the Brazilian frontier toward the Andes more effectively than ever.[67] According to Father Pablo Hernández:

Another consequence of the expulsion of the Jesuits has been the aggrandizement of the Portuguese in Brazil. While those possessed their missions, these did not usurp anything, and as many times as they tried it, by way of the Marañón, Paraná, and Uruguay, as many did they leave severely punished. But scarcely were the Jesuits removed when the Portuguese advanced by the Marañón, opening a road to invade Quito. A little later, with the foundation of Matto Grosso, they had established themselves almost within the Mojos and Chiquitos. Thirty days had not passed after the expulsion, when they made themselves masters of almost all the towns of the Guaraní Missions.[68]

That the temporal authorities recognized the value of the missions as checks to Portuguese expansion is shown by the recommendation of the viceroy of New Granada (1789) that twenty-five missionaries be sent to the region of the Putumayo River. "These missions," he said, "are more recommendable to the government not only because of the great fertility of their land, the excellence of their productions, and the docility and multitude of their converts, but also because the Portuguese introduce themselves into the Spanish dominions by means of the River Putumayo, with grave injury to our pacified Indians." [69]

With the successful termination of the wars for independence in South America, the boundary controversies were transferred to the new states. Disputes between Brazil and the Spanish-speaking nations continued, and the latter cited as proof of their claims many letters and other documents of Spanish frontier missionaries intended to show that the padres had voyaged and preached and established missions in the disputed territories east of the Andes. The Spanish padres of the interior jungles and grasslands of South America thus remained the bulwark of empire and the champions of Spanish civilization long after they had been buried in some bit of holy ground beneath the shade of a great tree or under the floor of a frontier church, and long after both tree and church had crumbled into decay.

BOOK III

Atmosphere and Achievements

STONES AND THORNS

I

VERYWHERE the Spanish padre went in his effort to carry the message of Christ crucified to his brown brothers steeped in the sins of the flesh, he found his pathway beset with obstacles. Difficulties assailed him the moment he entered the wilds, and pursued him until some friendly Indian, at the direction of the missionary, performed for him the sacrament of extreme unction, and his soul went forth to render an account of his stewardship. In 1567, after Philip II had requested the general of the Society of Jesus to send missionaries to the Indies, the general sent eight Jesuits to Peru with the following instructions:

Let them not place their lives lightly in grave danger among unconquered people, for although it may be profitable for them to die soon in this demand of the divine service, it would not be useful for the common welfare, owing to the great lack that there is of workers in that vineyard, and the difficulty that the Company would have in sending others in their place. Therefore, when they may have to make dangerous expeditions, let it be not without order of the superior.[1]

Difficulties, discomforts, and perils were inevitable on the frontier. The missionary accepted them philosophically, believing that the pains and penalties of this life would have their compensations in the life to come. Sometimes he gave thanks for the stones and thorns along his difficult road, believing that God in his wisdom had placed them before him to test his strength and courage.

II

One difficulty which caused much inconvenience and even suffering to the new missionary was the change in food and water. Much of the water that he drank while on the move beyond the frontier came from muddy streams. An item in the equipment of the modern explorer in tropical South America is a water filter, but this was something which the padre did not have. While the missionary may have boiled the water occasionally, the chances are that he drank it as he found it, sometimes with serious consequences. The food, in particular, was strange, often unsavory, and occasionally repulsive. Father Lucas de la Cueva, a Jesuit missionary to the Indians of Maynas, tells how the Indians ate monkeys, rats, lizards, ants, worms, and snakes, consuming even venomous serpents with relish. Father Lucas detested these delicacies at first; but as the Spanish soldiers ate them, and since it was eat or starve, he came to partake of them like an Indian gourmand. It was some time, however, before he could force himself to taste roasted monkey heads, being "horrified by that figure so like a man, which if one did not know what it was, one would judge to be a Negro, it being black after roasting." [2] On the Orinoco and the Meta rivers the Indians were accustomed to go out on great monkey hunts, kill large numbers of the animals, and preserve them by smoking them. Father Rivero was never able to overcome his disgust at sight of a pile of these smoked monkeys, resembling so many roasted boys.[3] Humboldt found missionaries on the upper Río Negro eating ants known as *vachacos*. The white, fatty hind part of the ants was separated from the legs and head, and mixed with cassava flour, making a food resembling rancid butter mixed with bread crumbs. This diet was nourishing if not tasty.[4] Sometimes missionaries could not obtain the food which ordinarily nourished the natives and were forced to use such fruits, nuts, or berries as they could find in the forest.[5] After the Marañón missions were well under way, the diet of the missionaries included beef, milk, cheese, corn, and honey; but during the early days smoked fish was almost the best thing that they had to eat. Father Francisco de Figueroa describes the food as repulsive:

the turtle eggs because of their bad odor, the monkey meat because of its figure, the forest birds on account of their dry meat, the forest hog because of its offensive smell, the green banana for what it is, for it serves as bread . . . and on getting dry hardens and becomes like wood more tasteless than before. . . . With all this, after one becomes accustomed to them, they are not as bad as at first they seem. The monkey, if one ignores the figure, has good and sound flesh, . . . and even the big mice or rats which are caught and grown in thickets and shrubbery are not so bad as the name sounds, but better than the rabbits of the country. Nor could we persuade ourselves that the eggs of turtles half hatched and with the little turtles forming, full of blood and the rest, may be endured or even seen without disgust, if experience had not taught us that it is tasty and refreshing food.[6]

According to Figueroa, no missionaries had starved to death in the oriente of Peru.

Living conditions on the frontier before and during the time that a mission was being established were extremely

Father Samuel Fritz suffered a prolonged illness, attended only
by an Indian boy, and visited by lizards, rats, and a crocodile

crude. If the padres had dwellings at all, they were uncomfortable little huts that may have served to keep out the rain,
but not the swarms of insects so common within the tropics.
When Father Samuel Fritz was suffering a prolonged illness,
he had to lie on his cot in a dingy abode with only an Indian
boy to serve him, while lizards came into his crude shelter
and a rat ate his food and gnawed on his spoon, plate, and
knife handle. A crocodile crawled into a canoe whose prow
reached into the hut, but it did not enter the dwelling.[7] Yet
the missionaries often gloried in such misery, confident that
their reward in the future life would be in proportion to their
sufferings in this. Father Chomé, a missionary to the Chiriguanos, wrote in June, 1732, that when he was traveling once
in Europe with another Jesuit, his companion pointed out a
miserable dwelling and laughingly said, "Such will be in the

Indies the house of Father Chomé." When the padre reached his field in America, he tried to find such a dilapidated place in which to live.[8]

The stoicism with which the padres were able to endure hardships is shown in the following letter, written by Father Arlet on September 1, 1698, to the general of the Society of Jesus:

There is no more Bread and Wine here than are requisite for solemnizing Mass. The River and the Forest furnish us with all our Food, the only Seasoning to which is some Salt, when we can get any; for often we have none, or very little. . . . I here enjoy sweeter Sleeps, on the bare Ground, and in the open Air, than I ever was bless'd with, when lying in the softest Beds in *Europe:* So true it is, that fancied Evils torment us much more than real ones.[9]

Yet at times the hardships seemed more than the missionaries could bear, particularly when their sufferings were combined with failure to bring the Indians into the fold; and there must have been many who, like Father Neira, begged God that their labors on this earth might soon be ended by death.[10]

Among the ranks of the ecclesiastical army were those who voluntarily increased their sufferings. Father Samuel Fritz was accustomed to eat the coarsest food, poorly cooked and unseasoned, even when he could get better. He seemed to encourage insects to bite him, not taking the trouble to drive mosquitoes away. Partly as a result of this self-torture his body became covered with ulcers. In addition to this abnormal practice—it should be said in his favor—he drove himself to constructive labor, loathing idleness more than disease, so that he became something of a painter, sculptor, architect, carpenter, and mason.[11]

The uncomfortable and unhealthful climate with its long periods of debilitating heat and frequent tropical rains, the myriads of insects, the vampire bats, the snakes, and other dangerous animals, and the storms and the floods, took the place of hair shirts in the lives of frontier missionaries. Father Figueroa speaks of deadly fevers, of the danger of drowning when a canoe overturns, of tempests, falling trees and branches, crocodiles, snakes, vipers, jaguars, big ants whose bite causes pain for twenty-four hours, little ants that get into beds and clothes, wasps whose stings cause running sores, and termites, as well as rats, cockroaches which crawl over the food, and large toads.[12] He tells of the almost unendurable heat on the Marañón and relates that a certain padre had twenty-seven sores on one hand as a result of mosquito bites. Lockman, in describing the climate and the animals of the Mojo country, says: "The raging Heat, joined to the almost continual Moisture of the Earth, produces a vast Number of Serpents, Vipers, Ants, Moskitoes, flying Bugs, and a numberless Multitude of other Insects which perpetually torment Man." He speaks also of "Bears, Leopards, Tygers, Goats, wild Hogs; and a great Number of other Beasts unknown in Europe."[13] Humboldt found near the boundary of Venezuela and Brazil an old missionary who said that he had spent "twenty years of mosquitoes in the forests of the Cassiquiare." His legs were so thoroughly covered with bites of insects that the original color of the skin could not be determined.[14] In Guiana and in many other places in tropical South America there were little insects, somewhat smaller than fleas, that went by the name of *niguas*. These insects would bore beneath the skin and lay their eggs there, causing infection and insufferable itching. In some places these niguas even entered people's noses and ears, so that Spaniards in particular sometimes died of the plague. The only remedy during the early days of missionary activity was to pick the insects and eggs out with needles or pins, but the padres finally discovered an ointment that was an effective cure.[15]

III

A stone of no small size on which all the missionaries stumbled, and over which some could not pass, was the variety of languages and dialects among the Indians. Among the Chiquitos, villages of a hundred families sometimes used a language that was entirely different from that of other natives in the vicinity. The Chiquitos, however, spoke only four languages, while there were in the upper Amazon valley some one hundred and fifty tongues as different from each other as French and Spanish.[16] Not only was there a great variety of languages, but they were exceedingly difficult to learn, consisting largely of grunts, grimaces, and gutturals. As Mozans has remarked:

To learn these tongues so as to construct a grammar that could be used by their associates and successors, and still more to find words to convey to the benighted Indian even the most elementary truths of religion, was, for the first missionaries, a tremendous task. Even so simple a word as "believe," which has no equivalent in many Indian tongues, offered enormous difficulties to the catechist.[17]

Some of the native languages lacked the sound of *r*, while others were full of *r*'s. Some were nasal, others guttural. The Saliva language was nasal; for example, "Friend, what will you eat tomorrow?" was *"Chónego, anda cuicuacá tandema?"* In the Situfa tongue, which was guttural and had no *r* sound, "What are your relatives saying to you?" was *"Madagena nefecola falabidaju?"* In the Betoye tongue, in which the *r* sound was very pronounced, "Why do you steal my corn? I am going to strike you," was *"Day ráaquirrabicarrú romú robarriabarrorrá ácajú."*[18]

In the late years of the colonial period, after many Indians had learned some Spanish, the padres still had difficulty in teaching them, the similarity of certain Spanish words confusing the poor neophytes. A missionary among the Chaymas had great difficulty in explaining the difference between the two Spanish words, *infierno* (hell) and *invierno* (winter). In the Orinoco valley the word "winter" was applied to the rainy season, which comes during the months of June, July, and August. As the Indians understood the padre's explanation, the white man's hell was a place where the wicked were constantly exposed to tropical storms.[19]

It frequently happened that after the missionary had learned the language of a particular tribe, his superiors transferred him to some other location, so that it was necessary for him to begin studying again, making use of interpreters in the meantime. The Jesuits in eastern Peru decided that the most practical solution of the language difficulty was to teach all the natives the Inca tongue, since they could learn it more easily than Spanish. But this plan was not successfully carried out on a large scale.[20]

IV

For the missionary there was always the danger of accident while he traveled through wild and trackless country, over mountains, in swamps, along flooded rivers, and across desert wastelands. In the llanos and Chaco during the wet season thousands of square miles might be flooded, while during the dry season one might travel for leagues without finding a drop of water to quench one's thirst. Father Lucas de la Cueva, while trying to find a shorter and easier route between Quito and the Marañón, was almost drowned when his boat overturned, but was saved by an Indian boy.[21] Lockman describes the hardships suffered by Father Cypriano Baraza

In Venezuela the padres usually traveled mounted

while trying to discover a route across the Andes between Lima and the Mojo missions:

He was exposed to great Dangers, and labour'd under a Variety of Sufferings, during the three Years that he endeavoured, but in vain, to find out the wish'd-for Road. He now wou'd wander thro' Places frequented only by wild Beasts; and which were rendred inaccessible, by tufted Forests and craggy Rocks. Another Time he wou'd be travelling on the Summit of high Mountains, benum'd with the extreme Rigour of the Cold; pierced thro' with violent Rains; unable almost to stand upon his Legs, occasioned by the Ground being so very miry and slippery; and seeing, at a vast Distance below, Vallies covered with Trees, under which Torrents were heard to flow with an impetuous Noise.[22]

In Venezuela, where much of the country was sufficiently open to permit riding on horseback, the padres usually traveled mounted.[23] They customarily used horses also in Paraguay and the Chaco. In the Amazon valley they employed *piraguas*, canoes hollowed out of logs, much of the forest being almost impenetrable. In these piraguas some of the padres journeyed thousands of miles, the sturdy Indian paddlers being able to average a hundred strokes a minute for hours at a time.

V

Lay Spaniards, desirous of exploiting the Indians, as frequently pointed out in this narrative, were another hindrance to the evangelization of the natives. Secular officials and encomenderos often interfered in the internal affairs of the missions, thereby disturbing their organization and sometimes causing the Indians to flee from the reductions in fear of being forced to labor on the plantations. Particularly after missions had become numerous and wealthy, did Spaniards interfere with the efforts of the padres, hoping that through elimination of the missionaries they would secure part of the land, herds, and buildings of the reductions. The missionaries wished to keep the natives under their tutelage as long as possible, while the lay Spaniards wanted them to be turned over speedily to the temporal authorities.[24] In speaking of a certain Captain Navarro, who had told a missionary to stick to his praying and Masses when the padre had reprimanded him for mistreating some Indians, Father Rivero accused him and his like of injuring the missions. He was

certainly a great head for the Government, when he did not give heed to such injustices. Heads such as this have driven away the heathen, caused the missions to decay, depopulated the Llanos, discredited the Faith, filled Hell with infidels, and the earth with so many difficulties and impediments for preaching

Jesus Christ, that only he can give his word on this matter who works among the heathen who are scandalized and terrified by such iniquities.

An interpreter of Father Alonso Neira told him that he should find some other expression for "Our Lord" than "*Nuestro Señor*," which also means "our master," or else the Indians would get the idea that God was a cruel slave-driver who would treat the Indians like dogs.[25]

VI

Of all the difficulties encountered by the missionaries the one which caused them the greatest heartaches was the inability of many Indians to understand the first principles of the Christian religion as the padres tried to teach it to them. The natives in many instances were careless, indifferent, and irresponsible. They acted like little children, sometimes willfully bad, at other times simply without forethought. Father Antonio de Orellana, writing in 1687, complained that many of his letters did not reach their destination because the Indian carriers frequently tore them up and used them for cigarette papers.[26] As for such teachings as those of the Immaculate Conception and the Holy Trinity, the average neophyte had no idea of what they meant. The immediate interests of the day appealed to the Indian more than theological concepts. A missionary in Venezuela was preaching to a group of natives when there appeared in a nearby tree a rat which in that section attains a huge size. This animal so distracted the attention of the converts that they could hardly listen to Mass; and as soon as the service was over, they rushed out, dispatched the animal with a few throws, and proceeded to eat it. One of the converts told the padre that God had granted them the rat as a reward for the Mass that they had so quietly sat through.[27]

The intelligence of the natives varied greatly, some tribes having a learning capacity virtually equal to that of whites, while others appeared to be morons. Their apparent mental dullness may have been, however, the result of their difficulty in understanding what the padre was saying to them in what he supposed was their language, rather than lack of intelligence. On the Marañón some Indians followed the instructions of the padres while in church, but others simply repeated what they saw the missionary do. If he raised his hands, they raised theirs; if he pointed downward to emphasize the idea of hell, they did the same; if he spread his arms, his whole congregation was likely to imitate him; if he slapped a mosquito that had alighted on his body, they would strike themselves at the same place, "actions which, if they move one to laughter or tire one, are an indication of their simplicity and of the will that they have, by the kindness of God, to learn." They even copied the movements of his mouth.[28]

Sometimes old squaws, who had come to doubt the Christian teachings or probably had never believed them, would burlesque the sermons of the padre. Talking in an undertone, a number of these old women scattered about over the church could make themselves heard by most of the neophytes at the service while the padre could not tell but that they were mumbling their prayers. They would ask whether the preacher had visited the hell of which he spoke or had received visitors from there, would complain that such a powerful God ought to feed them without their working, ask why the padre did not live the life of abstinence that he extolled, and accuse him of asking them questions in the confessional from curiosity and a desire to interfere in other people's affairs, "so that with such commentaries, the sermon is more prejudicial than favourable to the progress of the faith."[29]

The Jurimagua Indians of the Amazon basin objected to the

sacrament of baptism, thinking that it was some kind of injurious witchcraft.[30] On the other hand, the Achaguas of the llanos believed that baptism had mysterious healing powers. One woman brought her sick son, who had already been baptized once, in order that the padre might cure him by baptizing him a second time. When a child cried, the mother sometimes brought it to the missionary for baptism, saying, "Be quiet, child, with this you will get fat." [31] Some Indians in the first days of missionary activity in South America were said to have permitted padres to baptize the victims whom they intended to eat; but after a while they withdrew this permission, thinking that baptism injured the taste of human flesh.

Missionaries had numerous difficulties in connection with the confessional. Some Indians objected to confessing at all, while others worried the padres by confessing too frequently. On the Achagua missions the converts were so anxious to confess that if the padre was not at the church by daylight to hear them, they would go to his house, get him out of bed, and tell him of their sins. They were particularly desirous of freeing their consciences by confession prior to undertaking long journeys, thinking that thereby they would be made safe from dangers along the road. The Achaguas of New Granada even conducted prayer meetings in their huts.[32] Some converts who were willing enough to confess could not understand just what they were supposed to do. Father Francisco de Figueroa found that if he asked an Indian the question, "Have you robbed?" the answer would be, "Have you robbed?" To the question, "Have you become intoxicated?" the reply would be exactly the same. If the padre should say, "Tell me the sins that you have committed," the convert would command the missionary to tell him the sins that the padre had committed. When one old woman was very ill, a missionary came to her to receive her confession. She called two girls who were near and told them to answer the questions that the priest asked her. Figueroa exclaimed in exasperation, "Above all, it is no little torment to dispute with animated trunks and irrational men." [33] Some Indians seemed to think that the more heinous were the offenses that they confessed, the more worthy of praise was their confession; and so they were inclined to tell of crimes they had not committed. When a certain Indian on a Maynas mission was very ill, the padre went to him to hear his confession. Among other things he asked if the convert had killed anyone. The answer was, "*Ari, Padre, iscai passac quinca passac*," or "Yes, Father, two hundred, three hundred." After the Indian had given exaggerated answers to a number of queries, the padre told him to stop lying and to confess only the sins that he had actually committed. The sick man replied, "No, Father, in order to get well it is necessary to confess well." The Indian recovered, very likely attributing his good fortune to the falsehoods that he had told.[34]

Father Guillelmo D'Etre in a letter written on June 1, 1731, complained:

That which most troubles a Missionary who does not know the character of these Peoples is to hear their confessions: they make them with difficulty according to the manner in which they are questioned. For example: if they are asked, "Have you committed such a sin?" they answer "Yes", although not having committed it. If one says to them, "You have not committed such a sin?" they answer "No" even though having committed it many times. . . . They will confess what they have denied and will deny what they have confessed.[35]

There were other converts who objected to confessing at all. Father Juan Plaza, writing in January, 1578, stated that of three thousand Indians who had confessed in the town of Juli during the preceding year, two thousand had confessed only because they were forced to do so. Some of the natives who were living with women to whom they were not married according to the Catholic rites, and who were told to marry or separate, confessed in order to be eligible for the marriage ceremony. Others confessed only when they became ill. These people also objected to hearing sermons and preparing lessons in the doctrine, so that on Sundays it was necessary to appoint watchmen to see that the converts attended church instead of going to their fields or to hunt.[36] There were still others who, when forced to attend the confessional against their will, would argue with the padre. If the missionary, who very likely already had a fair idea of what sins the Indian had been committing, tried to get him to admit them, a debate would ensue, the neophyte stoutly maintaining to be false what the missionary knew to be true. If finally caught in a falsehood and compelled to admit his sins, the Indian would begin to curse those who had testified against him. During this combat of wits, the Indian, instead of kneeling as he was supposed to do, would squat down on the floor.[37]

Other examples of questions asked Indian converts in the confessional were:

When your ears ring, do you say that someone is talking about you? And when your right ear rings, do you say that they speak well of you, and when the left, do you say that they speak ill of you?

Have you hired some magician to aid you in anything?

Do you do what the witchdoctors command?

When you drink *chicha*, do you say: "Oh mother *chicha*, clear as gold, guard me well and do not make me drunk"?

Are you accustomed to worship the sun, saying, "Father sun"; and the moon, saying, "Mother moon, give me life"?

Have you deceived anyone by swearing?

Have you brought Indian men to your house in order that they may get drunk and gamble so that your wife may have occasion to offend God with one of them? [38]

Indians usually abhorred the drudgery of memorizing prayers and the catechism. When a mission was new, they were influenced either by the novelty of the procedure or by the hope of some gift to repeat the formulas of the Catholic ritual under the direction of the padres, even though they were unable to understand the meaning of the words. After the novelty had worn off and the padre's gifts had all been distributed, their interest quickly lagged. Figueroa wrote:

> It matters not that for remedy for these and other disorders the missionary use in fervent conversations all the efficacy of his zeal, emphasizing the greatest necessity of eternal salvation and demonstrating the existence of a Supreme and powerful Master, who is God; the rewards that he promises to those who obey his law; the punishments that are preordained for the sinners in hell and other such things. All this . . . is for these neophytes a matter of laughter.[39]

One old fellow in the Peruvian oriente said that he did not care to become a Christian, that Christianity was for children. This old heathen had been attending classes in the doctrine in company with some children, without much success in learning the catechism. The padre found that the reason that he objected to being converted was that he could not memorize the things which the children learned with comparative ease. The missionary told him that it was not necessary for him to memorize, that it was enough if he simply listened to the doctrine and catechism and believed them with all his heart. The old Indian then consented to be baptized, as did many others who were of short memory.[40] When two Jesuits went to the llanos of New Granada in 1659, they found an aged Indian cacique of the Tunebo tribe who refused to become a Christian on the ground that he was too old. The missionaries tried to show him that there was greater reason for an old man to become a Christian than for a young man, since the probability was that he would die sooner; but the old chief "remained obstinate in his errors and the blindness of heathendom, to the great sorrow and regret of the servants of God."[41]

Some Indians thought that the white man's God was inferior to their own gods and showed Him little respect. Others objected to worshiping inside a church, preferring processions in the open air. An Indian on the upper Orinoco told the missionary that the Christian's God kept himself shut up in a house like an old man, while his Indian god moved about freely through the forests and fields and "on the mountains of Sipapu, whence the rains come."[42] When Father Joseph de Gumilla told a Betoye Indian that whoever did not believe the doctrine of the Catholic Church would be burned forever, the Indian became sad from thinking of the fate of his ancestors, and complained that God was not fair to condemn them before he sent missionaries to show them how to live. Gumilla's answer was that "the cause of the perdition of his ancestors was not in God, but in the sins of those Heathens, by which they were made unworthy that his Majesty should send them Preachers."[43] The Christian God frequently met competition from gods of the jungle. When Father Cristóbal de Acuña was descending the Amazon, he heard of an Indian down the river who claimed to be a god. Acuña sent him word that he was bringing a more powerful divinity. On reaching the village of the man-god, he met that worthy, who was filled with curiosity to see his more powerful rival. But when the padre pointed heavenward, saying that his God was of the spirit, the Indian ridiculed the idea, claiming that he was a child of the sun and that he made a trip to the sun every night.[44]

VII

When Spaniards entered among wild Indian tribes, they carried countless disease germs, which were far more fatal to the natives than were the maladies of the Indians to Spaniards. The padres, who were partially or wholly immune to diseases which had existed in Europe for centuries, were ignorant of the fact that they were carriers of deadly germs. The most destructive disease which the Spaniards introduced was smallpox, which in time accounted for the death of hundreds of thousands of Indians. Syphilis was introduced among the natives probably by Spanish soldiers who escorted the padres. Even diseases such as measles and scarlet fever, which were not ordinarily dangerous to Europeans, proved to be fatal to Indians. These afflictions, added to the numerous maladies which the Indians already suffered, sometimes decimated the population of the reductions. When in 1665 dysentery was causing many deaths among the llanos Indians, the *mohanes* (native witchdoctors) told the converts that they had observed by the flight of birds, the swimming of fish, and the actions of wild beasts that everyone who remained on the reductions would die. The Jesuits had great difficulty in holding their missions together in the face of the superstition of their wards.[45]

Indians were inclined to believe that missionaries possessed unusual powers, that they led charmed lives, and that they were capable of the most preposterous machinations for evil as well as for good. Father Samuel Fritz was supposed by the natives to have caused an earthquake. While he was a prisoner at Pará, the tale was bruited about among his converts that the Portuguese had cut him into pieces, but that his soul had joined the bits back together, so that he was as well as ever. Some Indians would not believe he was a real man

until they had actually touched him.[46]   On one llanos mission
a cacique came to the padre and complained that God did
not love the Indians, that He repeatedly sent pestilences upon
them, of which they died like ants.   He pointed out that, on
the other hand, the missionaries remained well while plagues
raged about them.   This being the case, the convert wished
to become a friar so that he would be safe, for "the pestilence,
seeing one dressed in those black clothes, has fear of entering
in."   The Indian insisted that the padre give him an old cassock, and the missionary found difficulty in convincing him
that the cloak would be no more efficacious in frightening
away disease than any other dress.[47]   When a certain young
Indian on the mission of Tame in New Granada died, his
father, convinced that the missionary had killed him by some
magic, ran away to another mission, where he tried to persuade
the converts to revolt and flee back to the forest.   The missionary, notwithstanding the fact that the Indian had sworn
to kill him, started out to persuade the angry father to stop
his revolutionary activities.   When he overtook the insurgent
at Macaguane, the native was so afraid the padre had some
secret method of killing him that he attempted no violence,
and the missionary was able to persuade the new converts not
to leave their village.[48]

When a neophyte was very ill and apparently about to
die, the custom was for the padre to hear his confession and
perform for him the last sacrament of extreme unction.
Sometimes the Indian refused the sacrament because he did
not like the odor of the oil.   Sometimes he hid when the missionary came to receive his last confession or to administer
extreme unction, thinking that this religious ceremony was a
cause of death.[49]

Many Indian tribes buried their dead inside their huts, and
the missionaries found it difficult to persuade them to inter

the deceased either in the church cemetery or in some plot of holy ground. A certain Saliva Indian became ill, and the padre baptized him and gave him the name of Ignatius, but the malady continued, and the poor fellow became gradually weaker until finally he was only skin and bones. The padre again visited him and, seeing that he was not long for this life, consoled him by saying: "Well, Ignatius, good courage, for soon you are going to rest in Heaven." When the friar returned later in the day, he found the sick man's family digging a grave at the foot of his bed. They explained that they were taking the padre at his word and were going to bury the dying Indian. The padre persuaded them to wait until he had breathed his last before putting him in the ground, and tried to get them to make another grave outside the hut at the foot of a large cross. The Indians refused to do this because they thought that Ignatius would be made uncomfortable by the rains.[50] An old Indian of the village of Suay, an invalid for many years, called his sons to him one day and said to them: "No longer am I of use in this world except to disturb and fatigue you: I have been a good Christian, and I wish to go to Heaven to rest; I charge you to believe well in God, and that you do not depart from the teachings of the Fathers. . . . Now finish my grave, and bury me; and if the Father becomes angry, tell him that I have commanded you thus." They dug his grave, put him in it, and began to throw the earth on top of him, leaving his face free until the last. After a while the old man told them to wait a bit, for the dirt was heavy. But in a few minutes he ordered them to finish the job, and he was buried alive.[51]

Another Indian, however, an Achagua, when on the brink of death, was afraid that his family would fail to bury him in holy ground with proper rites; so he had them open a grave for him within the church. After this had been done, he became quiet, satisfied that his soul would not be weighted down by the ignominy of an unholy burial.[52]   And a good old Indian of the Otomacos, believing that his time had come, dug his own grave, lay down in it, and proceeded to make a speech to his assembled family in the presence of his "patron" and some Spanish soldiers.   He averred that he was happy, and commanded his family to stay with the padres and be good Christians.   Having completed his discourse, he stretched out in his grave and died.[53]

VIII

While new missions were constantly being added to the total number on the frontier, the padres often saw their reductions dissolve before their eyes, no matter how hard they might struggle to maintain them and increase their prosperity. The Indians on frontier missions seem always to have been ready, on slight provocation, to return to the wilds.   The viceroy of New Granada reported in 1789 that the Indians of new villages in New Granada were disposed to remain settled as long as the missionaries gave them knives, fishhooks, machetes, clothes, and the like, but that as soon as these gifts were no longer forthcoming, they were likely to disappear in the night, carrying all their gifts with them and perhaps setting fire to the village.[54]   There appeared to be something in the very blood of the Indians that made them love the free life of the forest, for young children would occasionally wander away from the missions for several days at a time, living on such fruits and herbs as they could find.   Sometimes villages would be temporarily deserted while their inhabitants were away hunting, fishing, or seeking the products of the forest.[55]   After a padre had died of the "humidities" or other causes, it was frequently the case that the Indians of his reduction would disperse if another missionary was not sent immediately to take his place.[56] Humboldt lists the following causes for the depopulation of missions: smallpox, unhealthful climate, objection of the Indians to mission regulations, poor food, high mortality of children, and the use of contraceptives made from herbs.[57] The Capuchin prefect of Guiana in 1761 listed the ways in which eight of his missions were lost as follows: (1) smallpox; (2) burned by Caribs; (3) invaded by the English; (4) destroyed by uprising of the converts; (5) padre and six Spaniards killed by Caribs; (6) Indian (Carib) uprising in which several Spaniards were killed and the missionary barely escaped; (7) Indian uprising; (8) Indian converts fled.[58] The Guiana mission of Purísima Concepción de Suay was devastated by the English and again by epidemics of smallpox and measles. The mission of Caroní had repeated epidemics, was atttacked again and again by Caribs, and was burned three times.[59] With what profound sentiments of melancholy must the missionaries have seen destroyed within a few hours the results of years of labor and suffering; for once the converts were dispersed through the forest, it was often more difficult to reduce them than it had been at the beginning.

In their efforts to control their wards, the missionary friars relied first on advice, exhortations, and admonitions. Corporal punishment was ordinarily resorted to only for the worst offenses or in cases where the Indians repeatedly disobeyed mission regulations or the commands of the padres. The threat of confinement, the stocks, or whipping did not always deter unruly converts from following at times the dictates of their own desires. An Indian of Peru, for instance, repeatedly failed to attend church on Sundays. When the priest learned that his truancy was due to his getting drunk every Sunday morning, he ordered that the delinquent be beaten. The punishment having been applied, the Indian thanked the priest, as was customary on such occasions, and requested that he be given another whipping since he had an appointment for another drinking match on the following Sunday.[60]

IX

On missions of the farthest frontier, such as those of the Mojos and the Chiquitos, loneliness was a thorn that made hardships more difficult to bear than would have been the case if the padre had been assisted by some kindly and sympathetic member of his order.   Padres on the Maynas missions would sometimes not see one another for a year; they would undergo great hardships to visit each other in order to talk over their successes or to borrow some wine and unleavened bread.   Yet when these missionaries were recalled to Quito, they would "sigh for their children in Christ" and wish to return to the scenes of their labors.[61]   There were times when a missionary spent years without hearing the sound of his native language from other lips than his own.   The barbarous people among whom he lived were so different from him that no strong feeling of comradeship could exist between teacher and pupils. In order to diminish the oppressiveness of solitude, the padre must needs drown himself in his labors.   "Only is there consolation in concentrating on the salvation of these poor people and on God for whom it is done, and with whom it is necessary to commune much in order to carry on.   His Divine Majesty succours him who for love banishes himself to such solitudes." [62]   After many years far from the cultural associations of civilization a padre might overcome his nostalgia and find complete satisfaction in his missionary labors.   One old missionary, who had lived for thirty years among the Indians, said to Abbé Raynal:

My friend, you know not what it is to be the king, almost even the God, of a number of men, who owe to you the small

279

portion of happiness they enjoy; and who are ever assiduous in assuring you of their gratitude. After they have been ranging thru immense forests, they return overcome with fatigue and inanition; if they have only killed one piece of game, for whom do you suppose it to be intended? It is for the Father, for it is thus they call us: and indeed they are really children. . . . It is among them that I will go and end my days.[63]

X

Father José Dadey, one of the founders of the New Granada mission towns of Morcote, Chita, Pisba, Támara, and Paya, was connected with the mission movement in northern South America for more than half a century, dying at the age of eighty-six years, seventy of which had been spent in the Society of Jesus.[64] Few padres, however, were able to give such a long life of service to the cause of converting savages. For many of them the hardships of frontier life were fatal; they died like brave soldiers out on some embattled salient of Spanish civilization: some of disease, others from accident, and still others by the hands of the savages whom they were trying so hard to lead to a better life.

One of these martyrs was Father Francisco de Figueroa, a native of Popayán, educated in the Jesuit college at Quito. After he had entered the Society of Jesus, Father Cujía, founder of the Jesuit missions on the Marañón, took him (1640) to this frontier. For twenty-four years Figueroa lived in the forests, converting savages, founding villages, and later governing other missionaries of Maynas as superior. During his quieter moments he studied and wrote. In 1663 several tribes revolted, including the Cocama Indians. Figueroa went to the rebellious reductions where by his kindly smile and winning personality he was able to quiet the natives. Later, however, he was killed.

Accounts of his martyrdom differ. According to a convoy

*Many padres died like brave soldiers out on some embattled salient
of Spanish civilization*

officer, Captain Marcos de Salazar, a group of Cocama Indians
encountered Father Figueroa at the confluence of the Apena
and Huallaga rivers. Some of them approached the missionary, saluted him, and began to take things from his canoe.
A friendly Indian boy resisted and was struck down by the
Cocamas. In reply to the padre's exclamation, "Jesus! what
has this boy done to you that you should mistreat him thus?"
an Indian struck the missionary. Father Francisco said to
him, "And this is the payment that you give me after I have
worked in teaching you the law of God?" Declaring that
they would fix the missionary so that he could no longer
preach, the Indians attacked him and the friendly natives of
his escort. In the ensuing battle Father Francisco was captured after forty-five of his Indians had been killed. They
tied the padre to a tree and, while he continued to exhort and
sing, cut him in pieces, prolonging the torture. When he
was dead, they roasted and ate him.[65]

Another account of his martyrdom is that while he was traveling with a few friendly Indians he came upon a great number of canoes loaded with Cocamas, Chepeos, Ucayales, and Maparimas. He approached the bank, disembarked, and made signs that they should come near. They accepted his invitation; and while one of the savages kissed his hand, saying, "Praised be the Most Holy Sacrament of the Altar," another knocked him down from behind by hitting him on the head with a paddle. The whole crowd of Indians then attacked Figueroa and his allies, killing the padre and a number of his companions. They decapitated him, threw his body into the river, and took his head along with them. When news of his death reached Quito, a padre and five soldiers were sent to look for his body in order to give it an honorable burial. They were able to find only his spectacles, a paten, and some pieces of torn paper. The next year a Spanish squadron "furrowed the waters of the Marañón, and punishing the sacrilegious assassins, gave peace to those regions." [66]

Another martyr was Father Pedro Suárez, also a missionary to the Marañón country, who was killed during his first year on the frontier, when he was but twenty-six years of age. Suárez was said to have written in his own blood the letter requesting that he be sent to the missions. This young padre was laboring among the Abijira nation, where polygamy was common. When he tried to do away with this practice, he found himself opposed by the cacique, Quiricuare, who had twelve wives. Quiricuare, with six other Indians who did not wish to lose their harems, went to the missionary's hut and wounded him with a lance. As he exclaimed, "My God! My God!" several of the savages ran him through the body, and one wounded him in the mouth. According to Father Juan Lorenzo Lucero, who reported the tragedy to his superiors at Quito, the assassins, unable to cut off his head, buried him in terror before he was dead.[67]

Father Cypriano Baraza, who had for twenty-seven years worked in converting Mojos, was murdered in 1702 at the age of sixty-one. A troop of Baure Indians, armed with bows, arrows, and hatchets, approached him, shooting arrows as they came. The friendly Indians who accompanied him fled, leaving him to the mercy of the infuriated savages. The attackers, after wounding him with their arrows, fell upon him with hatchets. They knocked his cross out of his hand and killed him by a blow on the head while he was calling upon Jesus and Mary for succor.[68]

In 1735 Caribs attacked the town of Guaya while the people were attending Mass, beginning the onslaught by setting the church on fire. Father Andrés López finished Mass while the battle raged in the plaza outside the church. Then, taking a crucifix in his hand, he went out and began to preach fervently to the enemy. Wounded by a ball in the leg, he paid no attention to the pain, but continued preaching until a Carib struck him in the mouth and knocked him down. The soldiers and converts were forced to retreat, leaving the padre stretched out on the ground. After sacking the village, the Caribs found the missionary still alive, whereupon they hit him on the head, hanged him, and lighted underneath him a fire "in which that soul, purified, we ought to believe, by the kindness of God, flew triumphantly to heaven." [69]

The courage with which a missionary could face such dangers is shown by the following letter written by Father Lucas de la Cueva at the mission of Concepción de Xeberos in eastern Peru on October 9, 1643:

I, Father of my soul, expect hourly to be killed at the hands of these Indians; and if not by them, then by being exhausted and worn out, for I am in poor health and am failing very rapidly. That which, with all the affection of my heart and in reverence for the most bitter Passion and precious blood of Our Lord Jesus Christ, I ask Your Reverence and my Father Francisco, is that although I may die at the hands of these barbarians, you may not leave them, nor abandon them, nor may Satan triumph.[70]

Sixteen years later Father Lucás was still living and thanking God for leading him safely through so many grave dangers.[71]

And so the padres labored, sweated, hungered, and suffered travail of body and anxiety of spirit in their life on the frontier in order to extend the empires of God and of His Most Catholic Majesty. They had little to hope for in material glory or reward. If they remained on their missions, the only formal title that they could expect was "preacher" (*predicador*). If they returned to the monastery after years in the field, it was to find that others who had enjoyed the quiet life of the cloister and had never undergone such hardships, had been promoted. If the missionaries wished to attain positions of honor within their order, they had to begin where they left off on going to the reductions. The viceroy of New Granada in 1794 cited this discrimination in favor of the less active as a reason why the missionaries sometimes refused to turn over their reductions to the secular clergy, preferring to live among their Indians rather than to return to the cloister.[72] In 1800 there was at Cumaná, on the coast of Venezuela, a home for old, infirm missionaries of the Aragonese Capuchins; but few padres were so fortunate as to end their days in the snug security of an old men's home. Most of them had to endure the cruel pricks of the thorns and the bruises from the stones even until the last.

Chapter XVII

DIVINE MERCY AND SATANIC MALICE

I

ENTURING forth into the heart of the South American wilds, the missionary friar went with full knowledge that Jehovah walked at his right hand. His was not the cold faith of one who believes that God is distant and impersonal, uninterested in the struggles of his mundane creatures, or incapable of changing the course of events in a universe that he has put in motion. The padre's God was close to his earth, intensely alive to the doings of mortal men, ever ready to intercede if the occasion seemed proper, especially if a holy man should raise his voice in supplication. But on the left of the advancing padre, just beyond the reach of God's avenging hand, crept the Prince of Darkness, breathing hatred and threatening calamity. Occasionally Satan would sneak off into the forest to seize some poor lost soul and hurl him to damnation, only to return to cast snares at the feet of the good friar and fling horrible oaths into the very teeth of the Almighty.

II

In December, 1720, Father Juan Rivero, having received permission from his superiors, started out for the llanos missions. The trail led through a place called "El volador de Cravo," a narrow path along the top of a mountain, skirting a precipice over which many travelers had fallen to their death. At the bottom of the cliff was a forest filled with wild beasts. Rivero had reached this dangerous part of the trail when he noticed his companions had disappeared. His repeated shouts brought no response. His guides, supposing that Rivero was in front, had hurried on in order to reach a settlement by nightfall. When they arrived at the village of Cravo, they discovered to their amazement that the padre was not there. In dismay they retraced their steps, and about midnight found the missionary's mule tied to a tree. They shouted and shouted, but received no answer save the hollow echoes from the cliffs. Returning in grief to the village— for they supposed that Father Rivero had fallen to his doom or had been killed by some fierce animal—they were surprised to see the padre entering from another direction. His clothes were torn and his body scratched and bruised, but he was not seriously injured. When darkness had come and the missionary's mule had refused to proceed, Rivero had dismounted, hitched his beast, and cut through the forest, scrambling over rocks, running into bushes, falling time after time as he advanced. But, thanks to his reliance upon the Virgin, he had reached Cravo without serious mishap. On first seeing him, his guides thought they beheld a ghost. His "miraculous" arrival was attributed to Divine Providence, and the Indians of the vicinity, who thereafter considered Rivero a holy man, came from far and near to see him.[1]

In colonial Spanish America superstition was the order of

the day among ecclesiastics and laymen alike. "All through life," says García Calderón, "the pious colonist is surrounded by marvels. He loves nature with an ingenuous faith, and attributes to the saints and demons a continual intervention in his placid existence. An unexpected sound reveals the presence of a soul in torment; a tremor of the earth, the divine wrath; sickness is a proof of diabolic influence; health, of the efficacy of an amulet." [2]

Heavenly beings appeared early in South America to throw in their lot with the Spaniards and aid them in their conquests; although occasionally the malicious interference of the devil and his cohorts temporarily checked their progress toward ultimate success. During a battle between Pizarro's men and the Indians of Cuzco, the Virgin Mary appeared in the air, holding in her arms the infant Jesus. While the native warriors were gazing at this astonishing spectacle, a fine dust fell into their eyes, so that they were blinded long enough to enable the Christians to win the battle. [3]

Lifeless objects, when inspired from above, were able to do wondrous things. According to legend the marble slabs comprising the pulpit of the cathedral at Cartagena reached the city after a series of miracles. The marble was sent to Cartagena on a Spanish vessel, which was attacked and plundered by a British ship, whose crew threw the marble overboard. But the heavy stones floated and were retrieved by the Spanish sailors. The Spanish vessel was again attacked, this time by a Dutch pirate, who killed all the crew and set fire to the galleon. The ship and its contents were destroyed, except the marble slabs, which floated to the very walls of Cartagena. Some enterprising merchants then seized the blocks, and when the bishop of Cartagena was unable to pay the exorbitant price that they asked, put them on a vessel bound for Spain. But this ship also sank, and the marble again floated to Cartagena, this time actually to be secured by the bishop for use in constructing the pulpit of the cathedral.[4]

The village of Nueva Barcelona on the coast of Venezuela was one time saved by a miracle. A squadron of English ships came into the harbor for the purpose of taking the town. When the Spaniards went out to resist the large landing party, which was more numerous than the defenders, they were surprised to see the English retire to their ships, weigh anchor, and sail away. The Spaniards soon discovered, however, that the bronze image of a saint had left her pedestal in the cathedral, and going out upon the sands of the beach, had so deceived the English that they had seen a vast army upon the shore. They were sure the saint had aided them, for, on investigation, it was discovered that the edge of the image's dress was wet and sandy, with some little plants that grew near the shore attached to it.[5]

In the village of Guaca in New Granada was a painting of the Lady of Sorrows with her infant. This picture had been privately owned, but when the image of the Virgin and infant, which had almost disappeared because of the great age of the painting, were miraculously renewed, the owner had given the painting to the church. It became famous for the miracles it performed. During an epidemic of smallpox it cured many. Indeed, out of sympathy for the afflicted, the Virgin herself contracted the disease, "and in order that there should remain the memory of the one who served them, she has in the face today signs of having had smallpox, to the admiration of all those who behold the marvel. Proof of her love, for her image sickened of smallpox when her devotees became ill." [6]

South America has its native Virgins even as Mexico has its Lady of Guadalupe. One of these is Our Lady of Coromoto, Protectress of the Indians of the llanos of Venezuela.

DIVINE MERCY AND SATANIC MALICE

In 1651 an Indian named Juan Sánchez reported that he had met in the forest an Indian chief whose tribe had been converted, but who had himself refused to accept Christianity. The cacique even admitted to Sánchez that a beautiful Lady had appeared to him, telling him to join his tribe in accepting the new religion in order that "the whites might pour water on his head and enable him to go to heaven." But the chief remained adamant while some seven hundred Indians of his tribe were baptized. The children of the converted Indians often saw the Holy Virgin when they went to a pool for water. At first the parents scolded the children for lingering at the pool, but when they learned of the Virgin's presence, they began to wear the pebbles from its bottom as jewels and to attribute miraculous powers to the water. But the chief still remained obstinate, and on the night of September 8, 1652, the Virgin appeared to him in his hut. When he abused her and ordered her to leave, his wife said to him, "Don't insult the Lady that way! What a hard heart you have!" Yet he refused to listen. He even started to shoot an arrow at the visitor, but she disappeared into the darkness, and the Indian chief found himself holding a small image of Holy Mary. Now thoroughly frightened, he hid the image in the straw roof of his hut and fled into the forest, where he soon died from snakebite. A little boy later found the image, however, and on November 11, 1652, it was placed in the church of the village of Guanare, in the jurisdiction of San Carlos, Venezuela.[7]

Another Mary indigenous to South America is Our Lady of the Bark of Acarigua. In January, 1702, a pious mulatto woman named Margarita la Perla went with her son to the festival of Our Lady of Coromoto. She went to compensate the Lady for having cured her son of an illness. She tarried several days at Guanare, praying before the image of the

Virgin, which, however, was placed so high on the wall that she could not see it well. Saddened by her inability to view the image at close range, she returned toward her village. On the way she stopped to rest beneath the shade of a huge tree beside a stream. After tying her donkey, she stretched her hammock, and lay down. After a while the child noticed that the mule appeared to be frightened. Searching for the cause of the disturbance, Margarita observed that a brilliant light came from a place on the bark of a tree. Examining the tree more closely, she saw that the light came from a little image, engraved in the bark, representing the Virgin with the Christ Child in her arms. Margarita cut the image out, wrapped it in a cloth, and placed it in a saddlebag. As they were proceeding on their way home, the mule suddenly bolted and ran to the church door at the village of Acarigua. There the image of the Virgin suddenly became so heavy that the animal was unable to walk. Friar Miguel de Placencia soon relieved the mule of its load and placed the image in the church, where it became the Protectress of the people of Acarigua.[8]

Many were the miracles performed in behalf of the missionaries and their neophytes, ranging from unseen hands guiding the footsteps of a mule to divine intercession to bring rain to a parched earth. Father Manuel de Yangués, grieving because his efforts to win souls for Christ had not met with greater success, was riding one day on the back of a little mule. Suddenly his mount stopped and could not be urged on even by the combined efforts of the padre and an Indian who accompanied him. Finally Father Manuel suggested that the mount be allowed to take its own course, whereupon the beast left the trail and made its way through the pathless forest for half a league. There the padre found a hut in which an Indian child lay at the point of death. Baptizing

Baptism was indeed a powerful medicine in purging souls of guilt

the baby, he resumed his mule, which was now ready to continue the journey. The friar had been the "guide and mute instrument of predestination for that soul, which will praise the Most High throughout eternities of glory." [9] Father Raimundo de Santa Cruz was directed by divine hand for three days through a dense forest in order that he might baptize a tiny Indian before it died.[10]

Baptism was indeed a powerful medicine in purging souls of guilt. The missionaries recount many instances of its efficacy. Father Fritz tells of an old Indian woman who was very ill and wished to be baptized. She expired shortly after the ceremony, but soon reappeared in wondrous attire and said to her infidel son:

You have no reason . . . to weep for my death, for scarcely did I expire before my soul, more resplendent than the sun, was borne to a land supremely pleasant, where I behold wonderful things that I am unable clearly to explain to you, and all this I owe to baptism, . . . without which I should irremediably have gone to the infernal regions.[11]

At the mission of Loreto de Paranapuras a padre administered baptism to an old squaw who was on the brink of death, and after he had explained the things of God to her fully, she "raised her hands . . . with tender passion, invoking God and the Holy Virgin." She then received other sacraments and "fled to heaven, as the pious can believe."[12] On another occasion, there came to the padre of this mission an Indian with face so ghastly that he almost frightened the missionary. Asked why he had come, the native replied that he was very ill, that with the aid of his wife and son he had traveled a great distance, and that he did not wish to die like a heathen. The padre catechized and baptized him, after which he soon expired, confident that he was bound for a land of eternal bliss.[13]

On another mission of the Maynas region an aged Indian woman was severely stricken with smallpox, and had taken a drug which was supposed by the natives either to kill or to cure in a short time. When the padre entered her hut, she was unable to hear or talk. The father went outside, where he and some Spaniards who were standing nearby committed her soul to God. A few minutes later he returned to her bedside and found her able to hear the catechism and answer correctly. He administered the sacraments of baptism and extreme unction, after which she soon passed to her reward.[14]

The padres were especially concerned lest infants should die without being baptized. Among the Cocamas of the Ucayali valley, a missionary received a celestial impulse to visit some huts apart from the village. In one of them he found a newly born Indian girl on the verge of death. He baptized her, giving thanks to God for leading him to her and thus enabling him to rescue her soul. On the mission of Santa María de Huallaga, a padre so afflicted with sores that he could scarcely move about nevertheless made his usual round of the village. He found two sick children and administered the efficacious water. A week later both of them died, but he experienced the joy of knowing that they were in heaven.[15]

Quite remarkable were the miracles of inanimate things shedding blood. The Indians of the pueblo of Calote in the oriente of Peru revolted, killed their padre, and burned the village. They seized some large stones and tried to break the bell that had called them to Mass; but the bell began to bleed, and the insurgents threw it down the mountainside. The Spaniards, who later subdued the Indians, often heard the sound of a bell during the frequent storms which disturbed the region, and finally decided to follow the sound to its source. Finding the bell at last, they returned it to the Indian village, where it became a protection against lightning and violent winds. Later, it was melted down, part of it being used to make a new bell and the rest for manufacturing relics.[16]

The governor of Nueva Barcelona, in Venezuela, an official who was supposed to be guilty of extortion and cruelty toward the Indians, invited Father Francisco de Pamplona to dinner. At the table, the padre, in violation of good manners but in keeping with the reputation which missionaries had for defending the Indians, reprimanded the governor. The official denied the accusations against him, and the friar replied: "Do not deny these deeds, Your Lordship, for the blood of Indians is being eaten here." To prove his words, Father

Francisco pressed the bread, and blood flowed from it. The governor was frightened, but one of his admirers urged him not to be upset, for Pamplona was a wicked friar, whereupon this friend of the governor was not only struck blind but afflicted with leprosy—and was soon assassinated.[17]

In order to achieve his divine purposes, God at times made use of broken tools. In the province of Charcas a wicked soldier, fearing punishment, fled to the wilds. The Indians among whom he took up his residence were in great need of rain, which they were unable to obtain by the usual rain-making ceremonies. The fugitive Spaniard made a large cross, which he set up on an eminence, and told the Indians to worship it and ask for rain. When they did so, the rain descended in such quantity that their crops were saved. The Indians were so deeply impressed by the power of the new God that they asked that preachers be sent to them. But the soldier who had thus been an agent in bringing men to the true religion failed to reform his ways, and was hanged at Potosí.[18]

In the valley of the Marañón the spirit of San Francisco Xavier, Protector of this region, was said to have performed marvels. Father Lucas de la Cueva, one of the heroes of this frontier, attributed his success to the intercession of this saint. Father Figueroa tells how an armada of converted Jebero Indians encountered an infidel boy who had climbed a tree after a monkey. The boy was so frightened by the sudden appearance at the foot of the tree of this crowd of Indians who were friendly to the Spaniards, that he lost his hold and fell to the ground. The Indians picked him up and carried him captive to the padre, who called on St. Francis to cure the youth. The next day the young Indian was so much better that it was necessary to keep him in confinement in order to prevent his escape. At another time, thanks to the saint, a soldier accidentally shot by a companion was not injured, though two balls struck him.[19]

According to the padres, the Christian religion was highly efficacious in protecting Indians from wild beasts. Before the arrival of Jesuits among the Mojos, the Indians of that region were frequently killed by jaguars, but after being baptized they were seldom molested.[20] The Payagua Indians of the Chaco erected huge crosses at their encampments in order to keep away the "tigers"[21] which were numerous in that region.[22] In the Chiquito country a converted Indian, Diego, who was noted for his saintly life, was hunting in the forest when he was attacked by a "tiger" so suddenly that he had no time to defend himself. Fortunately, however, he was able to speak the powerful names of Jesus and Mary, whereupon the fierce beast fled, after wounding him just enough to leave scars as a reminder of the miracle whereby he was saved.[23] A Mojo Indian who wore a medal of San Antonio reported to the missionary that it had saved him from being bitten by a rattlesnake.[24]

No less efficacious was Divine Providence in dealing with domestic animals. Father Juan Fernández Pedroche was traveling from one village to another on a young and easily frightened mule. The animal threw the padre and began to run and kick, dragging Father Juan, whose foot had been caught in the stirrup. The missionary, however, had the presence of mind to remember the Virgin of Pilar, whom he invoked. Scarcely had he spoken her name when the mule stopped dead still, and the padre found himself unhurt. To show his appreciation, the missionary named a village after the Virgin.[25]

While at times God or the saints intervened to save the lives of missionaries, at others they permitted them to be killed and afterwards exhibited their marvelous powers. Divine paradox! Indians of the Llanos of Caracas killed Friar Nicolás de Rentería and cut off his head, so that "he gave his spirit to God, achieving on that day what he had always desired: to lose his life for Jesus Christ, who had offered his to save us all." The savages dragged the body to a river with the intention of throwing it in. But when they reached the bank, the corpse became so heavy that they could not move it, whereupon the Indians became frightened and fled. Friends of the padre found the body next day and carried it to a neighboring village, where another missionary gave it decent Christian burial.[26]

Some missionaries achieved great reputations as healers of the diseases of the body as well as of the spirit. They seem really to have believed that they healed the sick, and the Indians certainly had faith that some padres had healing power. In Maynas an old Indian woman suffered for a long time with severe pains in her breasts, which were seriously infected. A missionary who was asked by the cacique of her village to visit her made the sign of the cross over her abscessed bosom. She immediately began to improve; and when the father saw her some time later, she was fully recovered.[27] In an Indian village of New Granada there lived a woman so seriously afflicted with scrofula that there were great open sores on her neck. She begged Father Luis Beltrán to heal her. He made the sign of the cross on her throat and bandaged it with a handkerchief, saying to her: "Go with God, and have confidence in him, for you will get well—and return tomorrow." The next day the Indian exhibited no sign of ever having had the disease, and she was baptized along with a number of others who had seen the miracle.[28] During the smallpox epidemic of 1719, however, thousands of Indians along the Orinoco died while God stood by without exerting himself on behalf of the stricken people; but Father Gumilla philosophized that the Divine Cultivator reaps his harvest when he wills.[29]

The missionary did not forget that God was ruler of the elements as well as of man. On one mission there was a great drought. The earth was dry and cracked, the corn was withering, and the cattle were dying of thirst and hunger. The natives, Christian and heathen, implored Father Luis Beltrán to ask his God to give them rain. The padre told them to pray to Santa Catalina, whose fiesta was to be celebrated the next day, and ordered them to prepare a great procession in honor of this saint.

The Indians did all that was commanded of them. More than a thousand persons, including many unbelievers, were present. The Mass over, he preached them a sermon. He showed them the lies with which the devil had deceived them. He told them of the life and martyrdom of Santa Catalina, and assured them that God would give them water in abundance. And . . . the air began to be troubled, the sky to darken, and the clouds to gather with such speed that the people had not returned to their homes when there began to fall a rain so copious that it lasted three days. . . . With this miracle the earth was so refreshed that they had a year of greatest abundance.[30]

In 1721 occurred a severe drought in the country of the Betoyes on the llanos of the Orinoco. The natives held a procession in honor of the Virgin Mary, after which it rained for eight days. At the end of this time another drought set in, and the missionary advised the Indians to celebrate a fiesta in honor of the Son. They made a great procession on Corpus Christi day, and again it rained; and they praised God for the mercy that he had shown them.[31] In 1659 God sent a thunderstorm to assist two Jesuits who were trying to convert the natives of the Orinoco llanos. The savages were frightened beyond measure, and began to beg for mercy. A bolt of lightning struck the house of a cacique and burned it to the ground, injuring five people, but the injured confessed that very night, the Jesuits aiding them with their medicines, so that none of them died. In this way "God knew how to contribute to the ministrations of our missionaries with this sermon of judgment, the clouds serving as pulpit and the thunder as voices, heated in the forge of divine fury, which penetrated like beams of light into the most obstinate hearts." [32]

The Lord of heaven and earth knew how to punish the evildoer as well as to heal the sick and aid the needy. He was a God of vengeance as well as of love. Certain Indians, after attacking a mission village and killing Father Pedro Suárez, robbed the church of its bells, ornaments, and vases. But all the natives who rang the bells or profaned the ornaments and vases died, and in the end the savages threw the whole lot of booty into the River Curaray. [33] When a missionary reprimanded a Spanish settler of New Granada for failing to pay his Indian laborers the wages due them, the Spaniard became angry and threatened to shoot him. But the Almighty planned the destruction of this wicked Spaniard. A short time afterward he was accidentally shot and killed by a companion, "this sad case leaving to posterity the conviction of how zealously God honors his Servants, himself avenging their wrongs." [34]

The Ruler of the universe knew also how to use wild animals in achieving his inscrutable purposes. While on an Indian slave-hunting expedition on the Meta River, a soldier, in the very sight of the captain of the company, was attacked, killed, and eaten by a huge crocodile—a clear indication of the intervention of divine justice. [35]

The missions also received supernatural aid in the enforcement of rules relative to monogamy. Father Matías Ruiz Blanco tells proudly of how, by the aid of God, he cured a polygamous Indian of his desire for a multiplicity of wives. The padre was working on a reduction of the Characuare Indians of New Granada, among whom was one man who had five wives. The missionary inveighed against this heinous sin, without results; he then resorted to prayer, asking that all five of the wives should die. The women were young and healthy, but the padre had faith, and baptized them all in anticipation of the journey that they were to take to the land beyond. They soon sickened and died, immediately ascending to heaven by virtue of the holy water, so that their death was not a punishment to them. The widower was sad-dened—not so much, however, by the loss of his wives as by the fact that no other women now had the courage to marry him. He therefore became a Christian and begged Father Matías to find him a Christian wife. The request was soon granted.[36]

Occasionally the mercy of the Almighty seemed to the missionaries to be misplaced. While working among the Chiquito Indians, Father Lucas Caballero, together with eleven of his neophytes, became ill, but the heathen Indians in the vicinity remained well. The good padre saw that the infidels were very unfavorably impressed by this turn of events. If Christians sickened while unbelievers remained healthy, what was the need of accepting Christianity? Caballero carefully reasoned with the Lord about the matter:

I know full well, Lord, that my sins deserve this and much more; but look, Lord, after your glory. . . . Observe, Lord, that the neophytes will have a horror of the labors and fatigues of the Mission, if when persecuted by savage heathen and afflicted by sicknesses, you do not hasten to aid them and free them. . . . If you work miracles to cure the infidels, why will you not do the same for Christians?[37]

Father Lucas received a message from heaven telling him to persevere and trust God.

299

The missionaries found difficulty in explaining to themselves and to the Indians why the death rate among their converts was so high. Indeed, the natives sometimes conceived the idea that the padres had persuaded them to settle in villages in order that they might kill them by disease. In times of plague the fathers would go among their wards baptizing the sick, receiving confessions, burying the dead, and comforting the living; yet, notwithstanding prayers and alleged miracles, numerous neophytes died. Father Figueroa estimated that two thirds of the Indians died after coming into contact with Spaniards. What divine paradox was this—that pestilence should enter the huts of the natives hard on the heels of the gospel? Figueroa offered some ingenious explanations: (1) God may choose this season to punish the Indians for their past sins, having postponed the punishment until the arrival of missionaries, who could baptize them before death and so save them from eternal perdition. (2) God may be punishing the Indians for feigning to accept Christianity while in their hearts they reject it. (3) By decreasing the number of people whom they wish to exploit, God may be punishing the Spaniards who desire to make an unjust profit out of the Indians. (4) God may be killing some as an example to others, so that in the end more will be saved.[38]

III

While God and the saints were busy hastening from one reduction to another—sending rain here and stopping it there, healing the sick and bringing afflictions to the healthy, calming the ferocity of wild beasts or spurring them on to greater fierceness—Satan and his ubiquitous demons never rested in their attempts to check or undo the good work of the padres. Devious as were the methods of the heavenly beings, they

The henchmen of Beelzebub were always maliciously destructive

always intervened to aid the missionaries; but the henchmen of Beelzebub were always maliciously destructive. And the devil's power reached from Spain to the farthermost corner of the South American forests, as was shown by the case of a native of Estremadura. The devil appeared to this man, who was desperate with poverty, and offered, in exchange for the man's soul, to take him to a forest where he could find much gold with little effort. The Spaniard immediately consented, and gathered some loaves of bread to sustain him on the long journey across the Atlantic. Almost before he knew it he was in Peru, where a creole, who recognized him to be a recently arrived *gachupín*, invited him to lunch. Observing that the guest had some Spanish bread, the creole knew that he had been brought from Spain to Peru by the devil.[39]

301

It must be understood that the devil had ruled the tribes of South America since the Indians had departed from the true faith as taught them by the ancient apostle. It is no wonder, then, that he resented encroachment upon his empire by shaven-headed little men from beyond the seas. Said Acosta:

The Pride and Presumption of the Divell is so great and obstinate that alwaies hee seekes and strives to be honoured as God, and doth arrogate to himself all hee can, whatsoever doth appertaine to the most high God, hee ceaseth not to abuse the blinde Nations of the world vpon whom the cleere light of the holy Gospel hath not yet shone. But in the end, although idolatrie had been rooted out of the best and most notable partes of the worlde, yet he hath retired himself into the most remote parts, and hath ruled in that other part of the worlde which, although it be much inferiour in nobilitie, yet is it not of less compasse.[40]

Some infidel Indians once came trembling to Father Ruiz Blanco. They said that as they were coming through the forest to the village with the intention of embracing the religion of Christ, they heard the sound of mournful cries coming from the depth of the woods complaining because they had decided to accept the Christian faith. These sounds came, as the padre was quite certain, from the devil himself, who was lamenting the loss of these souls, whom he had hoped to drag into his subterranean kingdom.[41]

Among the Maynas missions Satan also entered and tried to persuade the Indians that the padres were reducing them either in order to murder them or to hand them over to lay Spaniards as slaves. The Wicked One told them that when the padres knelt down or made the sign of the cross they were using this method to call cruel Spaniards into the country to seize the natives whom the missionaries had persuaded to come to the reductions.[42]

DIVINE MERCY AND SATANIC MALICE

Once an Indian was on his way to see a missionary for the good of his soul when there appeared to him a group of people whom he took to be Spaniards. They said to him: "You are a simple Indian, and it is easily seen that you are not well acquainted with that fellow whom you seek and call 'Holy Father.' Know and do not doubt that he is a demon who has come to deceive you all, and so do not continue the journey, nor believe his words any longer." But the Indian went on to the mission, where he told the padre what had happened and received the information that the Spaniards whom he had seen were really devils in the form of men, who had come to deceive him with lies.[43]

Soon after 1659, when three Jesuit padres were sent to the Llanos of San Juan (Colombia) to establish missions, they learned of a lake in which the devil dwelt in the form of a great serpent. Shortly before the arrival of the three Jesuits into the country of the Tunebos, some of these Indians had gone to the lake to consult the serpent. The repulsive reptile was hidden in the depths of the lake, the surface of which raged as though disturbed by a storm, although the air was calm. After a time the serpent came to the surface to warn the Indians against certain white men, liars and deceivers, who were coming among them to teach them views contrary to those he had always taught. They must, the serpent said, continue to come to him for counsel and aid. "With these diabolic advices and promises . . . the serpent plunged into the waves, giving forth horrible hisses."[44]

The devil one time actually attacked Father Luis Beltrán, beat him, and threw him upon some thorns. At another time he appeared to the padre in the shape and dress of a hermit and tried to persuade him that his work was in vain and that he should cease his attempts to convert the natives. But the missionary recognized the Evil One, notwithstanding his dis-

303

guise, and made the sign of the cross, whereupon the devil, uttering an awful cry, disappeared, leaving Father Luis triumphant.[45]

In what is now northern Argentina, in the province of Corrientes, there was found in a river an island which had the disturbing habit of moving back and forth from north to south and from south to north. Infernal spirits, who dwelt there, rent the air with their hellish yells whenever anyone approached, and terrified people with the most unearthly grimaces. A missionary friar, arriving in the vicinity one day, instead of becoming frightened and fleeing as the Indians were accustomed to do, stood his ground and blessed the floating island. Since that day the island no longer moves, nor do the demons find it a congenial dwelling place any more.[46]

The devil was sometimes more successful than in the cases just described. With the aid of Satan, witchdoctors of the llanos were able to kill distant Indians by incantations over a vile mixture of hair, saliva, and dust.[47] The devil visited the mission of San Andrés de los Parranos on the Marañón, entered the houses, dug up the decayed corpses which the Indians, after their custom, had buried there, and fled with them into the forest. Moreover, the evil spirit, taking the form of an Indian, would often threaten neophytes on the missions with death, after which the natives would actually die. The Christian Indians might shoot their poisoned arrows into the devil-man, but he would remain unhurt.[48]

Luckily for the missions, however, the devil had his limitations in changing himself or men into animals. According to Father Caulín the devil could not transform a man into a dog, tiger, or other animal; but he could so distort the vision of spectators as to make them think that they saw one of these animals in the place of a man. He could also throw the skin of a wild beast over a man in order to deceive the spectator, or cover the individual with dense air so as to make him invisible while he created a wild beast to place where the man was, thus deceiving the onlookers into thinking that the human had been transformed into the beast.[49]

A cacique of the Jurimaguas told Father Samuel Fritz that the devil was accustomed to come to their villages and chastise the Indians. After permitting the women and children to flee, the wicked spirit would take a whip made of the hide of a manatee and flog the men until blood flowed. As soon, however, as Father Samuel erected a cross in a village, this cruel apparition ceased to visit it.[50]

An Indian of Tame, while hunting with some friends for hogs in the forest, became separated from his associates, who soon heard a frightful cry. They rushed to the aid of their companion, but were unable to find him or any signs of him. There was no blood to show that he had been killed, nor were there any bones to prove that he had been eaten by a wild beast. Surely the devil must have seized and made off with him.[51]

After learning that the devil had been such a constant menace to the missions during the early days of missionary activity in South America, one might be relieved to be informed that in the end he was vanquished. Father Joseph de Acosta wrote toward the close of the sixteenth century:

And we cannot deny it (being most evident and knowne to all the world) that the Divell dareth not hisse, and that the practises, oracles, answers, and visible apparitions, which were so ordinary throughout all this infidelitie, have ceased, whereas the Cross of Christ hath beene planted, where there are Churches, and where the name of Christ hath been confessed. And if there be at this day any cursed minister of his, that doth participate thereof, it is in caves, and on the toppes of mountaines, and in secret places, farre from the name and communion of

305

Christians. The Soveraigne Lord be blessed for his great mercies, and for the glory of His holy name.[52]

But unfortunately this was not entirely true, for Satan continued to appear at not infrequent intervals during the entire epoch of colonial missionary activity.

THE BLIND SHEPHERDS

I

F the thousands of Jesuit, Franciscan, Dominican, Augustinian, and other religious who went to the Spanish colonies in America during the three hundred years of the colonial period, even the most zealous Catholic would expect to find some who were not fitted for the high calling of ambassadors of God to the infidel. The records reveal that there were a number of religious who achieved a modicum of success and some who wrote books, inspired huge crowds of worshiping Indians, or established numerous successful reductions. There must also have been many humble padres, whose names were scarcely known even in their own time, who served to the limit of their abilities in the fields assigned to them. The reward of the best of them was small in worldly fame.

To these true apostles fell in America the magnificent enterprise of reducing the natives to the civil and Christian life, which in great part they accomplished, doing prodigious acts of extraordinary self-denial and charity; by them the untilled forests were converted into orderly towns and beautiful and productive fields, the thickets into easy roads, many large and unexplored rivers into navigable waterways of easy communication, and a multitude of ferocious savages into humble subjects of the Church.[1]

All honor to these plain but godly men. Nevertheless, it is an undeniable fact that there were not a few who lacked the vision of a divine mission and who, moved by the impulses of their baser passions, wished more for the satisfaction of their appetites and the aggrandizement of their own fortunes than for the salvation of their fellow men. Blind leaders of lost sheep, they cast a black shadow upon the otherwise glorious achievements of the frontier missionary movement.

II

Probably the least objectionable of these blind leaders were those who had no conception of the true meaning of Christianity. To them the religion of the Carpenter of Nazareth meant a body of dogma, a set of stereotyped prayers, a worship consisting of kneelings and bowings and mumblings and the counting of beads. Religion for them was void of inspiration, a sort of combination of mental and physical calisthenics which must have become exceedingly tiresome in the course of time. The principles of brotherly love, of unselfish service, and of sincere devotion, not to mention the experience of spiritual ecstasy, were unknown to them. In their work of proselyting they doubtless considered themselves successful if the Indians substituted the forms of the Catholic worship for their old pagan rites, even though the savages had no idea what it all meant. If such missionaries as these were of upright morals, they very likely did no harm, even if they never caught the true spirit of Christianity.

There was also the missionary who, while possessing exalted character and sincere devotion to the cause, lacked those qualities of leadership, tact, and insight so necessary in dealing

with a crude and savage people. These men were most unfortunate. Their aspirations exceeded their capacities. "Not
to all is conceded that special grace which is required to walk
with the heathen. Men have been seen, holy and very
zealous for the conversion of souls in the missions, but without that attractiveness which God is accustomed to concede
to those whom he chooses for this employment, and which
captivates the wills of the savages."[2] Some missionaries,
through their lack of diplomatic skill or because of their hasty
rebuke of their wards, caused the Indians to rise against them
and flee from the reductions. Such a padre, a man unable to
"permit the loss of one piece in the game of backgammon in
order to win the whole game," caused a rebellion of Cocama
Indians in the Peruvian oriente and the death of Padre Francisco de Figueroa.[3] Due respect should be given to these
missionaries who did their best and failed; perhaps after all
they were not really blind leaders, but leaders with the clear-
est vision who, perceiving their goal far in the distance, must
needs rush forward in too great haste.

Others there were who failed to abide closely by the teachings of the church they represented and refused to obey the
commands of their superiors. The Jesuits in particular were
inclined to become restless under the restraining reins of lay
and ecclesiastical authorities. While claiming to be subject
to the commands of the pope, they sometimes reinterpreted
Catholicism if by so doing they could increase their own
power and prestige and secure more converts. Their missions
once founded, they were apt to challenge the ecclesiastical
and lay authorities if their methods were criticized. As for
their teachings, "They forged a new instrument which
changed the destinies of races. It was a subtle commingling
of diplomacy and religion, knowledge and inspiration, gold
and grace. They boasted of wearing hair-shirts under their

gay apparel, and of conveying religious instruction through the elegancies of Horace and Tibullus." [4] Justly or not, the Jesuits in Paraguay were accused of planning to create an independent Indian empire. And individual missionaries of the different orders were disposed, after years on the frontier, to assume a degree of independence out of harmony with their professed humility. The viceroy of New Granada reported in 1789 that missionaries in the field sometimes refused to return to the monasteries when ordered to do so by their superiors and that, when they did return, they often refused to abide by the strict discipline of the cloister, thereby setting a bad example for their brothers. [5] Prelates and religious were specifically ordered by a law of January 17, 1590, not to interfere in matters of government. [6] But they did not fail to violate this statute. It should be said in their favor, however, that the missionaries often accomplished more by thwarting the secular officials, disobeying their superiors, and placing a liberal interpretation on the Catholic dogma than they could have done by servile obedience.

The Abbé Raynal's prejudiced criticism of the friars in America may be correct for some of them, but it cannot apply to all. His accusations are directed mainly at the friars in the cities rather than at the padres on the frontier:

Can any thing be more absurd than this authority of the monks in America? They are a set of men without knowledge and without principles; their independence tramples upon their institutions, and makes them regardless of their vows; their conduct is scandalous, their houses are so many places of evil resort, and their tribunals of penance so many trading shops. From thence it is, that they insinuate corruption into innocent minds, and that they seduce women and girls into debauchery: they are a set of simonists, who make a public traffic of holy things. . . . There are no crimes which they cannot commit with impunity. [7]

THE BLIND SHEPHERDS

A criticism almost universally applicable is the one that the
several missionary orders were jealous of each other, their
jealousy sometimes reaching a degree of hatred that made
them blind to the welfare of the very people whom they were
supposed to Christianize, civilize, and protect. It is sufficiently
difficult to understand the fierce rivalry between the Spanish
and Portuguese missionaries on the frontier; but it is even
more difficult to comprehend the antagonism of the various
Spanish orders toward each other, if they really thought that
any interruption of or hindrance to the work of the missionaries would result in the eternal loss of souls. It was the
opinion of Thomas Gage, an English Jesuit who spent a
number of years in Spanish America but later abandoned the
order, that

> no Hatred is comparable to that which is between a Jesuite
> and a Fryer, or any other of Romes Religious Orders; and above
> all yet, between a Jesuite and a Dominican. The Ambition and
> Pride of Jesuites is inconsistent in a Kingdom or Common-wealth
> with any such as may be equal to them in Preaching, Counsel,
> or Learning. . . . Which Policy and Ambition in them being
> so patent and known to all the World, hath stirred up in all other
> Religious a Hatred to them uncapable ever of Reconciliation.[8]

So friendly was Gage's father to the sons of Loyola that he
said he would rather see Thomas a scullion in a college of
Jesuits than general of the Dominican Order. The rivalry
among Spanish religious orders in the colonies must have been
more apparent in the cities than on the frontier, for once an
order had obtained permission to reduce the Indians of a particular area, it had a virtual monopoly there.

III

More serious criticisms of the religious in America are
those which concern their moral character. Such criticisms

In the convents themselves, sprightly abbés and licentious monks
were ruled by the passion of Andalusia

applied to padres on reductions as well as to those in religious houses. Living in an enervating and demoralizing tropical climate far from the restrictive influences of the cloister where the eyes of his superiors or his fellow religious were constantly upon him, surrounded by hundreds of savages addicted to polygamy and an intemperate use of alcoholic beverages, oppressed by the monotony of existence in the heart of the forest often with no one within a hundred miles capable of carrying on a conversation in Spanish or an intellectual conversation in any language, the frontier missionary was indeed of strong character if he could adhere unflinchingly to a high idealism, and without stumbling or retreating, work unremittingly to raise his wards to his own level. It was much easier, after a few years of repeated failures to reform the natives, to lower one's ideals and actions more nearly to the level of those of the Indians. The average level of character of churchmen in tropical America deteriorated during the colonial period. While in the early years of missionary endeavor most of the missionaries were no doubt spurred on by a noble incentive to a blameless life, toward the close of the colonial period they were inferior in character and spiritual idealism to religious of the United States and Europe.[9] This is far from being a blanket criticism, however, for even to the day when the wars for independence caused the breaking up of so many of the frontier reductions, numerous padres held courageously to the highest standards of their orders, receiving their reward in the firm conviction that the all-seeing eye of the Heavenly Father was observing them with approval, His recording hand noting upon the scroll their labors and sacrifices.

In the matter of sexual morality the friars could see about them the lax standards not only of their Indian wards, but also of Spaniards. The loose sexual habits so common among many races were most pronounced in colonial South America. Married men frequently kept concubines. Domingo Irala, governor of Asunción, married seven daughters of one chief. In Chile it was not unusual for one Spanish soldier to have four to six women. At least one of the conquistadores had fifty illegitimate sons.[10] With such examples about them, the religious were encouraged to depart from the straight path of virtue and tread the devious byways of amorous intrigue.

Sensuality and mysticism were the pleasures of the colonists. The convents themselves, despite their high walls, were not able to shut out these violent delights. Licentious monks, nuns with lovers, sprightly abbés, figure in the chronicles of the period as in the Italian *contes*. The cloister, with its rich arabesques, the patio [courtyard] perfumed with orange-blossom, the murmuring jet of the fountain: these evoke the passion of Andalusia. A devout society pays the insatiable convents a tribute of gold

313

and virgins; and love, fleeing the dead cities, takes refuge in cells quick with ambition and unruly desires.[11]

Thomas Gage, evidently a prejudiced writer, stated that three-fourths of the friars who went to America were men of lewd lives who had been punished in Spain for their lascivious conduct, for gambling, or for violating the vow of poverty. He told of one friar, Juan Navarro, who left Spain in 1632 because he feared that his escapades would be discovered. In 1635 he was caught in Guatemala by the husband of one of his lovers and was wounded in the face by the enraged spouse. The friar escaped without fatal injury, while the husband proceeded to cut his wife's throat. Even Gage, however, gives some of the padres credit for being "men of Sober Life and Conversation, moved only with a blind Zeal of increasing the Popish Religion."[12] Juan and Ulloa in their report on conditions in Peru during the early part of the eighteenth century told of a religious in the jurisdiction of Cuenca who kept as concubine the daughter of an Indian chief. He had deceived both her and her father by faking a marriage ceremony.[13] In New Granada toward the end of the colonial period prostitution was frequently practiced in the convents. Wealthy religious lived in houses of their own, scorning the scant comforts of the monasteries and begetting a numerous progeny of illegitimate offspring apparently without loss of their ecclesiastical positions. Drinking, dancing, and gambling were freely indulged in at some of these houses. The civil authorities, having no jurisdiction over the clergy, could not prevent these or more serious dissipations. Such looseness of morals in the colleges and monasteries was injurious to the distant missions on the frontier, both because funds needed to develop the reductions were spent in debauchery and because the missionaries were sometimes disposed to follow the example set for them by their

314

A devout society pays the insatiable convents a tribute of gold and virgins; and love, fleeing the dead cities, takes refuge in cells quick with ambition and unruly desires

superiors. The Jesuits, because of the strict enforcement of the rules of the order and the expulsion of unworthy members, were much less inclined to improper behaviour than were members of other religious orders.[14] While the clergy were probably less dissolute than the laity, the licentiousness of their behaviour as compared with their elevated pretensions may have caused the observer to reach an opposite conclusion.

After recounting the sordid story of the impure lives of one class of religious, it is appropriate to relate here an experience of the good missionary, Father San Luis Beltrán. The Indians of this padre's reduction, in order to tempt him, introduced one night into his humble dwelling a beautiful Indian girl, entirely nude. Using such wiles as nature had given and the wicked savages had taught her, and inspired also by the devil, she approached Father San Luis.

> The Saint, desirous of guarding the treasure of his most pure virginity, which he had kept inviolate all his life, seized the belt with which he was girded, and giving the Indian great blows, drove her from his presence. The wench, more ashamed of the audacity that she had displayed than of her nakedness, said to him: "Father, pardon me, for the blame was not mine but theirs who forced me to do this uncivil thing," and she told all that the Indians had commanded her to do.[15]

Thereafter the missionary was looked upon by the natives as truly an angel from heaven.

Probably more common than libertinism among religious was their covetousness, the latter being a defect of character that age does not remedy. A report on the condition of the Venezuelan missions in 1755 stated that while the frontier missionaries in that region were noted for their good moral character, there not having been a single case of violation of the vow of chastity, they resented having to serve under anyone, and were constantly asking their superiors to allow them to found a town of their own and to receive the benefice attached to it.[16] The missionaries on the frontier often found it possible to add comforts and luxuries to their fare by commerce and sometimes by direct exploitation of the natives. Sometimes they endeavored to fill their own pockets, sometimes to augment the material wealth of their orders. In either case they profited by the increase in the wealth of the mission.

A law of 1595 prohibited priests and religious from trading, acting as factors for others, employing persons to traffic for them, or participating in mining.[17] In 1635 religious were ordered not to have stores.[18] The canon law also prohibited commerce to members of religious orders, as did bulls of Urban VIII, Clement IX, and Benedict XIV. The canon law, however, defined as commerce the purchase and sale of an article without adding to its value, and permitted ecclesiastics to purchase raw materials for manufacture and sell the finished product, and to market commodities that they produced with their own labor.[19]

As early as 1582 Don Francisco de Toledo, viceroy of Peru, complained to the king that clerics and friars were not only masters of spiritual affairs in the viceroyalty, but were attempting to usurp temporal authority as well. He accused them of coming to America not to preach to and teach the Indians, but to exploit the natives for the purpose of enriching themselves.[20] Thomas Gage claimed that the Dominicans, especially those of Peru and New Granada, were very wealthy, "and they all live above their Vow of Poverty, abounding in Wealth, Riot, Liberty and Pleasures."[21] In Peru the Jesuits acquired vast estates, entered commerce on an extensive scale, accumulated such great wealth that they were able to send some of it to Europe to aid other members of the Society of Jesus in their political intrigues, insinuated themselves into positions of influence in the temporal government, and used the confessional to acquire material advantages. In 1767 the Jesuit Order in Lima owned 5,200 slaves, a noticeable contrast to their policy of protecting frontier Indians from enslavement. It should be said to their credit, on the other hand, that the Jesuits expended large sums in education and charity.[22]

It is reasonable to suppose that missionaries on the frontier employed the methods of the religious and clerics of more densely settled and more highly civilized parts of the colonies. The Indians were made to pay for every service performed by the church under threat of punishment in the next life; and an indication of the success of ecclesiastics in persuading the natives of the truth of their teachings about hell is indicated by the alacrity with which the Indians paid as ordered. One curate of the province of Quito was said to have collected annually more than six thousand hens and chickens, fifty thousand eggs, four thousand guinea pigs, and two hundred sheep; [23] and this was considered to be a not very lucrative position. Many priests made over five thousand pesos a year by collecting commodities from the Indians and sending them to neighboring towns and mining camps for sale, although their customary fees of a legitimate nature were only seven or eight hundred pesos. Monks in charge of curacies sometimes had Indian concubines, who exploited the women and children of the parish by making them work for them.[24]

On certain holy days, celebrations were held in which priests made huge gains. For each festival several Indians were appointed as majordomos, and they were held responsible for the success of the celebration. Any Indian refusing to accept an appointment as majordomo ran the risk of receiving a beating. These Indian officials obtained fees from the other natives, but the fees were offset by payments that the majordomos had to make to the priests. The Indians of the parish had to pay for Mass, for the sermon in praise of the saint, for wax and incense, and for the procession in honor of the saint. The *visitadores*, Juan and Ulloa, explained:

All this has to be paid in cash . . .; to this is added then the gift that the majordomos have to make to the Cura . . . which amounts to two or three dozens of hens, and as many young chickens, guinea pigs, eggs, sheep, and a pig if they have it. Thus, when the Saint's day arrives, the Cura gets hold of every-

318

thing that the Indian has been able to save in money all year long, and the birds and animals that his wife and children have raised in their huts, living almost deprived of food, and reduced to wild herbs, and the seeds that they gather from the little farms that they cultivate.[25]

The bishop of Paraguay, Bernardino de Cárdenas, wrote in 1651 to the Count of Salvatierra, viceroy of Peru, accusing the Jesuits of failing to instruct the Indians as they ought, of stealing fourteen million crowns from the royal treasury over a period of forty years, of defrauding the church and disobeying instructions of ecclesiastical authorities and of the king of Spain as well.[26]

The Jesuits of Paraguay engaged extensively in commerce, having stores as far away as Buenos Aires. River fleets were sent down the Uruguay and Paraná carrying tobacco, maize, wheat, sugar cane, hides, linseed, and yerba maté. Some of these commodities found markets as far away as Brazil, Chile, and Peru, while a near-by market of some importance was developed at Santa Fé. While this commerce was a violation of the laws of 1595 and 1635, it was not a violation of the canon law, since these products were produced by the Jesuits themselves with the aid of their Indian converts.[27]

Missionaries in Venezuela were permitted to have a private income in addition to the stipend paid them by the state. They were allowed to charge a fee of four reales a Mass and to earn money by the sale of rice, Indian corn, tobacco, poultry, and cassava. Some padres had their Indians extract from forest plants certain oils, which the padres sold, and some carried on a traffic in hammocks with the Caribs.[28] The Jesuits in New Granada, more than the other orders, aroused the hostility of lay authorities by engaging in commerce. The encomenderos of the llanos charged that the Jesuits obliged the Indians to buy from them rather than from ordinary merchants and that this traffic was injurious both to commerce in general and to the welfare of Indian souls. Another charge, namely that the Jesuits were becoming rich with the aid of Indians, was dropped, since this argument might be directed against the encomenderos themselves. Groot gives his opinion that the Jesuits of New Granada engaged in commerce in order to prevent the lay merchants from cheating the Indians. The Jesuits sold clothes to Indians practically at cost.[29] The Society of Jesus did build up vast property holdings in New Granada, farms, buildings, cattle, churches, and jewels; and poor Indians on the frontier may have contributed in part to the purchase of the jewels confiscated from the principal church in Bogotá in 1767 (there were 1483 emeralds, 64 pearls, 26 diamonds, 169 amethysts, 1 large topaz, and 13 rubies).[30] The commercial activities of the Jesuits were a cause for the dissolution of the order and the expulsion of the members of the Society of Jesus in 1767.[31]

Toward the end of the eighteenth century, missionaries of Venezuela were reported to have acquired fortunes of sixty to eighty thousand dollars, but it is likely that at times the wealth of the missions was confused with the personal property of the padres. Nevertheless, abuses were sufficiently frequent to cause the Indians at times to go to Caracas to complain to the bishop and captain general of the treatment accorded them and to request the recall of certain missionaries. There were cases in which the audiencia at Caracas called missionaries before it to answer charges which included smuggling. Franciscan missionaries were less frequently guilty of abuses than those of some of the other orders.[32]

IV

No less serious than the charges already discussed is that of cruelty to the Indians. Missionaries acted as judges in minor cases, while the passing of judgment on Indians guilty of severe crimes was left to the secular authorities. Antonio Astrain maintains that "to impose some paternal correction for the light and everyday faults seems necessary, considering the laziness and servile character of the natives."[33] On missions where the padre had almost unlimited power and where he was supported by a strong force of Spanish soldiers, it must have been easy to resort to the use of unnecessarily harsh treatment in dealing with fractious neophytes. Juan and Ulloa charged that the mistreatment and injustices prepetrated by both lay and ecclesiastical Spaniards were responsible for the escape of many Indians into the wilds:

Many have rebelled and have gone to the unconquered lands in order to continue in the barbarous customs of heathenism. . . . The doctrine which is taught to them cannot make any impression on them, if they see all to the contrary in the conduct of their teachers, because although it is preached to them that they obey the precepts of the law of God with all their hearts, loving the Lord above all things, . . . if they do not see fulfilled either the one or the other by those who should teach them the way, it is not strange that they are so indifferent to religion.[34]

There were numerous degrees of mistreatment of the natives. Some of the first missionaries to America required the Indians to submit to having their hair cut off prior to baptism. This practice was so objectionable to some natives that they preferred to risk perdition rather than lose their crowning glory. A royal edict of March 5, 1581, prohibited this useless practice of the friars.[35] Father Cristóbal de Acuña accused the Portuguese of setting up wooden crosses in Indian villages and enslaving the Indians if they permitted them to fall.[36] Missionaries would sometimes transfer individual Indians from one reduction to another, thereby permanently separating them from their families. A royal order of August 5, 1701, forbade this practice.[37] Whipping seems to have been an almost universal practice on the missions. In Peru the following method of corporal punishment was used by both laymen and ecclesiastical authorities: When an Indian had been guilty of some infraction of rules or had disobeyed orders, he was stripped and made to lie face downward on the ground. He was then scourged with a whip made of cowhide or of the hide of the manatee (which was said to be thick enough to stop a musket ball). The Indian was required to count the lashes until the number prescribed had been imposed. When the punishment was over, he had to kneel before the man with the whip, kiss his hand, and say to him, "May God bless you." Such punishment was inflicted for minor offenses, though probably less frequently by religious than by lay Spaniards.[38]

On the Mojo missions it was customary for the Jesuits to beat the Indians. The converts seem to have become reconciled to this punishment, for those who had committed some fault would go voluntarily to the padre's house, kneel down, and ask for a beating. They probably thought that in this way they would arouse the compassion of the missionary, thereby escaping with a light punishment. One Indian brought his nine-year-old son to the padre and asked him to give the boy a beating for going to examine fish traps on Sunday instead of attending Mass. If the Indian men objected to the behaviour of their wives, they took them to the missionaries for chastisement.[39] One Mojo Indian, becoming angry at his wife, wished to punish her. Since she threatened to tell the padre if he struck her, he took her to the missionary, who commanded the husband to give his wife a sound thrashing. Greatly to his own satisfaction he did as ordered:

The punishment finished, which she suffered with much silence, she began to cry and say: now you will hurt and kill me, or you will leave me; to which the husband replied very affectionately: don't say that. Am I some mad man, that our Father having punished you, I should dare to touch you? No, don't fear, for I respect you much; it is finished; I have forgotten everything. Both very humbly kissed the hand of the Father and departed in peace.[40]

On the Paraguay missions a system of public penance was established. The missionaries appointed some of the Indians to observe the others to see if they violated the rules of the mission. If a convert was caught in any serious infraction of the laws, he was dressed in a penitential habit, conducted to the church, and required to confess publicly. After this he was led to the public square and whipped. "The criminals always receive this correction not only without murmuring, but with thanks; and scarce ever relapse." [41] Whipping could not be employed on the new reductions because of danger of causing a revolt or an attempt at retaliation, and some tribes were so fierce that beating was never a satisfactory method of punishing them.[42] The employment of harsh punishments caused a critic of the Society of Jesus to say that the Jesuits held Indians in intolerable slavery.[43]

Humboldt tells of how missionaries on the Orinoco imprisoned Indians in stocks, called the *cepo*. The native's legs were placed between two blocks of wood so notched as to enclose the ankles, and were fastened together by a chain. One morning Humboldt was awakened by the cries of an Indian who was being beaten with a whip made of manatee hide. When he inquired about this form of punishment, the missionary told him that such methods were absolutely necessary for the preservation of the missions, for, if given complete liberty, the Indians would soon desert the reductions. Humboldt disagreed with the padre on the subject of corporal punishment, his opinion being that,

Man, in order to enjoy the advantages of a social state, must no doubt sacrifice a part of his natural rights, and his original independence; but, if the sacrifice imposed on him be not compensated by the benefits of civilization, the savage, wise in his simplicity, retains the wish of returning to the forests that gave him birth. . . . A government founded on the ruins of the liberty of the natives extinguishes the intellectual faculties, or stops their progress.[44]

On the lower Orinoco about 1800 it was customary for the padre to dispense justice after the celebration of Mass on holidays. At this time the missionary would receive gifts of plantains, wood, and other necessaries for his household. He would instruct his Indian officials to apportion the work for the following week, and would reprimand some converts, and give orders that others be whipped.[45]

In passing judgment on the use of corporal punishment by the missionaries, one should keep in mind that the padres were more than religious leaders. Preaching, teaching, and administering sacraments were not the most difficult of their duties. They were also the civil, financial, and not infrequently the highest military authority on the reduction. Their missions were sometimes located hundreds of miles from the nearest Spanish secular official. Fear of corporal punishment was probably the only restraint that kept many Indians, just passing from a state of savagery into one of semicivilization, in hand at all. They were like unruly children, and it was difficult for them to give up entirely their savage practices. A few blows might accomplish more in persuading an Indian to forget the ways of his fathers than hours of kindly exhortations or threats of punishment in a future life. Borda justifies the cruelty of Spaniards by ultimate results:

Great have been the crimes of the white race, as great also and heroic their services to humanity. It has been the first, if not the only actor, in the laborious and bloody drama of civilization.

In America, where the three races have been given a dwelling place, all the greatness in heroism and crime is due to it. It has decimated and tyrannized the native race; but it also has reduced it to a civil life, granting to it the scraps from the banquet of civilization and opening its eyes to the light of the true religion.[46]

V

Political intrigues—actual or alleged—of Jesuits in Europe resulted in injury to the Jesuit missions in America and finally in their total destruction or transfer to other religious orders. On September 2, 1758, Joseph I of Portugal, while driving to his Palace of Belem, was shot in the arm from ambush. The Jesuits were suspected, their houses were placed under guard, and within the next two years they were expelled from the Portuguese dominions.[47] In Spain their alleged intrigues caused their expulsion from all Spanish territories in 1767, as the reader will recall. Members of the order were even suspected of poisoning Pope Clement XIV, though there is no clear evidence of their having committed this crime.[48] Whether the Jesuits were or were not guilty of the crimes attributed to them, the spiritual blindness of some members of the order aroused the suspicion which caused their expulsion and the consequent decline of missions which Jesuit padres had proved so skilful in creating and maintaining. E. Boyd Barrett, a former Jesuit, thinks that the efficiency and aggressiveness of the Jesuits has been injurious to the Catholic Church as a whole. He says:

The Church has suffered in many ways from the presence of the Society of Jesus in its ranks, and from the influence it has exercised. There has been disturbance of peace and ill-will aroused, in every place where the Jesuits have been. But worse than this the Society has awakened a spirit of rivalry, competition, and hustling in religion that has not told for good.[49]

325

VI

Toward the end of the colonial period, as already intimated, the level of character and ability of the frontier missionaries in South America declined. Few of them retained in 1800 the enthusiasm and high idealism characteristic of padres of the seventeenth century. Mission life had been reduced to a more simple routine, so that the missionary friars performed a round of duties varying but slightly from day to day, and their lives were not greatly different from those of the curas (priests) in the Indian towns. On the whole, missionary work on the frontier in 1800 was not so perilous as it had been in earlier times, the fiercest and most dangerous tribe, the Caribs, having been conquered. As a consequence, padres of weaker courage than Francisco de Figueroa, Juan Rivero, and Samuel Fritz were attracted to the missions. The viceroy of New Granada complained in 1789 that the missionaries did not have sufficient ability to perform their duties properly for "the religious orders destine for this grave ministry the most inept, and those who only serve to clutter up the cloisters." [50]   Humboldt, after his visit to Guiana about 1800, reported that of the ten missionaries whom he met in this region only Father Ramón Bueno seemed to be sincerely interested in his wards and attentive to their welfare.[51]   On the Orinoco Humboldt came across a group of padres with shaven heads and long beards playing cards and smoking pipes. They were kindly, however, and advised him as to the character of the country through which he intended to go.[52]   Depons, whose respect for the earlier missionaries was profound, had little praise for the friars in Venezuela at the beginning of the nineteenth century. He says:

Contempt, sooner or later, succeeds to admiration, and enthusiasm gives place to indifference. . . . Thus it is that the holy fervour of the missionary has become chilled, and no longer exists but on his lips. The religious orders of Spain still furnish individuals who offer their voluntary services to replace those missionaries who die in America. It is doubtless their intention, on leaving Spain, to devote themselves to the spiritual conquest of the Indians, without anticipating any reward for their labours except the crown of the martyr or the recompence of the apostle. But on their arrival in America, finding the lives of their brethren rather fashioned according to the sprit of man than the spirit of God, the frailty of their natures deems it more convenient to follow than to furnish an example.[53]

Such, then, were the blind shepherds: the spiritually dull, the impatient, the rebellious, the jealous, the licentious, the covetous, the brutal, the delvers in political intrigue, the assassins. The difference between their actions and their teachings must have seemed a strange inconsistency to the Indian, to whom the ways of the white man were always inscrutable enough. It is difficult to speak in, defense of such missionaries except to say that the padre, notwithstanding his vestments, his crucifix, his breviary, and his Latin, was yet a man moved by ambitions and passions like other men. Nor should the evil deeds of the blind leaders be permitted to obscure the glorious achievements of their less worldly brothers.

MATERIAL ACHIEVEMENTS

I

Y the sincere Spanish Catholic, the work of the missionary friar in bringing into the Church untold thousands of wayward souls was considered of such great importance that his more worldly accomplishments attained by comparison a position of relative insignificance. According to Don Juan Nuix, the uncompromising protagonist of the Spanish system in America, the conversion of the natives was the outstanding accomplishment of Spain in the western hemisphere. He says:

Even if it had not done another thing than carry and establish Christianity there, who but the boldest Atheist or Deist will be able to deny, that for this benefit the Indies owe to Spain the origin of all of even their temporal felicity? The Spanish missionaries were the Apostles chosen by God to announce the Gospel in those unknown countries. They were the ones who demolished the empire of the devil in all those lands, and who instilled the knowledge of the only and true God, and the belief in our Redeemer, into those most stupid and barbarous nations, converting into men, or, better said, into Angels worthy of heaven those insensate savages, who seem to the eyes of our philosophers little better than beasts.[1]

One must admit that it was a labor of no little magnitude to drive the devil himself out of the great continent of South America, where he had been entrenched for some thousands of years, and where he had built up the most formidable army of diabolical spirits that could be found anywhere this side of Cathay. Alonso de Zamora claimed that the Franciscans and Dominicans alone in two centuries catechized and baptized ten million Indians.[2]

But the modern observer is inclined to judge the success of the missionary movement not so much by the number of savages sprinkled with the holy water of baptism, nor even by the success with which the padres persuaded the Indians to substitute processions for ceremonial dances and the adoration of wooden figures of saints for obeisances to trees containing spirits, as by other contributions which possibly could have been made by men with little formal religion at all if they had been genuinely interested in the welfare of the natives. Such an observer is prone to maintain that the missionaries most worthy of renown were those who strove to make life here on earth better for their converts while they were preparing them for the life to come.

II

Not the least of the contributions of frontier missionaries were those in the field of exploration. Carrying with them rude instruments, they estimated latitude and longitude, and drew numerous maps, which, although lacking the accuracy of the products of modern cartographers, showed the relative positions of the more important natural and artificial features of the area. They blazed trails which were later followed by lay Spaniards carrying civilization to points far east of the

Andean cordillera. By virtue of the efforts of the missionaries the dark interior of South America came to enjoy at least an era of twilight, although, with the passing of the great colonial missionary movement, huge areas reverted to oblivion until in recent years they were again opened to view by modern explorers. The modern scientific explorer gliding up some hidden stream in western Brazil no doubt derives a feeling of satisfaction from the belief that he is the first white man to ride those turbid waters; but the chances are that two or three hundred years ago a missionary father traveled that very route. Moreover, the tonsured explorer of those early days carried with him neither canned foods, nor camp furniture, nor mosquito netting, and even his medicines were a mixture of impurities and superstitions.[8]

III

Of greatest importance was the intensely practical training which the padres gave their wards. On their reductions the missionaries introduced plants and animals of European origin, taught the Indians how to raise them, and strove to improve the crude agricultural methods of the natives, furnishing them with metal implements for farming and metal weapons for hunting and fishing. They also taught their neophytes to construct not only pretentious churches, but capacious storehouses, strong fortifications, and comfortable dwellings. In wet country they taught them drainage, and in arid lands irrigation. They introduced improved methods of manufacture, so that the Indians became skilled handicraftsmen, making the missions almost independent of the outside world.

What a task it must have been to transport three calves across the Andes and down the streams by canoe to the Maynas reductions! Yet the padres managed to build up a little herd of a hundred cattle in this region, which furnished them for a time with butter, meat, milk, and cheese. The Indians, however, often shot the animals with poisoned arrows; and the climate and herbage were unsatisfactory, so that the livestock industry here was unsuccessful.⁴ Great credit is due Father Baraza for introducing the first herd of cattle into the Mojo missions and undergoing many hardships in driving them after most of his Indian helpers had deserted.⁵ In 1810 there were 72,863 cattle and horses in the Mojo region.⁶

In 1755 the Guiana missions had cattle farms which supplied fresh and jerked beef to the missionaries, overseers, servants, cowherds, and dependents, and even to any needy Indian who might apply for it. The padres also supplied meat at six pesos the head to the inhabitants and garrison of Santo Tomás de Guayana, and at five pesos the head to workmen engaged in labor for the government. The friars sold soap, hides, tallow, butter, and cheese, although the greater part of these commodities was consumed on the missions. With the hides they manufactured a number of commodities, including halters, trunks, and straps for tying packs. Hides then sold at sixteen reales the arroba (25 pounds) and cheese at eight reales the arroba. At this time a horse farm, called the *Yegüera*, belonging to the Capuchins, had a herd of three hundred mares and a number of jacks and stallions. Enough horses were raised to supply a mount for each padre besides enough for the cowboys. In addition the mission made a profit by selling pack mules at fifty pesos a head. Fifty pack mules were continually in use carrying goods between the missions and the settlement of Santo Tomás. Horses and mules were also hired out to other missions to carry loads to this town. In his report on industries for the benefit of the common funds of the missionaries, Don Eugenio de Alvarado, on April 20, 1755, listed among the possessions of the padres in Guiana the Divina Pastora cattle farm, the Yegüera, two

331

sugar mills, and several plantations. "The plantations of the community . . . supply the Fathers with all the bread they need for themselves, their servants, overseers, and other dependents, the surplus being sold for the benefit of the community and the proceeds thereof handed over to the Father Procurator. . . ."[7] In the middle of the eighteenth century droves of wild horses grazed on the llanos of Venezuela, and it was estimated that the herds of wild cattle contained as many as from ten to twenty thousand animals.[8]

Miguel Marmión, governor of Guiana, reported on July 10, 1778, to the secretary of state for the Department of the Indies that during the previous year the Catalonian Capuchin fathers had made an offer to give for the service of the king twelve thousand head of cattle. It was proposed that these cattle be used to encourage the settlement of white people in Guiana, a small herd to be granted to each poor settler. After the colonist had built a house, thereby giving evidence that he intended to be a bona fide farmer, he should be given twenty-five to thirty cows "with the corresponding bulls" on condition that he would not kill, sell, or otherwise dispose of them within three years.[9]

The governor of Guiana estimated in 1788 that out of a total of 220,000 head of cattle in his province the Capuchin missions owned 180,000.[10] This may have been an exaggeration, for Humboldt in 1804 estimated that the Catalonian Capuchin missions in Guiana had something over 60,000 head of cattle. He told how in 1768 Don Manuel Centurión had driven off 20,000 head belonging to these missionaries in order to distribute them among the poor.[11]

Father Caulín wrote of the Observant missions in Nueva Andalucía:

Besides the cities, villas, and towns to which I have referred, there are found innumerable ranches of horses, mules, and cattle that multiply with abundance in all the area of the llanos, which stretch from the base of the sierra and the edges of the forest along the coast to the Orinoco, and whose terrain consists of very pleasant and broad pasture grounds, in this country called *sabanas*, of fresh and thriving grasses; of beautiful meadows; and of broad valleys in which the inhabitants cultivate and produce abundant harvests of sugar, honey, brown sugar, bananas, Indian corn, cassava, rice, beans, and other things. . . .[12]

With the coming of the revolution against Spain and the abandonment of the missions in Venezuela, the cattle that had been under the care of the llaneros of the reductions ran wild. Shortly after 1800 it was estimated that there were some 150,000 head scattered over the llanos. The followers of Bolívar in the Orinoco region subsisted largely on these herds and on the remains of plantations that had been established by the padres.[13]

While in Paraguay there were great farms worked by gangs of Indians, and while on the Orinoco there were huge cattle ranches, it was commonly the policy of frontier missionaries to encourage their wards to operate little farms or *conucos* of their own. Under the direction of the padres the Indians were able to produce more of the necessities of life than ever before. There was no longer the danger of famine, which had formerly stalked even in regions having many natural advantages for agriculture. Possessing a regular supply of food, the converts no doubt gradually abandoned their old habit of gluttonously gorging themselves after periods of existing on short rations.

The padres became manufacturers and possibly miners. A Franciscan friar, Francisco Alvarez Villanueva, wrote in 1777 that the Jesuits of Maynas had been accustomed to mine annually from three and a half to four million dollars worth of gold, which they used to purchase goods from the Portuguese. They may have mined some gold, but this statement

Some of the Indians, before being reduced, were skilled in making blowguns—lethal weapons some seven feet long, from which poisoned darts were ejected

as to the amount appears to be a gross exaggeration similar to many others in regard to Jesuit activities in South America.[14] Besides manufacturing sugar, the missionaries in Venezuela made molasses and rum. While chocolate and lemonade were popular drinks, the habit of "taking an eleven o'clock" created a demand for the more potent beverage, which was also used as a liniment for bruises. The padres employed rum, distributed in small quantities at psychological moments, to persuade Indians to run errands.[15]

Missionaries on frontier reductions performed a valuable service by educating their wards to make things with their hands. Some of the Indians, before being reduced, were skilled in making wooden tools, blowguns and other weapons, canoes, pottery, baskets, and ornaments. Possessing the inherent musical instinct of the savage, they easily became interested in learning the construction of and the method of playing new types of musical instruments. José Diguja, governor of Cumaná, wrote in 1761 of the Capuchins of Guiana:

The Fathers try their best to provide them with iron utensils for the cultivation of their fields. . . . The Indians . . . are well instructed in the Christian doctrine and sufficiently conversant with the Castilian language. Many of them learn music and play several instruments skilfully, and most of these are applied to the service of the Church, where the solemn functions are carried out with genuinely satisfying ceremonies.[16]

On the Paraguay missions the Jesuits had workshops for painters, sculptors, gilders, and gold and silver smiths, as well as for workers in the baser metals, carpenters, and weavers. Converts learned to make brick, lime, glass, shoes, hats, lace, organs, and trumpets. Children entered these shops at an early age to learn a trade. Some of them became highly skilled in the handicrafts, retaining their knowledge and skill after the expulsion of the Jesuits. The women became proficient in spinning; each woman was given at the beginning of each week a supply of cotton or wool, which she must make into thread by Saturday night. Churches constructed in Paraguay by Indians under the direction of the padres rivaled those of Peru and Spain.[17]

The missionaries added enormously to the material wealth of the regions in which they established reductions. Whereas in 1724 Guiana was so impoverished that the missionaries could not maintain themselves unassisted, by 1755 they were self-supporting, and soon after this date were able to furnish supplies to other colonists.[18] There were said to have been at one time on the Paraná River two thousand boats carrying the commerce of the Paraguay missions, while the value of the property of these reductions has been rated as high as twenty-five million dollars.[19] Borda says that the Jesuits contributed greatly to the total wealth of New Granada, founding during their career in that region over a thousand towns, and that they gave large quantities of alms and food to the poor, besides educating them without pay.[20]

Humboldt's description of a fat, jolly missionary on the upper Orinoco represents him as an altruistic country gentleman, mainly interested in the material success of his estate:

The missionary of San Fernando was a Capuchin, a native of Aragon, far advanced in years, but strong and healthy. His extreme corpulency, his hilarity, the interest he took in battles and sieges, ill accorded with the ideas we form in northern countries of the melancholy reveries and the contemplative life of missionaries. Though extremely busy about a cow which was to be killed next day, the old monk received us with kindness, and permitted us to hang up our hammocks in a gallery of his house. Seated, without doing anything, the greater part of the day, in an armchair of red wood, he bitterly complained of what he called the indolence and ignorance of his countrymen. Our missionary, however, seemed well satisfied with his situation. He treated the Indians with mildness; he beheld his Mission prosper, and he praised with enthusiasm the waters, the bananas, and the dairy-produce of the district. The sight of our instruments, our books, and our dried plants, drew from him a sarcastic smile; and he acknowledged, with the naïveté peculiar to the inhabitants of those countries, that of all the enjoyments of life, without excepting sleep, none was comparable to the pleasure of eating good beef. . . .[21]

IV

Another noteworthy achievement of the missionaries was their translation into Indian languages of Spanish writings—especially prayers, the catechism, songs, and the like—and their compilation of dictionaries and grammars of the native tongues. In Peru as early as 1576 a beginning was made in arranging vocabularies, writing grammars, and translating the catechism into the native languages. By 1596 the Jesuits were translating catechisms into the Aymará and Quechua languages, the chief tongues of the old Inca empire. The plan was to have these translations printed at public expense.[22] Spanish law required that missionaries learn the languages of the Indians among whom they worked. The study of such strange dialects must have been exceedingly exasperating to the average padre; but some of them took up the task with such determination that they succeeded in learning several languages.[23] In less than a year after reaching the New Granada missions Father Juan Rivero learned three Indian languages so well that he wrote sermons in them. He also learned, though imperfectly, two other Indian tongues. Chided once by another padre for the care with which he studied the native dialects, Rivero answered: "I, my Father, look at each word . . . as a grain of gold which I gather greedily, because when watered it later will produce among these heathen fruits of life eternal." Rivero wrote grammars of the Indian dialects to aid the missionaries who should succeed him.[24] Concerning the study of the native languages, Father Joseph de Gumilla wrote:

It is certain that, at the beginning, the study of new languages has very bitter roots, but as afterward the fruit, in the salvation of many souls, is so delicate and abundant that the cost is very slight, in view of so much gain; and if the eternal salvation of only one of those souls were superabundant recompense of many years of Apostolic tasks, what will it be on seeing a continuous gain of souls for glory, not only for the present, but also for the future.[25]

While some indigenous dialects were simple, having only a few hundred words, others were quite complex. Father Ignacio Chomé, who was well versed in European languages and had some knowledge of African and Asiatic tongues, expressed his admiration for the Guaraní language. In his opinion it was not inferior to any European language. Each word expressed a clear, distinct idea. The Guaraní had so many subtleties of expression that years were required to learn them. Yet this language was so widely spoken by the Indians that if a missionary once learned it he could converse with natives inhabiting the vast territory between the Atlantic and Bolivia. A knowledge of Guaraní was practically indispensable to the missionary on the Charcas, Río de la Plata, and Paraguay frontiers.

The padres who labored among the Chiquitos translated the formulas used in worship, confession, and other Catholic ceremonies and sacraments into the native tongue. The proper thing to say on making the sign of the cross was, "By the sign of the Holy Cross our God defends us from those who hate us, in the name of the Father and of the Son and of the Holy Ghost." The translation into Chiquito was, "*Oi naucipi Santa Crucis oquimay zoychacu Zoichupa mo unama po chineneco zumanene au niri naqui Yaytolik ta naqui Aytotik ta naqui Espíritu Santo.*"[26] It is interesting to note that while the words, "Holy Cross" and "Holy Spirit" are not translated from Spanish, the word, "God," is translated. The inference is that the Chiquitos had some powerful god named *Zoichupa* and that the missionaries gave the Christian God this Indian name in order to facilitate conversion. The neophytes very likely thought that they were being taught a new way to worship their old god. A precedent for such procedure on the part of the missionaries was set by St. Paul at Athens when he acclaimed himself the representative of the Unknown God.

Among the Mojos, where there was a great variety of dialects, the padres chose the one which appeared to be most widely used. This was made the universal language of the

Mojo missions, and Indians as well as padres were required to learn it. Some missionaries compiled a grammar, which was used as a textbook in the reduction schools. All preaching and catechizing were done in this language.[27]

V

The eyes of the padres on the South American frontier were not closed to the marvels of nature about them. This country, with its strange men, its queer animals, and its luxuriant vegetation, was very different from the bare plateau of Castile, the mountain-shadowed valleys of Granada, the plains of Andalusia, or the craggy heights of Navarre. Living for decades beyond the pale of any civilization except that which they carried with them, the Spanish missionaries became intimately acquainted with the animal and vegetable life of chaco, pampas, selvas, and llanos. Possessing more literary ability than the average soldier or trader, they became not only the chroniclers of their own achievements, but also amateur anthropologists, zoölogists, and botanists who described the plant and animal life of this exotic world. They carried into the wilds with them some knowledge of the crude medical science of the time; and, combining that knowledge with what they learned of the healing practices of the Indians, they concocted marvelous and potent remedies that sometimes failed to kill. They recorded the action of volcanoes, the character and changes of climate, the habits of insects, and the customs, beliefs, and physical characteristics of the natives. They frequently displayed astounding superstition, but occasionally they exhibited a lucidity of intellect and a scientific precision that demand respect.

The scientific writings of frontier missionaries are thus intensely interesting, though hardly scientific in the modern sense. Much of what they wrote was doubtless quite accurate. If they erred, it was often in the matter of interpretation, and in their naïve credulity, rather than in defects of observation. They were too much inclined to accept as truth statements of Indians concerning the habits of animals and the efficacy of remedies. An investigator wishing to obtain authoritative information on subjects of a scientific nature on which the padres wrote could hardly afford to depend on their books; but if from curiosity he should compare their productions with those of later more careful and less superstitious observers, such as Alexander von Humboldt, F. Depons, and twentieth-century explorers and scientists, he would find them surprisingly accurate, considering the paucity of general scientific knowledge available from the sixteenth to the eighteenth centuries. Scientific writings of missionaries of the latter part of the eighteenth century are more nearly accurate than similar productions written two hundred years earlier.

The Jesuits are credited with the introduction of the use of quinine. Shortly before 1629 an Indian communicated to a Jesuit the knowledge of the healing qualities of this drug, and Peruvian Jesuits began to use it in treating sick Indians on the missions. In 1630 the wife of the Count of Chinchón, viceroy of Peru, became ill of an intermittent fever. After her doctors had given up all hope for her recovery, the count's confessor, a Jesuit named Torres Vázquez, administered quinine, after which she completely recovered her health. The drug was known as "Jesuit powder" until 1742 when its name was changed to *chinchona* in honor of the countess whom it had cured.[28]

In the field of medicine the colonial period in South America was in the main, however, one of quacks and strange cure-alls. Apothecary shops sold such medicines as condor's grease, claws of the tapir, and unicorn's horns.[29] Remedies still used among Indians of northern Argentina and Paraguay were then in vogue among white people as among the natives. Tapirs' hoofs ground or pulverized and drunk in the form of tea were excellent for heart troubles and hemorrhages. Spiders preserved in alcohol were also considered efficacious in curing the latter malady. Wax mixed with flies, if applied to a thorn wound, would facilitate the removal of the thorn. A fresh mouse hide applied to a bullet wound would make possible the easy extraction of the ball. If one should be bitten by a venomous snake, the proper procedure was to cut off the serpent's tail and apply it to the wound. A little cross over the door was considered effective in keeping away disease.[30] The muddy waters of the Río Grande were said to be good for diseases of the bladder.[31]

With such medicines in vogue it is not surprising that the padres, who usually had no special training in medical science, should advise the use of strange medicaments. When the remedies were not poisonous, they may have helped to put the patient in an optimistic state of mind, one of the prerequisites of improvement. Friar Francisco de San José was said to have cured "many sick with grave accidents and distinct illnesses" by means of three bananas, some holy water, and the gospel of Saint John.[32] Father Caulín told of a cureall of the Orinoco region; namely, balsam of Copaiva, which, besides being a purgative and nerve bracer, was good for apoplexy, convulsions, rheumatism, colic, liver pains, fracture, dislocation, gonorrhea, white flux, delayed menstruation, and ills of the kidneys and lungs.[33] He advised the use of tobacco in cases of snakebite and told of a mule which, after being bitten by a rattlesnake, found some cured tobacco leaves, ate them, and was well the following day.[34] The Napo Indians of the upper Amazon valley, when bitten by a snake, used tobacco and salt, refrained from eating fish that had teeth, ate no butter, and avoided passing the house of a pregnant woman.[35] Father Charlevoix related that poisonous snakes were very common in the Chaco, but added that antidotes for their venom were still more common, including the viper's herb, the eyetooth of a viper, the stalk and ear of Indian corn, and tobacco leaves. The shank bone of a cow broiled and applied to the wound was highly efficacious in drawing out the poison, especially if the bone had first been bathed in milk and wine.[36] If one should see a snake in time to avoid being bitten by it, and should wish to kill it by a safe and effective method, one should catch the reptile and put tobacco in its mouth. Iguanas might be killed in the same manner.[37] Father Charlevoix suggested also that in case of snakebite the victim might apply a poultice of garlic, "St. Paul stone," or a bezoar stone; or he might apply brimstone to the wound after making an incision; or he might eat the head and liver of the serpent.[38] Father Martin Dobrizhoffer advised for use in snakebite: nard mixed with brandy or wine, gunpowder mixed with brandy, or a mixture of radish juice and garlic. Tobacco smoke blown upon the wound, or the odor of radishes, was helpful. In order to keep serpents at a distance, garlic should be carried on one's person. Father Martin also related, though he did not vouch for the effectiveness of the cure, how certain people used rattlesnakes for medicine. The head of this venomous serpent, tied to the neck of a sick man, was good for pains of the throat. The fat was an excellent ointment to relieve swellings. A person suffering with headache might easily cure himself by pricking his neck with a rattlesnake tooth.[39] Poultices made of certain snakes were reported to have healed ruptures.[40]

Missionaries had numerous opportunities to observe the use of the poison known as curare, in which Indians dipped the points of the darts that they used in their blowguns. Borda reported that this poison, while deadly to an animal even slightly wounded, might safely be taken internally, provided there were no abrasions in the mouth or alimentary system. Animals killed with the poisoned arrows were edible. Indians often put the tips of their arrows into their mouths to moisten them, thereby making the poison more active. When the poison came into contact with the blood stream, death was almost instantaneous.[41] Father Joseph de Gumilla gave the following account of how curare killed an animal. An Indian companion having shot a monkey,

I ran, although I was near; and not finding heat on the exterior of his body, I commanded that he be cut open from the breast downwards, [and] (O great prodigy of the hidden causes of which we are ignorant!) I did not find a trace of any heat, not even in the heart itself. About this he had much black and cold blood; in the rest of the body he had almost no blood, and the little that I found in the liver was in the same condition as that of the heart, . . . and I inferred that the exceedingly intense cold of the curare instantaneously cooled the blood.[42]

A powerful antidote for all kinds of poisoning was the eyetooth of a crocodile worn so as to make it touch the skin. The efficacy of this amulet was supposed to have been discovered by a Negro slave in the vicinity of Caracas.[43] In case of earache the sufferer should insert in his ear a bone from the tail of an armadillo. Gumilla told of a diuretic that was made by taking a small white rock from the stomach of an iguana, grinding it into a powder, and mixing it with water.[44]

Some missionary friars, particularly the better educated ones, must have used medicines that were superior to most of those just described. The Jesuits of New Granada were accustomed to go about the country with saddlebags filled with food and medicines for sick people in the villages.[45] Father Ruiz Blanco exhibited more wisdom than many of his fellow padres when he advised that the way to preserve one's health in the hot lands along the coast of Venezuela was to eat little, bathe frequently, avoid getting the feet wet with dew, keep out of the sun as much as possible, and permit no blood lettings.[46] Nevertheless, it is no wonder that Indians were often afraid to take medicine offered them by the padres, believing that either their illness would be prolonged or that they would be killed outright. Using their own remedies, the natives were freer from toothache, kidney ailments, and rheumatism than the Spaniards; and some of them lived to a very old age.[47]

VI

In their descriptions of the indigenous animals of South America the padres often either allowed their imaginations to run riot or depended too much on absurd tales told them by their converts. One missionary described a little animal whose feet turned to roots and whose body became a plant which grew into a tree.[48] Father Rivero related the following story, but did not vouch for its accuracy: A Spanish convoy captain, Don Domingo Zorilla, a truthful man, had gone into the country of the Betoyes. On his return he encountered a strange, manlike animal, having two feet, a huge head, arms like those of a man, and body entirely covered with hair. Before the captain could collect his wits to shoot, the animal fled.[49] Humboldt reported that missionaries as well as Indians on the upper Orinoco believed in the existence of a hairy man of the forest, called *salvaje*, *achi*, or *vasitri*, who was accustomed to eat human flesh and to carry off women. Father Gili told of how this ape-man carried off a woman of the town of San Carlos in the llanos of Venezuela. She lived with him in the forest for several years, having some children that were only slightly hairy. In the end she returned to civilization in order to be near the church.[50] Perhaps the *salvaje* of Venezuela was related to the ape (*caraya*) of Paraguay, which Father Martin Dobrizhoffer described in the following charming, though not very definite manner:

> Their hair is tawny, they are full of melancholy, always querulous, always morose, always snappish. As they howl incessantly day and night no one chooses to take them home and tame them. They sit in crowds on trees, and wander about in search of food. When they howl with most pertinacity it is a sign of rain or storms; the sound they utter resembles the creaking of waggons with ungreased wheals, and as hundreds howl in concert, may be heard many leagues off. They are of a middle size.[51]

In Paraguay and the Chaco of Argentina dwelt a terrible monster called in the Guaraní language *Ahó Ahó*. This beast in some respects resembled a sheep, but it had the teeth and claws of a tiger, and surpassed that animal in ferocity and cruelty. It particularly liked to devour Indians who wandered from their missions without permission of the padres. If chased by one of these creatures, the miserable Indian need not seek safety by climbing an ordinary tree, for the Ahó Ahó would fell it with powerful blows of his claws, pull it up roots and all, or, if he were not inclined to exert himself, would simply lie down at the base of the tree until the Indian, exhausted from hunger, would fall into his ravenous jaws. Neither could the wandering neophyte find safety by taking to the water, for the animal was amphibious.[52] According to the missionaries, the only way of escape was to climb the "sacred tree of Calvary," which was a tall, thin tree, quite difficult to climb and a very unattractive perch for a man. The padres very likely invented this animal to keep Indians on the reductions, but in time they also came to believe in its existence. This belief in the fierce Ahó Ahó was preserved by the Paraguayan Indians to the middle of the nineteenth century.[53] Father Martin Dobrizhoffer, who worked for many years among Indians of the Chaco, believed in the existence of this animal, though he admitted never having seen it. "I never saw even the shadow of such a beast. From which I infer that they cannot be very numerous, nor common to the whole province. Would that they were banished from every part of Paraguay!"[54]

The "tigers" of the Chaco were said to be extremely vicious, though particular in the choice of persons to eat. They generally picked out of a group the person who smelled strongest. If a Spaniard, an Indian, and a Negro were traveling together, the "tiger" would always attack the Negro. If two people of the same race were together, it would attack the elder. If the person attacked should jump into a river to escape, the beast would follow him and have him within "six Ave Marias."[55] The Indians happily discovered a most ingenious method of driving away these animals without the use of weapons, for Father Charlevoix relates:

if they have no arms to defend themselves, they hurry up into a tree; the animal, unable to pursue his prey, surveys him with greedy eyes from the bottom of his asylum, and would there remain, it is probable, long enough, to oblige him to surrender at discretion, or let himself fall to the ground through weakness, had it not been happily discovered, that this animal cannot bear the smell of human urine; the Indian takes advantage of this discovery, and the tiger immediately flies to a sufficient distance, to give him an opportunity of making his escape.[56]

"Tigers" customarily scratched the bark of trees in order to relieve their claws of the great heat that tormented them.[57] They would catch fish by swimming out into a lake or river and blowing froth on the surface. Fish would be attracted to this froth, and the jaguars would catch them and toss them on shore.[58] Father Joseph de Acosta tells of fierce combats between alligators and jaguars.[59]

The tapir, called by the Spaniards the "great beast," was accustomed, when it felt itself to be too full of blood, to open a vein with a piece of reed and allow itself to lose enough to regain its normal state. Indians were supposed to have discovered the art of bleeding by observing the habits of this animal.[60] Water-dogs, very likely a species of otter, also exhibited surprising intelligence. A missionary observed that when one of these, which was on the bank of a river, was wounded with an arrow, several of its friends came and carried it to the opposite bank.[61] Then there were little "foxes" with fine and beautiful coats. "Nothing can be prettier than this animal, which besides is of so friendly a nature, that he comes out of the woods to fawn upon travellers; but it is proper to be on one's guard against him, for when you think least of it, he discharges his urine, the stench of which is not to be equalled, and which is besides of so penetrating a quality, that no scouring can get it out of anything it falls upon."[62] The *quinquinchón*, the armadillo of the Chaco, was a useful little animal, its scales, when half burnt and pulverized, being excellent for treating horses with sore backs.[63] When hungry, the armadillo would lie on its back until its shell was filled with rain water. Then, when some thirsty deer came along and began to drink out of its shell, the clever beast would seize it by the lips, stifle it, and make a meal of the victim.[64]

Whatever they might think about armadillos, jaguars, tapirs, and the Ahó Ahó, it was in their descriptions of the sizes and habits of snakes that the good padres suppressed their credulity and restrained their imagination least of all. Friar Pedro Simón told of a snake so monstrous that eighteen men sat on it, thinking that it was a huge log.[65] Father Jacinto de Carvajal said that there were snakes in the Orinoco valley as big as an ox.[66] In Paraguay the snake called the *Yacariná* "raises itself upon the last joint of its tail, and leaps upon people almost as if it were flying." [67] In the forests of the Marañón dwelt the great reptile called the *Amarón* or *Yacumama* ("mother of the water"), which was said to attain a length of fifteen yards and a circumference of a yard or more. This snake had the ability of charming people and other animals with its breath, so that they could not flee, and even of attracting its prey to it from a distance by the same method. The only remedy in such a case was to cut the air with an iron weapon. This snake would swallow a man half way, beginning at the head, and at the end of three days vomit him. [68] In order to kill their prey more quickly, these reptiles "introduce the tail, which is sharp at the end, by the ordinary way into the intestines, tearing them in search of the heart, with which the victim dies, not only crushed, but as though impaled." [69] Boas were said to be able to throw a poisonous vapor some distance. [70] Sometimes these constrictors would crush and swallow an ox or a cow. [71] On such occasions the serpent might find difficulty in digesting its dinner and become dangerously ill. If such should be the case, the monster would turn over on its back. The heat of the sun would make its belly putrify, and worms would then eat away its flesh so that birds, coming to the serpent's assistance, could consume a part of the animal that had been swallowed. When the animal had been reduced to a digestible size, the boa would frighten the birds away. His abdomen would then heal, and he would soon be as well as before. "But it often happens, they say, that the skin of the serpent closes upon the branches of trees upon which he has been in too great haste to station himself; this is a . . . [predicament] out of which he must find it a much more difficult matter to extricate himself than the former." [72] These huge snakes were said to attack women. One of the missionaries was summoned to a river bank to administer the last rites to an Indian woman. She confessed that as she had been washing some clothes in the river, a serpent had attacked and raped her. Soon afterward she died.[73] In Paraguay, according to Father Martin Dobrizhoffer, lived a great serpent that resembled the trunk of a very large tree covered with moss. Fortunately this reptile was perfectly harmless to man. In the padre's description of his one experience with this serpent, the *Ampalaba*, is perhaps found the solution of many a snake story. Although within a few feet of the reptile, really a log, he did not take the trouble to examine it, and he depends entirely on his imagination in describing it:

> As I was travelling through the territory of St. Iago, at the banks of a lake near the river Dulce, my horse suddenly took fright. Upon my enquiring of my companion the occasion of the animal's terror, he replied, "What, Father! did you not see the Ampalaba snake lying on the shore?" I had seen him, but had taken him for the trunk of a tree. Fearing that the horse would be alarmed and throw me, I did not think proper to stay and examine the great sparkling eyes, short but very acute teeth, horrid head, and many-coloured scales of the monster.[74]

Then there were smaller snakes that would climb trees and grunt like monkeys, so that the monkeys would flock to them, to be seized and consumed by the wily reptiles.[75] There were still other reptiles that could jump from tree to tree, and snakes with two heads, one at each end of the body. If the latter serpents were cut into several parts, the sections would reassemble. The most effective way of killing these hardy animals was to tie them to a reed and hold them in smoke until they were suffocated. When dried, powdered, and drunk mixed with water, they were a powerful cure for fractures.[76] New generations of snakes were constantly being created by heat and moisture.[77]

349

The crocodile, too, attracted the attention of the missionary zoölogist. Father Jacinto de Carvajal told of having seen a cayman twenty-five feet long, not counting the head and tail.[78] Father Alonso de Zamora was sure that some of these reptiles had four eyes.[79] Gumilla described the cayman in the following manner:

What definition can be found which adequately comprehends the frightful ugliness of the crocodile? It is ferocity itself and an uncouth monster of the greatest hideousness, horror of all the living; so formidable is the crocodile that if it should look at itself in a mirror, it would flee from itself trembling. The most lively imagination cannot conceive a more proper picture of the devil, portraying him with all the signs.[80]

Gumilla related that the crocodile swallows rocks to serve as ballast so that it can sink to the bottom of a river and sleep there in safety. Humboldt supported this statement concerning crocodiles swallowing rocks, but gave his opinion that they consumed them as an aid to digestion.[81] Another dangerous denizen of South American rivers is the caribe, a small fish with very sharp and strong teeth. Father Carvajal told how caribes were accustomed to castrate bulls and stallions that swam the rivers, and averred that there were many steers castrated in this manner on the llanos bordering the Apure River.[82]

Those ancient servants of man, the horse and the mule, were not entirely forgotten by missionary zoölogists. Father Dobrizhoffer, in discussing their comparative merits, pointed out that while the mule is fearful and treacherous, it has an easy pace, a sure foot, great endurance and strength, and can thrive on food that would kill a horse. He mentioned one mule, already past thirty years old, "which would bear a rider, and sometimes contrive to kick him off too."[83]

VII

In describing natural phenomena, the padres were sometimes quite accurate. Father Manuel Rodríguez believed that certain trees were composed partly of wood and partly of stone.[84] Caulín observed the changes of seasons on the Orinoco, the comparative rainfall of winter and summer, and the length of days at different seasons of the year.[85] Gumilla reported that the Orinoco rises for five months, is at its height for one month, falls for five months, and is at its low point a month. According to him, the river rises one yard higher than the average once every twenty-fifth year. The rise and the fall occur regularly without regard to the amount of precipitation in the lower Orinoco valley. He explained that there is a lag in the rise after the coming of the rains along the headwaters of the Orinoco and its tributaries because much of the water soaks into the parched banks or fills the lakes through which the rivers flow.[86]

When in 1698 Father Samuel Fritz observed that the Marañón became muddy for several days, he decided that the condition of the river was caused by a tornado upstream. He later discovered that the mud came from a volcano that had recently erupted. The Jurimagua Indians, among whom Fritz was working at the time, thought that the missionary had made the water turbid as a sign of his vexation with them.[87]

When Father Gumilla found difficulty in persuading the Betoyes that the sun is fire and not a god, he gathered the people of the village together in the plaza, took the hand of the highest ranking captain among them, and asked him if the sun was a god. The answer was "Yes." Remarking that "the sun is nothing but fire," Gumilla held a lens between the sun and the arm of the captain so that the focused rays burned a blister on his arm. The Indian cried, "It is true! It is true!

The sun is fire!" The other natives crowded around to experiment with the lens. When his neophytes were frightened by an eclipse of the moon, thinking that the moon was sick and about to die, Gumilla took a lighted candle, a mirror, and an orange, and proceeded to explain in a scientific manner the cause of the eclipse. "This same I made them see with the demonstration of the candle, and its light reflected from the mirror. . . . Some of the principal ones perceived the explanation, and striking themselves on the thighs, they spent much time in explaining to their people the cause of the eclipse, with such good outcome, that soon there were no tears, nor cries, nor any ceremony in the eclipses that followed." [88]

Father Joseph de Acosta explained the milky way by noting that, being the thickest part of heaven, it receives more light than the darker portions of the sky, which are thin and transparent. His opinion was that it rains most when the sun is near the zenith because the hot sun draws up vapor from the ocean, which later "doth suddenly dissolve . . . into raine." As for the winds:

there are some windes which helpe to the generation of creatures, and others that hinder and are opposite. There is a certaine wind, of such a quality, as when it blowes in some country, it causeth it to raine fleas, and in so great aboundaunce, as they trouble and darken the aire, and cover all the sea shoare: and in other places it raines frogges.

The summits of mountains, thought Acosta, are colder than the lowlands because sunbeams have greater repercussions on lower levels. Father Acosta made the mistake, however, of saying that the Amazon flows into the sea near the island of Trinidad. [89]

THE FRONTIER MISSIONARY MOVEMENT:
AN ESTIMATE

I

AS the frontier missionary movement in South America a success? Were the efforts and sufferings of the padres and the expenditure of so much gold by the state worth while? Were the Indians made better men and women by virtue of their contact with the missionaries, or did they merely mask their innate savagery with a veneer of religion and civilization? When the padres were obliged to retire from the field because of the wars for independence and the withdrawal of the material aid of the Spanish government, were the mission Indians able to carry on without the assistance of the friars? And finally, one may ask that unanswerable question, "Were the souls of the lost sheep of the llanos, the selvas, and the jungle really saved?"

II

To the inquiry, "Was the missionary movement a success?" the immediate reply is another question, "What is success?"

In the opinion of the devout and courageous friar laboring among his flock, his work was successful if he managed to assemble a few hundred human beasts from the jungle, baptize them, and persuade them to say that they believed all that the Holy Catholic Church "holds and teaches." In his heart he felt that the souls of these savages were now saved, and that the future held for them eons of bliss. The possible state of his mission a century or two later was of slight importance as compared with the great question of how his wards might be guided safe into heaven. He did not doubt that his success was in direct proportion to the number of Indians whom he baptized.

To the king, the missionary movement was successful in proportion to the number of Indians, the square leagues of land, and the wealth of material resources brought under his jurisdiction, although he too was interested in the spiritual conversion of the American natives.

To the lay Spaniard, the activities of the padres were successful in direct ratio to the speed with which the missionaries reduced the Indians to a settled form of life and turned the missions over to the secular authorities, for thereafter the natives, no longer under the protection of the good fathers, were subject to exploitation by the *vecinos* and miners.

To the Indian, who was the object, often unwilling, of all this solicitous regard, the whole idea must have seemed of doubtful value. If the mission Indian profited by an improved standard of living, he lost much that to the savage must have been precious: his freedom to wander at will through the forest, to abandon his village and build another in some distant place, to stalk his enemy, to indulge his passions. Formal worship in a church may have seemed to him a poor substitute for the wild abandon of a drunken dance at midnight while the ghoulish light of a tropical moon

354

sifted down through the forest canopy and the glare of huge fires turned sweating brown bodies to burnished copper.

In reviewing two centuries of evangelistic enterprise in South America, one may envisage for a moment a scene on the great Marañón in the year 1760. There on a high bank is a village of neatly arranged huts. The ground is clean. The few short streets converge on a little plaza where stands a small, well-constructed church with mud walls and thatched roof. In the tower is a bronze bell cast in Arequipa or perhaps in Spain. Life moves placidly about this toy cathedral. Men bring fish from the stream and game from the forest. Women and children gather corn and beans from the well-kept fields back of the village, and plantains from the neighboring grove. Some of these they bring to the padre, who stops his task of teaching the children long enough to thank them for the gifts and to give them his blessing. Later the good man goes the round of the huts, giving comfort to the sick, showing one Indian how to make sun-dried bricks and another how to milk a cow that has been brought to the mission by canoe with much tribulation to all concerned. Toward evening the bell rings to summon the Indians to worship. They crowd into the church, humble, in their white clothes, their bare feet making no sound on the packed clay floor. They hear from the padre a few words of love and encouragement. They sing a hymn. Then they file out silently to their homes. Soon the crackle of numerous fires and the pungent odor of burning wood mixed with the tempting aroma of cooking food indicate that the villagers are preparing their evening meal. The fires die down; the dense night embraces the village in loving arms. Soon all is quiet as the Indians rest in peace until the dawn of a new day.

Decades pass. In the great world beyond wars are fought.

If the padres succeeded in winning one generation of Indians from savage practices to a degree of civilization, they were a success for that generation

New states come into existence, and old ones pass from the earth. The padre dies, is recalled by his superiors, or is forced out by the cold hand of the law. The mission, no longer having the directing oversight of the missionary, withers away. The thatched roofs crumble in. The huts lean and fall. Tropical growth encroaches upon the clearing; and once again the site becomes the home of the slinking jaguar, the sinuous boa, and the jabbering monkey.

What was the use? The mission was an ephemeral thing, a flower that bloomed but a day. From Paraguay to Guiana the crumbling ruins of mission buildings denoted the ultimate bankruptcy of a vast undertaking. The attempts after 1820 to reënact the drama of the colonial padres seldom had the force of the efforts of former times. But did the ultimate disappearance of the missions mean that the missionary movement was a failure? It does not seem so to us. For if the mission was ephemeral, so is all life. The Catholic padres contributed in their day to the transfer of much that was best in European civilization to people who were steeped in savagery. If they succeeded in winning one generation of Indians from the practice of torture, cannibalism, and internecine warfare, they were a success for that generation. The fact that in the end the natives of subsequent generations often reverted to their old ways of living should not in the least diminish the glory of the missionaries who succeeded in carrying some of the principles of Christianity and of higher civilization to a large number of the South American savages. The colonial evangelistic movement must be judged by what it accomplished in its day and not by what it failed to accomplish in the end, just as a great surgeon must be judged by the number of people he cures and not by the number who die after his hospital has burned and he has passed to his reward.

III

From the standpoint of the state, the mission movement was undoubtedly a success. The Spanish padres succeeded in extending the domain of the crown far into the interior of the continent. That they were not more successful in this respect was due to the failure of the secular authorities to give them adequate support. The Portuguese government sent large bodies of troops to the Brazilian frontier, while Portuguese filibusters took their toll of land and Indians at the expense of Spain. The odds against the padres in their attempts to reach out as far as the Line of Demarcation were too great. But if these representatives of God and king had not organized their reductions on the frontier, the Portuguese would very likely have pushed as far west as the foothills of the Andes. Professor Bolton says of the frontier missionary:

Whoever . . . undertakes to interpret the forces by which Spain extended her rule, her language, her law, and her traditions, over the frontiers of her vast American possessions, must give close attention to the missions, for in that work they constituted a primary agency. . . . In the Spanish colonies the men to whom fell the task of extending and holding the frontiers were the *conquistador*, the presidial soldier, and the missionary.[1]

It may be said that, since the military and civil authorities could have carried on the task of frontier expansion, the missionary was superfluous as an imperialist. But the principal theater of the padre's activities was among Indians who were so poor that they offered no inducement to conquest by private soldiers of fortune, and who were so widely scattered over inhospitable regions that their conquest by armies of the state would have involved an outlay of money entirely out of proportion to the material returns.

In their work of civilizing the Indians the missionaries performed a great service to the state, since they made useful, tax-paying citizens of destructive savages. The more highly civilized native races, such as the Chibchas, Quechuas, and Aymarás, could be enlisted in productive enterprises immediately after their conquest. They were already skilled metallurgists, successful farmers, and builders of irrigation projects, elaborate terraces, bridges, roads, and stone edifices. But before the wandering tribes of the interior lowlands could be employed in the creation of an opulent material civilization in South America, it was necessary to teach them self-control and the manual arts. The task of instructing these savages was a slow one, hardly to be undertaken by Spaniards seeking immediate results in the form of profits. In cases where the padres taught the Indians the Spanish language, they were preparing them to understand orders and instructions that were to be given them by lay Spaniards when the time came for them to take their places as productive units in the colonial

economic system. Christianity made the Indians more obedient and tractable. From the purely political standpoint the
religious teachings of the missionaries were valuable, since
the padres emphasized the command, "Render unto Caesar
the things which are Caesar's and unto God the things which
are God's." Professor Priestley says of the influence of the
mission on the Indian:

The missions did fail to bring him to the cultural stature of
the whites; but, on the other hand, they furnished him a refuge
from the more selfish exploitation by the lay conquerors. They
were the schools in which the native learned more, and enjoyed
greater peace and security, than in any other institution devised
for his improvement. . . . As a social institution the mission
compares favorably indeed with the modern reservaton or Indian
school. Its disappearance was as much due to the cupidity of
its competitors, the lay Spaniards, as to any weakness inherent
in its conception. Its accomplishment challenges the result of
any other system of control of dependent peoples developed in
the field of modern colonization.[2]

The disciple of Rousseau will undoubtedly say that the
Indian would have been better off if permitted to remain in
his primitive state. He can assuredly adduce a battery of
arguments to support such a view. But granted that the
conquest was to be accomplished, the Indian was very likely
brought under the dominion of the Spanish crown by the
missionaries with less bloodshed than would have been the case
if he had been conquered entirely by men-at-arms. Even in
those cases where the conquest was primarily carried on by
the conquistadores, it is reasonable to suppose that the presence of ecclesiastics made the yoke of the conquered easier
to bear. The padres were almost invariably the champions
of the Indians against the extortions and cruelties of lay
Spaniards. The work of Las Casas is well known, but there
were many others. Shortly after 1500 the Jeronymite fathers

attempted to improve the condition of the natives, and as early as 1541, several Dominican friars of Peru, New Spain, and Cartagena pleaded at the court of Charles V that steps be taken to check the cruel treatment of Indians by conquistadores, and received from His Catholic Majesty the command to promote the enforcement of the laws relative to protection of Indians. The laws of 1512 and 1542 were largely the result of the padres' efforts. On May 1, 1543, the emperor sent the following command to the provincial of the Dominican Order in New Granada: "I pray you and charge you that, as all that they [the laws] contain is dedicated to the service of God and the conservation, liberty, and good government of the Indians, . . . you and the other religious of your order . . . work to the best of your ability in order that these our laws may be guarded and obeyed." [3] The friars in general maintained that the Indians should be directly under the protection of the crown or of themselves as representatives of the crown. The Jesuits in particular were implacable opponents of secular authorities and individual Spaniards who attempted undue exploitation of the Indians. A Jesuit in Paraguay wrote to a lay Spaniard:

We do not mean to oppose those advantages you may draw from the Indians in a lawful manner; but you know it never was the king's intention that you should consider them as slaves; and that, besides, the law of God strictly forbids it. As to those we are commissioned to gain over to Jesus Christ, and upon whom you can have no claim, since they were never conquered by force of arms, our design is: first, to labour to make them men, that we may be the better able to make them Christians. We shall then endeavour to induce them, from a view to their own interest, to submit chearfully to the king our sovereign; and hope, with God's blessing, our endeavours will be crowned with success. [4]

IV

In the field of pure religion, it is very difficult to measure the success of the padres. It is a fact that the missionaries baptized vast numbers of savages. But it must have been extremely difficult for these simple people to understand the complexities of the Catholic dogma (such ideas as those of the Holy Trinity, the Atonement, and the Immaculate Conception), although stories of the Garden of Eden, the Deluge, and the Crucifixion may have been easy enough for them to grasp. It is unlikely that many Indians caught the spirit of apostolic Christianity. The viceroy of Peru, in 1565, stated that of three hundred thousand baptized Indians, not more than forty were Christians, the rest still retaining their ancient forms of worship.[5] Two centuries later Juan and Ulloa gave as their opinion in regard to the converted Indians that

their religion does not resemble the Christian religion . . .; for if we examine the subject with care, it will be found that, notwithstanding the nominal conversion of these tribes, the progress they have made in religion is so inconsiderable that it will be difficult to discover any difference between the condition they now live in and that in which they were found at the time of the conquest.[6]

Christianity became for the Indians a hybrid religion. While partially accepting the teachings of the padres, they did not entirely give up the beliefs and superstitions of their ancestors. They tended to identify the God of the missionaries with the chief deity of their pantheon, and the devil with one of the many demons who peopled the dark places of the forests and the depths of the waters. The padres, instead of trying to destroy their beliefs entirely, often took what they considered best among them in order to build on this foundation the Christian structure. Religion was made attractive to the natives by the use of ornaments, candles, music, flags, sky-rockets, processions, and images, and by the firing of guns. Christianity was that which the Indians could see, hear, and discuss, while they preserved within their hearts the religion of their fathers, clinging to it with firm grasp because its practices were prohibited.[7] A Bolivian blacksmith once made a silver crucifix depicting Christ as an Indian with a beard of three hairs.[8] David Rubio, an Augustinian, admits

that some aborigines of Peru were not converted to the Christian religion nor to civilization, and that a considerable number of them simply confessed it with their lips, it never penetrating into the depth of their hearts; that is to say, that many of those who received baptism did it simply for human considerations or in order to ingratiate themselves with the missionaries and conquerors, remaining as attached as before to their idolatries and wicked vices.[9]

It was the opinion of Alexander von Humboldt that

The missionaries may have prohibited the Indians from following certain practices and observing certain ceremonies; they may have prevented them from painting their skin, from making incisions in their chins, noses, and cheeks; they may have destroyed among the great mass of people superstitious ideas, mysteriously transmitted from father to son in certain families; but it has been much easier for them to proscribe customs and efface remembrances, than to substitute new ideas in the place of the old ones.[10]

In criticizing the religion of the converted Indian, one should remember that to the average colonial Spaniard religion was not so much a matter of the spirit as of the senses. This being the case, one can hardly expect the simple Indian to have caught the vision of a higher spiritual order. To the average Spaniard or creole, religion was mainly a matter of Masses, processions, genuflections, obeisances to painted saints and wooden figures of hideous Christs blotched with red paint, of admiration for altars decorated in the style of circus wagons of a later day, of intolerance and bigotry. The Indians did learn in some instances the Catholic procedures and catechism so well that many years did not efface them from memory. When some Jesuits explored the llanos of New Granada thirty years after Father Diego Molina had proselyted there, they found one old man among the Tunebos who could still repeat the catechism.[11]

In the realm of personal morals the missionaries certainly made life more complicated for the denizen of the South American wilds. The primitive Indian lived a simple life, almost completely free from the inhibitions placed upon individuals in a Christian community. In the course of centuries he had become mentally and physically adapted to his environment, so that he was seriously injured if suddenly transferred to another climate. Because of the tropical heat he wore almost no clothes, anointing himself with oil as a protection against insects. When angry, he fought. When hungry, he ate, if he had the food; and if he had none, he stalked his prey as would another carnivorous animal. He took unto himself a plurality of wives. He became gloriously drunk on *chicha* without qualms of conscience. In a word, he lived a life not greatly different from that of the other animals in the forest about him. Then came the friars with their stock of taboos to tell the Indian that the practices which he had considered right and natural were evil and abnormal. It is to the credit of the padres, whose vows obliged them to live abnormal lives, that they often took into account the weaknesses of the natives and did not place upon them moral burdens which were impossible for them to bear. They did not try to make monks out of the Indians. The difficulty that the natives had in understanding the moral code of the padres is shown in Father Joseph de Gumilla's account of the introduction of clothes:

Many Missionaries, before being practiced in the ministry, have carried and divided some linen, especially among the women, for some decency; but in vain, because they throw it in the river, or hide it in order not to dress themselves; and if told to cover themselves, they answer: "We do not cover ourselves because it makes us ashamed." And here you see another unheard of thing! They understand shame and bashfulness; but the meaning of the expression is changed, because on dressing themselves they feel ashamed and run, and are satisfied and contented with their accustomed nakedness. . . . But this repugnance to dress themselves in a short time ceases to be a great trouble to the Fathers because as they progress, hearing and perceiving the Mysteries of our Holy Faith, their inner eyes become clear; they recognize their nakedness, they receive as much linen as the Missionary is able to give, and they beg for more and more with great aggravation, men as well as women.[12]

So solicitous were the missionaries in their efforts to cover the nakedness of their wards that they spent the alms they collected and part of their stipends, and even tore up the sheets and blankets of their beds to divide among the Indians.[13] The outcome of all this was that many converts on the reductions went about "decently clad." (Recent photographs of some Maynas Indians show them clothed from neck to heel in yards of sheeting reminiscent of the ample robes of ancient patriarchs.)

The missionaries were quite successful in abolishing polygamy among their neophytes. It is likely, however, that the elimination of polygamy promoted immorality (immorality being defined as extra-marital sexual intercourse). Juan Rivero reported in 1736 that the natives settled in mission villages on the Meta and the Orinoco had almost completely given up the practice of polygamy.[14] The principal contribution of the padres in the field of domestic relations was their protection of wives, who had formerly been considered the slaves of their husbands, from excessively brutal treatment by their "lords and masters."

The padres worked hard to diminish the evil of drunkenness; and on the better conducted missions, such as those of Paraguay, they succeeded in virtually abolishing it. They helped to eliminate head hunting, tribal warfare, and the use of torture. But while the missionaries were carrying on a crusade against the improper practices of the natives, these natives learned from lay Spaniards, and from missionaries who were unworthy of the trust placed in them, the arts of lying, stealing, cheating, and profiteering. If the Indians possessed discerning minds, they no doubt at first wondered at the discrepancy between the teachings and the actions of "Christians"; but in the end they tended to take the easier course of emulating the questionable practices of the Spaniards. Taking all things into consideration, one may safely say that the missionary fathers were often successful in making better men and women of the savages whom they reduced. While some of the restrictions imposed upon the Indians were absurd and contrary to a normal mode of life in a tropical environment, others were fundamental in character and contributed toward making the Indian a saner and happier person. Humboldt was of the opinion that, although the missions were in the early colonial period useful in reforming the Indians to a better way of living, in the end the close regulation and supervision to which the converts were subjected on the reductions crushed their individuality, tending to make them stolid and dependent. He wrote:

Their number has considerably augmented, but the sphere of their ideas is not enlarged. They have progressively lost that vigour of character and that natural vivacity which in every state of society are the noble fruits of independence. By subjecting to invariable rules even the slightest actions of their domestic life, they have been rendered stupid by the effort to render them obedient. Their subsistence is in general more certain, and their habits more pacific, but subject to the constraint and the dull monotony of the government of the Missions, they show by their gloomy and reserved looks that they have not sacrificed their liberty to their repose without regret.[15]

Depons, writing of the Venezuelan missions about 1800, gave his opinion that after three centuries of missionary activity the Indians were only superficially reformed, and that with the slightest suspension of control they would resort to the practice of drunkenness, stealing, incest, lying, perjury, and idleness.[16]

V

In 1654 the royal patronage had been extended to the Jesuit mission system, and thereafter the Jesuit padres constantly labored under the threat that if they failed to obey the royal mandates their missions would be placed in the care of other religious orders.[17]   After this threat was carried out in 1767, there was a general decline in the missions that had been under the control of the Society of Jesus.   Half a century later the wars for independence drove practically all missionaries from the field.   The several hundred thousand Indians found themselves without their leaders and masters. Once again they were free as in the days before the coming of the men of God with their crosses, their little books, their queer ways, and their strange talk of other worlds.   Some of the natives had been born on the reductions, and knew of the carefree, nomadic life in the forest and of the ancient gods only from stories told them in the quiet of huts beyond hearing of the padres.   What became of the sheep now that the shepherds had left them?

Most of the reductions fell into decay.   In Paraguay the elaborate mission buildings were abandoned or transferred to new uses.   They were sometimes razed by dictators of the new republic.   As late as 1846 services were still being held in one of the great Jesuit churches, which was eighty by three hundred and twenty feet in size. At another place a military officer was living in a house that had formerly been the home of a Jesuit padre. The house was in a perfect state of preservation although it had never been repaired, and the bamboo slats that were laid across the rafters to support the tiles appeared to be as new as ever.[18] Little is now left of the extensive missions of Paraguay except ruins and the legend of the lost city of *Emboré* supposed to have been secretly built by the Jesuits. Here, according to the story, in houses without doors and windows and which can be entered only through tunnels whose entrances are carefully hidden, is buried the treasure abandoned by the Jesuits when they were forced out of America.[19] After the proclamation of independence in 1821 the Franciscan missions on the Ucayali suffered a complete eclipse.[20] On the Paranapura, the Huallaga, and the Amazon, where "during the heyday of missionary activity, there were flourishing towns and villages, there are now but a few rickety huts tenanted by a few wretched Indians, or a riot of tropic growth, which conceals every trace of former human habitations."[21] Throughout the viceroyalty of New Granada the missions vanished with the disappearance of Spain's colonial empire in South America.

With the passing of the padres and the missions, did the Indians, now dispersed, hold within their hearts the teachings of the friars? Did they abhor the devil and all his ways and continue to worship the one God? Did leaders rise among them to take the place of the padres who had left them? Did they shun savage practices, or did they again become unbridled children of the forest as of old? Sir Robert Schomburgk, who visited Venezuela in 1841, stated that it was evident that the Indians who had formerly lived on the reductions were an improved race, more industrious and possessing better manners than the other natives, although a quarter of a century had passed since the missionaries of Spanish Guiana had been massacred.[22] The Indians often continued to wear clothes. In Paraguay, where the Jesuits had required all reduction Indians to wear the same style of clothes, the successors of the missionaries had great difficulty in persuading them to wear clothing that expressed a greater degree of individuality.[23]

In the matter of religion the natives partially reverted to paganism, but they were still influenced by the Catholic dogma. After telling of head hunting, tattooing, and lip boring among the modern Jíbaros, K. G. Grubb says of their religion:

> Invisible forces, however, play the chief part in the life of the Indian. The substance of his relations to the invisible is found in animism. The dominant motive in his religion is evidenced in his fear of the human dead. Spirits are attributed to inanimate objects, to plants, to trees and to stones. Masked dances, magical ceremonies, the operations of the medicine man, ceremonial mutilation and numerous other ritual activities are essential to placate these mysterious beings. . . . The definite conception of the preternatural supremacy of a single deity is generally lacking.[24]

Juan B. Ambrosetti, while traveling in northern Argentina about 1900, found a curious custom among the Indians and mestizos of that region. It was customary for children and even adults to ask a blessing of their older brothers, uncles, fathers, grandfathers, godfathers, and travelers. With his hands together and his head uncovered, the petitioner asked this benediction, sometimes several times a day—on rising, before and after dinner, and before going to bed. Frequently he would kneel down before the person who was to give the blessing and pray for a time before the benediction was granted. The whole process was very annoying to Ambrosetti, but he carried it out as patiently as possible. In one home he blessed a child with his left hand, since he was holding a teacup with his right, saying, "May God make you a saint." The child was not satisfied, so that Ambrosetti had to repeat the formula, this time giving the blessing with his right hand.[25]

In regard to the permanent influence of the missionary on the Indians of the Bolivian oriente Colonel George Earl Church says that the Mojos have not yet recovered from the harsh treatment of the Jesuits: "joy had been wrung out of them, they were gloomy, silent, and depressed."[26] His interpretation is hardly a rational one. People are seldom gloomy over the sufferings of their ancestors. The aspect of these Indians must have been due to some inherent psychological condition, to climate, disease, or present oppression. H. J. Mozans (J. A. Zahm), a Catholic priest, claims that the pleasant memory of the missionaries of former days still lingers in the minds of the natives of the montaña:

Even to-day, after an absence of a century and more, the father-priest, as he is called, is a name to conjure with among many Indian tribes of the *montaña*, who know of him only through the traditions which have come to them from their forefathers. Wherever his ministrations have been felt, his memory is still green. They still long for his return, and wonder why he remains away from them so long. And if he were to return again, he would be joyfully acclaimed by young and old, as he was generations ago.[27]

If this statement is true, the Indians of the oriente must have forgotten the strict discipline of the reductions.

In the interior of tropical South America are today many Indians living in a wild state hardly different from that in which the Spaniards found them four hundred years ago. While the ancestors of some of these were never converted, those of others once lived on frontier reductions. Besides these savages, there are a number of Christians whose religion is scarcely more than a "baptized paganism." The Catholic Church of late years has concentrated its attention on the European communities of South America more than on the several million Indians of the interior.[28] Among such Indians as the Mojos, where some semblance of worship is still carried on under the direction of Catholic priests, the worship is often lifeless and dull. The priest goes through the mechanical motions of the Mass, while the Indians look on, stolidly indifferent as to whether the sacrament they are beholding is "the embodiment of a blasphemous fable and dangerous deceit, or whether they were, in very deed and truth, spectators of the offering at the hands of erring and sinful man of the actual Body and Blood of the Son of God as a sacrifice for the living and the dead."[29]

In attempting to estimate the success of the missionary movement in South America, one might wish that the millions of Indians whom the padres brought into the fold of Mother Church actually received the reward in heaven which the missionaries predicted. Not sure that they did, one must limit oneself to the conclusion that the missionary movement on the frontier of South America was a noble effort to improve the spiritual and material well-being of a large portion of the continent's population; that it was as successful as many other great movements altruistically conceived; and that its agents, the humble padres, deserve all honor for their courage, their self-immolation, their patience, and the magnificence of their aspirations.

NOTES

CHAPTER I

1. *El mar del norte,* or Caribbean Sea.

2. Father Joseph de Gumilla, *El Orinoco ilustrado* ... (Madrid, 1741), p. 7.

3. Quoted in E. G. Bourne, *Spain in America* (New York and London, 1904), pp. 47-48.

4. Juan Nuix, *Reflexiones imparciales sobre la humanidad de los españoles en las Indias* (Madrid, 1782), p. 257.

5. Frances Gardiner Davenport (ed.), *European Treaties bearing on the History of the United States and its Dependencies to 1648* (Washington, 1917), pp. 62-63.

6. Bernal Díaz del Castillo, *The True History of the Conquest of New Spain,* 5 vols. (London, 1908), I, 73.

7. Alonso de Zamora, *Historia de la provincia de San Antonio del Nuevo Reyno de Granada* (Barcelona, 1701), p. 16.

8. Fernando Pallarés and Vicente Calvo, *Noticias históricas de las misiones de Santa Rosa de Ocopa* (Barcelona, 1870), p. 164.

9. Bourne, *op. cit.,* pp. 302-3.

10. Fray Bernardino Izaguirre, *Historia de las misiones Franciscanas y narración de los progresos de la geografía en el oriente del Perú,* 9 vols. (Lima, 1922-1929), VI, 31.

11. Fray Pedro Nolasco Pérez, *Religiosos de la Merced que pasaron a la América española* (Seville, 1824), pp. 9-10.

12. Juan Solórzano Pereyra, *Política Indiana,* 2 vols. (Madrid, 1739), II, 2.

13. *Recopilación de leyes de los reynos de las Indias,* 4 vols. (Madrid, 1774), I, 1. (Henceforth cited as *Recopilación.*)

14. *Ibid.,* p. 2. June 26, 1523.

15. *Ibid.,* Oct. 4, 1563.

16. *Ibid.,* Oct. 5, 1607, and Aug. 16, 1614.

17. Zamora, *op. cit.,* p. 303.

18. *Ibid.,* p. 23.

19. Bernard Moses, *South America on the Eve of Emancipation* (New York, 1908), p. 139.

20. Luke 10:3, King James Version of the Bible.

21. Floyd Keeler, *Catholic Medical Missions* (New York, 1925), p. 17.

22. Gumilla, *op. cit.,* pp. 286-87.

CHAPTER II

1. J. Patricio Fernández, *Relación historial de las misiones de Indios Chiquitos que en el Paraguay tienen los padres de la Compañía de Jesús,* 2 vols. (Asunción, 1896), I, 127-28.

2. J. B. Francesia, *Nuestros misioneros de Quito en el Ecuador* (Barcelona, 1902), p. vi.

3. *Recopilación,* IV, 3.

4. *Ibid.,* I, 32. May 31, 1552.

5. *Ibid.,* IV, 4. Sept. 24, 1518.

6. *Ibid.,* I, 26. Feb. 20, 1583.

NOTES

7. *Ibid.*, p. 62. Nov. 9, 1530.
8. *Ibid.*, p. 61. Sept. 8, 1546.
9. *Ibid.*, p. 63. Aug. 19, 1552.
10. *Ibid.*, pp. 62-63. Nov. 9, 1592.
11. *Ibid.*, p. 62. Sept. 19, 1588, and March 29, 1601.
12. *Ibid.*, p. 61. March 11, 1553.
13. *Ibid.*, p. 60. Sept. 27, 1574.
14. Pérez, *op. cit.*, pp. 10-11.
15. *Recopilación*, 1, 61. May 7, 1570.
16. *Ibid.*, pp. 60-61. July 10, 1607.
17. *Ibid.*, p. 61. Dec., 1607.
18. Pérez, *op. cit.*, pp. 11-12.
19. Manuel Rodríguez, *El Marañón y Amazonas* (Madrid, 1684), p. 224.
20. Pérez, *op. cit.*, pp. 13, 15-16.
21. *Ibid.*, p. 16.
22. *Recopilación*, I, 53. June 17, 1563.
23. *Ibid.*, IV, 11. Oct. 17, 1575.
24. *Ibid.*, I, 74. Feb. 27, 1610.
25. Baltasar de Lodares, *Los Fran-*

ciscanos Capuchinos en Venezuela, 3 vols. (Caracas, 1929-1930), III, 352.
26. *Recopilación*, I, 63. March 24, 1572.
27. *Ibid.*, p. 62. Jan. 19, 1562.
28. Jorge Juan and Antonio de Ulloa, *Noticias secretas de América* (London, 1826), p. 359.
29. Juan Rivero, *Historia de las misiones de los llanos de Casanare y los ríos Orinoco y Meta* (Bogotá, 1883), p. 350.
30. José Joaquín Borda, *Historia de la Compañía de Jesús en la Nueva Granada*, 2 vols. (Poissy, 1872), I, 33-37; J. M. Solá, *Vida de San Pedro Claver* (Barcelona, 1885). Solá is no doubt too eulogistic.
31. Francisco Jarque, *Ruiz Montoya en Indias*, 4 vols. (Madrid, 1900), IV, 46.
32. Robert Southey, *A Tale of Paraguay* (London, 1825), canto III, stanza 21.

CHAPTER III

1. J. Lucio D'Azevedo, *Historia de Antonio Vieira com factos e documentos novos*, 2 vols. (Lisbon, 1918), I, 238.
2. K. G. Grubb, *The Lowland Indians of Amazonia* (London, 1927), pp. 20-21; Clark Wissler, *The American Indian* (New York, 1922), *passim.*
3. For a detailed discussion of the origin of the American natives see *Origen de los Indios de el nuevo mundo e Indias Occidentales, averiguado con discurso de opiniones por el Padre Presentado Fr. Gregorio García de la Orden de Predicadores* (Madrid, 1729).
4. Zamora, *op. cit.*, p. 14.
5. *Ibid.*, pp. 15-16.
6. Gumilla, *op. cit.*, p. 323.
7. *Ibid.*, pp. 56-57.
8. Father Joseph de Acosta, *The Natural and Moral History of the Indies*, 2 vols. (London, 1880,

Hakluyt Society Publication), I, 55, 62, 68.
9. *Ibid.*, p. 57.
10. *Ibid.*, II, 360-64.
11. Sebastián Lorente, *Historia antigua del Perú* (Lima, 1860), p. 286.
12. *Ibid.*, pp. 96, 97.
13. Webster E. Browning, *Roman Christianity in Latin America* (New York, 1924), pp. 64-65.
14. Fray Bartolomé de las Casas, *De las antiguas gentes del Perú* (Madrid, 1892), p. 51.
15. Fr. Antonio Caulín, *Historia coro-gráphica, natural, y evangélica de la Nueva Andalucía provincias de Cumaná, Guayana, y vertientes del río Orinoco* (Madrid, 1779), pp. 96-97.
16. Gumilla, *op. cit.*, p. 292.
17. Rivero, *op. cit.*, p. 56.
18. Gumilla, *op. cit.*, pp. 291, 292. Theos appears to be a Greek word.
19. Rivero, *op. cit.*, p. 116.

NOTES

20. *Ibid.*, p. 113.
21. Gumilla, *op. cit.*, p. 307.
22. Padre Anello Oliva, *Historia del reino y provincias del Perú* (Lima, 1895), pp. 130, 131, 134-35.
23. *Ibid.*, p. 126.
24. Francisco de Figueroa, *Relación de las misiones de la Compañía de Jesús en el país de los Maynas* (Madrid, 1904), pp. 234-35, 236, 240, 241, 243.
25. Diego de Eguiluz, *Relación de la misión apostólica de los Mojos en esta provincia del Perú* (Lima, 1884), p. 7.
26. *Cartas edificantes, y curiosas, escritas de las missiones estrangeras, y de Levante por algunos missioneros de la Compañía de Jesús,* 16 vols. (Madrid, 1753-1757), VII, 101-2. (Hereafter cited as *Cartas edificantes.*)
27. John Lockman, *Travels of the Jesuits,* 2 vols. (London, 1762), II, 448.
28. *Cartas edificantes,* VII, 405.
29. Father [François Xavier de] Charlevoix, *The History of Paraguay,* 2 vols. (Dublin, 1769), II, 98-99.
30. Fernández, *op. cit.*, I, 59.
31. Charlevoix, *op. cit.*, II, 95.
32. F. Depons, *Travels in South America,* 2 vols. (London, 1807), I, 238-39.
33. *Op. cit.*, pp. 45-46.
34. Charlevoix, *op. cit.*, I, 203-4.

35. Pallarés and Calvo, *op. cit.*, p. 76.
36. Grubb, *op. cit.*, p. 77.
37. Lockman, *op. cit.*, II, 459, and many others.
38. Figueroa, *op. cit.*, p. 150.
39. Borda, *op. cit.*, I, 64-65.
40. Víctor M. Maúrtua, *Juicio de límites entre el Perú y Bolivia; prueba peruana presentada al gobierno de la República Argentina,* 12 vols. (Barcelona, 1906), II, 5.
41. *Journal of the Travels and Labours of Father Samuel Fritz in the River of the Amazons between 1686 and 1723* (London, 1922, Hakluyt Society Publication), pp. 47-48. (Hereafter cited as *Journal of Father Samuel Fritz.*)
42. Pallarés and Calvo, *op. cit.*, note on p. 74.
43. Eguiluz, *op. cit.*, p. 9.
44. Gumilla, *op. cit.*, pp. 345-49.
45. Alexander von Humboldt, *Personal Narrative of Travels to the Equinoctial Regions of America,* 3 vols. (London, 1852), III, 75.
46. II, 390.
47. *Op. cit.*, pp. 230-31.
48. *Op. cit.*, p. 247.
49. Zamora, *op. cit.*, pp. 133-35.
50. Enrique Torres Saldamando, *Los antiguos Jesuítas del Perú* (Lima, 1882), pp. 125-26.
51. Oliva, *op. cit.*, p. 127.
52. Charlevoix, *op. cit.*, I, 316-17.
53. *Op. cit.*, pp. 579-80.

Chapter IV

1. Sebastián Lorente, *Historia de la conquista del Perú* (Lima, 1861), p. 496.
2. Solórzano Pereyra, *op. cit.*, I, 188.
3. Bourne, *op. cit.*, pp. 258-60. This, the ideal, was rarely attained.
4. *Recopilación,* II, 221. Aug. 14, 1509. For a good discussion of this phase of Spanish Colonization, see Lesley Byrd Simpson, *The Encomienda in New Spain* (Berkeley, 1929).
5. *Recopilación,* II, 222. Oct. 20, 1545.
6. Quoted in Charles S. Braden, *Religious Aspects of the Conquest of Mexico* (Durham, 1930), p. 213.
7. *Recopilación,* II, 256. Dec. 4, 1528.
8. *Ibid.*, p. 190. Aug. 23, 1538.
9. *Ibid.*, p. 198. March 21, 1551.

373

10. *Ibid.* April 16, 1618.
11. *Ibid.* June 21, 1604.
12. *Ibid.*, p. 199. Feb. 19, 1560.
13. *Ibid.* Dec. 1, 1573.
14. *Ibid.*, p. 208. June 26, 1523.
15. *Ibid.* July 5, 1578.
16. *Ibid.* Jan. 30, 1607.
17. Zamora, *op. cit.*, p. 253.
18. *Recopilación*, I, 7. Aug. 28, 1552.
19. *Ibid.*, II, 268. July 16, 1622.
20. *Ibid.*, I, 9. April 3, 1534.
21. *Ibid.*, p. 6.
22. *Ibid.*, II, 188. July 13, 1530.
23. *Ibid.*, p. 190. June 5, 1552.
24. Bourne, *op. cit.*, p. 260.
25. *Recopilación*, II, 188. Dec. 24, 1580.
26. *Ibid.*, p. 217. Jan. 10, 1589.
27. Browning, *op. cit.*, pp. 23-24, 195.
28. *Recopilación*, II, 192. Feb. 23, 1575.
29. Henry Charles Lea, *The Inquisition in the Spanish Dependencies* (New York, 1922), pp. 319, 332. See J. T. Medina on this subject.
30. Figueroa, *op. cit.*, p. 336.
31. *Recopilación*, II, 195. Oct. 10, 1618.
32. *Ibid.* July 7, 1550.
33. *Ibid.* Sept. 12, 1628.
34. *Ibid.*, p. 196. Jan. 25, 1569.
35. Jarque, *op. cit.*, IV, 8-9.
36. Depons, *op. cit.*, I, 227-28.
37. *Recopilación*, I, 3. Oct. 5, 1541.
38. *Ibid.*, p. 4. Sept. 21, 1541.
39. *Ibid.*, p. 3. Oct. 10, 1618.
40. *Ibid.*, II, 198. Oct. 8, 1560.
41. *Ibid.*, p. 229. Nov. 20, 1536.
42. *Ibid.*, p. 265. July 17, 1622.
43. *Ibid.*, p. 271. April 10, 1609.
44. *Ibid.*, I, 4. March 5, 1581.
45. Lodares, *op. cit.*, III, 339-40.
46. *Recopilación*, I, 13. Oct. 7, 1541.
47. *Ibid.*, p. 89. July 18, 1593.
48. *Ibid.*, p. 91. May 10, 1554.
49. *Ibid.*, II, 190. June 7, 1550.
50. Lodares, *op. cit.*, III, 317.

51. *Recopilación*, I, 26. Dec. 2, 1578.
52. *Ibid.*, p. 76. March 8, 1603.
53. *Ibid.*, p. 55. March 17, 1619.
54. *Ibid.* March 2, 1634.
55. Torres Saldamando, *op. cit.*, pp. 37-38.
56. *Recopilación*, I, 47. Feb. 7, 1560.
57. *Ibid.* May 26, 1613.
58. *Ibid.*, p. 79. July 3, 1627.
59. *Ibid.*, p. 72. June 18, 1594.
60. *Ibid.*, II, 223. July 12, 1530.
61. *Ibid.*, p. 236. Oct. 19, 1595.
62. *Ibid.*, I, 56. Oct. 8, 1631.
63. *Ibid.*, II, 248. Oct. 10, 1618.
64. *Ibid.*, I, 56. March, 1663.
65. *Ibid.* Nov. 8, 1608.
66. *Ibid.*, p. 32. Nov. 25, 1578.
67. *Ibid.*, p. 33. Nov. 25, 1578.
68. *Ibid.* May 17, 1582.
69. Zamora, *op. cit.*, p. 156.
70. Bourne, *op. cit.*, pp. 253-54.
71. Humboldt, *op. cit.*, I, 297.
72. Figueroa, *op. cit.*, p. 180.
73. *The Counter-Case of the United States of Venezuela before the Tribunal of Arbitration to Convene at Paris*, 4 vols. (New York, 1898), I, 62-63. (Hereafter cited as *Counter-Case of U.S. of Ven.*)
74. *Ibid.*, II, 198.
75. *Recopilación*, II, 199. Oct. 10, 1618.
76. Domingo Muriel, *Historia del Paraguay desde 1747 hasta 1767* (Madrid, 1919), pp. 382-83.
77. William Spence Robertson, *History of the Latin-American Nations* (New York, 1932), pp. 96-97.
78. *Recopilación*, I, 78. Dec. 29, 1587.
79. Herbert E. Bolton, "The Mission as a Frontier Institution in the Spanish-American Colonies," *The American Historical Review*, XXIII (October, 1917), 47, 48.
80. Figueroa, *op. cit.*, p. 399.
81. *Recopilación*, II, 201. Nov. 20, 1536.
82. *Ibid.* May 2, 1563.

83. *Ibid.*, I, 66. Sept. 14, 1543.
84. *Ibid.* Feb. 21, 1609.
85. *Ibid.* Sept. 7, 1543.

86. *Ibid.*, p. 82. Aug. 1, 1558.
87. *Ibid.*, p. 66. Aug. 17, 1636.
88. *Ibid.*, p. 26.

CHAPTER V

1. Solórzano Pereyra, *op. cit.*, II, 156.
2. Pedro Joseph Parras, *Gobierno de los regulares de la América*, 2 vols. (Madrid, 1783), II, 122.
3. Charlevoix, *op. cit.*, I, 219-20.
4. *Op. cit.*, II, 454.
5. Lodares, *op. cit.*, I, 125.
6. T. J. Page, *La Plata, the Argentine Confederation, and Paraguay* (New York, 1859), pp. 496-97.
7. Caulín, *op. cit.*, pp. 243-44.
8. Depons, *op. cit.*, I, 234.
9. *Cartas edificantes*, VII, 395-96.
10. Page, *op. cit.*, p. 498.
11. Quoted in Lockman, *op. cit.*, II, 175.
12. *Noticias auténticas del famoso río Marañón y misión apostólica de la Compañía de Jesús de la provincia de Quito en los dilatados bosques de dicho río* (edited by M. Jiménez de la Espada, Madrid, 1889), p. 167. (Hereafter cited as *Noticias auténticas.*)
13. Ricardo Beltrán y Rózpide (ed.), *Colección de las memorias o relaciones que escribieron los virreyes del Perú acerca del estado en que dejaban las cosas del reino*, 2 vols. (Madrid, 1921–), I, 75. (Hereafter cited as *Memorias de los Virreyes.*)
14. Matías Ruiz Blanco, *Conversión de Píritu, de Indios Cumanagotos, Palenques, y otros* (Madrid 1892), p. 101.
15. Humboldt, *op. cit.*, II, 138.
16. Gumilla, *op. cit.*, pp. 238-54.
17. Jacinto de Carvajal, *Relación del descubrimiento del río Apure hasta su ingreso en el Orinoco* (León, 1892), pp. 111-13.
18. Borda, *op. cit.*, I, 84-85.
19. *Op. cit.*, II, 219.

20. Zamora, *op. cit.*, p. 304.
21. Figueroa, *op. cit.*, pp. 178-79.
22. *Op. cit.*, p. 6.
23. *The Counter-Case of the U. S. of Ven.*, III, 55-56.
24. *Ibid.*, p. 107.
25. Humboldt, *op. cit.*, II, 337.
26. *Ibid.*, pp. 346-49.
27. Rivero, *op. cit.*, p. 359.
28. José Amich, *Compendio histórico de los trabajos, fatigas, sudores, y muertes que los ministros evangélicos de la seráfica religión han padecido por la conversión de las almas de los gentiles . . . del Perú* (Paris, 1854), p. 81.
29. *The Counter-Case of the U.S. of Ven.*, III, 43.
30. *Op. cit.*, pp. 168-75.
31. *Ibid.*, pp. 319-20.
32. *Ibid.*, p. 181.
33. *Op. cit.*, p. 30.
34. *The Counter-Case of the U. S. of Ven.*, III, 19-20.
35. *Ibid.*, p. 22.
36. *The Case of the United States of Venezuela before the Tribunal of Arbitration to Convene at Paris under the Provisions of the Treaty between the United States of Venezuela and Her Britannic Majesty Signed at Washington, February 2, 1897*, 4 vols. (New York, 1898), II, 280, 281. (Hereafter cited as *Case of U. S. of Ven.*)
37. Villaroel, *Enfermedades políticas*, I, 55-70, quoted in H. I. Priestley, *The Coming of the White Man* (New York, 1929), p. 137.
38. Lodares, *op. cit.*, I, 117-18.
39. Rivero, *op. cit.*, p. 24.
40. Gumilla, *op. cit.*, pp. 160-61.
41. Nuix, *op. cit.*, p. 214.
42. *Cartas edificantes*, XIV, 49-50. Other illustrations abound.

CHAPTER VI

1. Humboldt, *op. cit.*, I, 245-46.
2. Bourne, *op. cit.*, pp. 305-6.
3. Canto IV, stanzas, 6-7.
4. Figueroa, *op. cit.*, p. 167.
5. Rivero, *op. cit.*, p. 244.
6. Antonio Alcedo, *The Geographical and Historical Dictionary of America and the West Indies*, 5 vols. (London, 1812), I, 302, 365; II, 94-96, 380-82; and Robertson, *op. cit.*, pp. 128-29.
7. *Relaciones de Mando* (Bogotá, 1910), p. 310. Such colleges had already been established in Peru, Ecuador, and Venezuela.
8. Thomas Gage, *A New Survey of the West Indies, or the English American his Travel by Sea and Land* (London, 1677), pp. 15-16; *Enciclopedia universal Europeo-Americana*, XL, 171-84. For bibliography, see each order.
9. Charlevoix, *op. cit.*, II, 33-34.
10. W. H. Koebel, *Paraguay* (London, 1917), pp. 134-35.
11. A. F. Frézier, *A Voyage to the South-Sea and along the Coasts of Chili and Peru, in the Years 1712, 1713, and 1714* (London, 1717), pp. 327-28.
12. *Noticias auténticas*, p. 162.
13. Rodríguez, *op. cit.*, p. 166.
14. *Op. cit.*, pp. 71-72.
15. Humboldt, *op. cit.*, I, 220.
16. Eguiluz, *op. cit.*, pp. 26-27.
17. *Ibid.*, p. 40.
18. Rivero, *op. cit.*, p. 121.

19. Quoted from a letter of Father Fauque, S. J., in *Cartas edificantes*, XII, 89-90.
20. Charlevoix, *op. cit.*, I, 269-70.
21. *Op. cit.*, I, 218.
22. Quoted in Lodares, *op. cit.*, II, 213-14.
23. Charlevoix, *op. cit.*, I, 270.
24. *Ibid.*, pp. 266, 268-69.
25. Page, *op. cit.*, p. 504.
26. *Cartas edificantes*, X, 119.
27. *The Counter-Case of the U.S. of Ven.*, III, 54-55.
28. Caulín, *op. cit.*, pp. 439-40.
29. Depons, *op. cit.*, I, 337-38.
30. Theodor Griesinger, *The Jesuits: a Complete History of Their Open and Secret Proceedings from the Foundation of the Order to the Present Day* (London, 1885), p. 142.
31. Fray Marcos Salmerón, *Recuerdos históricos y políticos de . . . la religión de nuestra Señora de la Merced* (Valencia, 1646), p. 303.
32. Charlevoix, *op. cit.*, I, 282.
33. *The Case of the U.S. of Ven.*, II, 290-91.
34. *Op. cit.*, p. 245.
35. *Op. cit.*, pp. 79-80.
36. Charlevoix, *op. cit.*, I, 289-90.
37. Lockman, *op. cit.*, II, 168.
38. Frézier, *op. cit.*, pp. 330-31.
39. G. Desdevises du Dezert, "Les Missions des Mojos et des Chiquitos de 1767 à 1808," *Revue Hispanique*, XLIII (1918), 375.

CHAPTER VII

1. *Relaciones históricas de las misiones de padres capuchinos de Venezuela. Colección de libros raros ó curiosos que tratan de América* (Madrid, 1928), p. vii. This work is vol. 22 of *Libros raros*.
2. Lodares, *op. cit.*, II, 5-21; Depons, *op. cit.*, I, 15; F. A. McNutt, *Bartholomew de las Casas* (London,

1909), pp. 116-73; Abbé G. T. F. Raynal, *A philosophical and Political History of the Settlements and Trade of the Europeans in the East and West Indies*, 8 vols. (London, 1783), IV, 84-85.
3. Lodares, *op. cit.*, II, 21. There were only four Spanish settlements in the region: Cumaná, Barcelona,

Cumanacoa, and Cariaco (*ibid.*, I, 169).

4. *Ibid.*, III, 146-68.
5. *Ibid.*, I, 23-29, 36; III, 214-17.
6. Ruiz Blanco, *op. cit.*, pp. 76-77.
7. Lodares, *op. cit.*, I, 39-40.
8. *Relaciones históricas de las misiones de padres capuchinos de Venezuela*, pp. xxviii-xxix.
9. Lodares, *op. cit.*, I, 45.
10. *Ibid.*, 49, 52.
11. *Ibid.*, pp. 52-58.
12. *Ibid.*, III, 383-84, 387-88.
13. *Ibid.*, pp. 384-89.
14. *The Case of the U.S. of Ven.*, III, 375.
15. Lodares, *op. cit.*, II, 97-100.
16. *The Case of the U.S. of Ven.*, II, 351.

17. *Historia coro-gráphica*, p. 376. Father Antonio Caulín labored in this region.
18. The full report of Torrelosnegros is printed in *Relaciones históricas*, pp. 147-256. Extracts are given in Lodares, *op. cit.*, II, 107 ff.
19. *Ibid.*, p. 142.
20. Caulín, *op. cit.*, pp. 376 ff.; Lodares, *op. cit.*, III, 383-84, 387-89, 391-92; Ruiz Blanco, *op. cit.*, pp. 120-31.
21. Caulín, *op. cit.*, p. 8.
22. Lodares, *op. cit.*, II, 141-43.
23. Caulín, *op. cit.*, pp. 300-01, 421-22.
24. Lodares, *op. cit.*, II, 99-102.
25. *Ibid.*, pp. 97 ff.; III, 245-56.
26. *Ibid.*, II, 141-43.

CHAPTER VIII

1. R. B. Cunninghame Graham, *José Antonio Páez* (Philadelphia, 1932), p. 10.
2. Lodares, *op. cit.*, I, 220.
3. *Ibid.*, p. 98.
4. *Ibid.*, p. 71.
5. *Ibid.*, pp. 263-64.
6. *Ibid.*, pp. 77-79.
7. *Ibid.*, pp. 122, 162.
8. *Ibid.*, p. 124.
9. José Gil Fortoul, *Historia constitucional de Venezuela*, 3 vols. (Caracas, 1930), I, 56-57.
10. Depons, *op. cit.*, I, 356; Lodares, *op. cit.*, I, 157.
11. *Ibid.*, p. 254.
12. *Ibid.*, pp. 166, 375.
13. *Ibid.*, p. 374.

14. *Ibid.*
15. *Ibid.*, pp. 160-61.
16. *Ibid.*, p. 164.
17. *Ibid.*, pp. 115-16.
18. *Ibid.*, pp. 244-51.
19. *Ibid.*, p. 303. There were only thirteen Spanish towns in the province of Caracas at the beginning of the seventeenth century. Among them were Coro, Caracas, Valencia, Barquisimeto, and Trujillo (*ibid.*, p. 169).
20. *Ibid.*, p. 206.
21. *Ibid.*, p. 217.
22. *Ibid.*, pp. 263-88.
23. *Ibid.*, p. 284.
24. *Ibid.*, p. 303.
25. *Ibid.*, pp. 345-59.

CHAPTER IX

1. H. J. Mozans (pseud. for J. A. Zahm), *Up the Orinoco and Down the Magdalena* (New York and London, 1910), p. 209.
2. J. M. Henao and G. Arrubla, *Historia de Colombia* (Bogotá, 1929), p. 67, *passim;* Borda, *op. cit.*, I, 81-82; J. A. Zahm (H. J. Mozans),

The Quest of El Dorado (New York, 1917).
3. Mozans, *op. cit.*, pp. 202-04.
4. Borda, *op. cit.*, I, 6-8.
5. *Ibid.*, pp. 10-12.
6. Rivero, *op. cit.*, pp. 83-84.
7. *Ibid.*, pp. 84-85.
8. *Ibid.*, p. 209.

9. *Ibid.*, pp. 54-55.
10. *Ibid.*, p. 101.
11. *Ibid.*, pp. 95-96, 171-73.
12. *Ibid.*, pp. 23-25.
13. *Ibid.*, pp. 223-25.
14. *Ibid.*, pp. 230-37.
15. *Ibid.*, pp. 288-89.
16. Borda, *op. cit.*, I, 149.
17. Rivero, *op. cit.*, p. 55. See also José Cassani, *Historia de la provincia de la Compañía de Jesús en el Nuevo Reino de Granada* . . . (Madrid, 1741), *passim*.
18. José Manuel Groot, *Historia ecclesiástica y civil de la Nueva Granada*, 5 vols. (Bogotá, 1889), II, 14-16.
19. Rivero, *op. cit.*, p. 335.
20. Borda *op. cit.*, II, 54-55.
21. Rodríguez, *op. cit.*, pp. 63-64.
22. Lodares, *op. cit.*, III, 277-95. See likewise Antonio Astrain, *His-*

toria de la Compañía de Jesús en asistencia de España, 7 vols. (Madrid, 1909-1925), VI, 651, and also *passim*.
23. Bernard Moses, *Spain's Declining Power in South America, 1730-1806* (Berkeley, 1919), pp. 146-47.
24. Borda, *op. cit.*, II, 57-61, 72-74.
25. *Ibid.*, pp. 109-10.
26. Groot, *op. cit.*, II, 101.
27. Moses, *op. cit.*, pp. 66-67.
28. Groot, *op. cit.*, II, 213-14.
29. *Ibid.*, p. 329.
30. *Relaciones de mando*, p. 308.
31. *Ibid.*, p. 224.
32. *Ibid.*, p. 308.
33. *Ibid.*, p. 307.
34. *Ibid.*, p. 548.
35. Cunninghame Graham, *op. cit.*, p. 87.
36. Mozans, *op. cit.*, p. 155.
37. *Ibid.*, p. 185.

Chapter X

1. Lodares, *op. cit.*, II, 148.
2. *Ibid.*, p. 149; III, 274.
3. *Ibid.*, pp. 274-75; Rivero, *op. cit.*, pp. 95-96, 171-83.
4. *The Case of the U.S. of Ven.*, II, 269, 338.
5. Lodares, *op. cit.*, II, 153-54.
6. *Ibid.*, pp. 154-58.
7. Caulín, *op. cit.*, pp. 9-10; Lodares, *op. cit.*, II, 173.
8. *Ibid.*, pp. 181-82, 184-85.
9. *Ibid.*, I, 182-83.
10. *The Case of the U.S. of Ven.*, II, 344.
11. Depons, *op. cit.*, I, 349; Lodares, *op. cit.*, II, 188.
12. *Ibid.*, pp. 188-89.
13. *Ibid.*, III, 385, 389-90.
14. *The Counter-Case of the U.S. of Ven.*, II, 218-19.
15. Gumilla, *op. cit.*, pp. 338-39.
16. *The Counter-Case of the U.S. of Ven.*, III, 25.
17. *Ibid.*, pp. 26-27.
18. *Ibid.*, p. 32.
19. *Ibid.*, p. 30.

20. *Ibid.*, p. 40.
21. Lodares, *op. cit.*, II, 207, *passim*.
22. *The Counter-Case of the U.S. of Ven.*, II, 191.
23. *Ibid.*, p. 192.
24. *Ibid.*, p. 193.
25. *The Case of the U.S. of Ven.*, II, 343.
26. *The Counter-Case of the U.S. of Ven.*, III, 69-70.
27. *The Case of the U.S. of Ven.*, II, 345.
28. Lodares, *op. cit.*, II, 232-33.
29. *The Case of the U.S. of Ven.*, *A Reply to the British Blue Book* (Atlanta, 1896), pp. 103-4.
30. Lodares, *op. cit.*, II, 241-42.
31. *Ibid.*, pp. 254-55.
32. *Ibid.*, pp. 269-71.
33. *Ibid.*, p. 331.
34. *Ibid.*, pp. 222-26.
35. *Ibid.*, pp. 226-27.
36. *Ibid.*, pp. 304-5.
37. *Ibid.*, p. 336.
38. *Ibid.*, p. 304.

39. *The Case of the U.S. of Ven.*, II, 287.

40. Lodares, *op. cit.*, II, 216-17.

41. *The Counter-Case of the U.S. of Ven.*, III, 62-63. Quoted from a report of Don Eugenio de Albarado, April 20, 1755.

42. Lodares, *op. cit.*, II, 336.

43. *Relaciones históricas de las misiones de padres capuchinos de Venezuela*, pp. 45-47.

44. *The Counter-Case of the U.S. of Ven.*, III, 83, 84.

45. Lodares, *op. cit.*, II, 308-10.

46. Humboldt, *op. cit.*, I, 303.

47. Lodares, *op. cit.*, II, 308-9.

48. *The Case of the U.S. of Ven.*, II, 405, 407.

49. *Ibid.*, p. 408.

50. Lodares, *op. cit.*, II, 247.

51. *Ibid.*, pp. 247-48.

52. *Ibid.*, p. 250.

53. *Ibid.*, pp. 254-57. These figures include the missions of the upper Orinoco as well.

54. *Relaciones de mando*, pp. 97-98. Perhaps he did not mean that his statement should apply to Venezuela.

55. *The Counter-Case of the U.S. of Ven.*, III, 120-21.

56. *Ibid.*, p. 105.

57. *Ibid.*, pp. 338, 344.

58. G. Desdevises du Dezert, "L'Eglise Espagnole des Indes à la Fin du XVIIIe Siècle," in *Revue Hispanique*, XXXIX (1917), 273-74. This is a good survey.

59. Lodares, *op. cit.*, II, 298-99.

60. Humboldt, *op. cit.*, I, 280, and III, 19.

61. Lodares, *op. cit.*, II, 322.

62. *Ibid.*, p. 332.

63. *Ibid.*, pp. 299, 313-40.

64. *The Counter-Case of the U.S. of Ven.*, III, 312-13.

65. Mozans, *op. cit.*, p. 98.

66. Lodares, *op. cit.*, III, 5.

67. *Ibid.*, II, 323.

68. *Ibid.*, III, 126, 127.

Chapter XI

1. Rivero, *op. cit.*, pp. 253-58.

2. Quoted in *ibid.*, p. 280.

3. *Ibid.*, pp. 296-300, 309.

4. *The Case of Venezuela. A Reply to the British Blue Book*, pp. 102-5.

5. *The Case of the U.S. of Ven.*, II, 293; Astrain, *op. cit.*, VII, 462-78. Lodares, *op. cit.*, III, 276, gives 1733 as the date of the pact. He is probably in error.

6. *Ibid.*, p. 277.

7. Moses, *Spain's Declining Power in South America*, pp. 146-47.

8. Lodares, *op. cit.*, I, 305-26.

9. *Ibid.*, pp. 327-33. The quotation is from p. 333.

10. *Ibid.*, pp. 334-46; II, 254-57.

11. *Ibid.*, III, 286, 358-59.

12. Humboldt, *op. cit.*, II, 337.

13. *Ibid.*, I, 191, 282-83.

14. Mozans, *op. cit.*, p. 143.

Chapter XII

1. Gumilla, *op. cit.*, pp. 52-53.

2. Borda, *op. cit.*, I, 218.

3. Humboldt, *op. cit.*, III, 87.

4. Gumilla, *op. cit.*, pp. 360-61.

5. Caulín, *op. cit.*, p. 373.

6. Gumilla, *op. cit.*, p. 361.

7. *Senate Document* No. 91, 55th Congress, 2nd Session, Part 2, pp. 153-54. This is taken from a report of Abraham Beekman, Commander in Essequibo, submitted to the West India Company, on March 2, 1682.

8. *Noticias auténticas*, pp. 75-76.

9. Depons, *op. cit.*, II, 356.

10. *Sen. Doc.* No. 91, 55th Cong., 2nd Sess., Part 1, pp. 154-56.

11. Depons, *op. cit.*, II, 355.

12. *Sen. Doc.* No. 91, 55th Cong., 2nd Sess., Part 1, pp. 388-89.

13. The Case of Ven., A Reply to the British Blue Book, p. 160.
14. The Counter-Case of the U.S. of Ven., I, 60-61.
15. Borda, op. cit., I, 131-32.
16. The Counter-Case of the U.S. of Ven., III, 18-19.
17. The Case of the U.S. of Ven., II, 295-96.
18. Sen. Doc. No. 91, 55th Cong., 2nd Sess., Part 2, p. 261.
19. The Case of the U.S. of Ven., II, 96.
20. Ibid., p. 284.
21. Ibid., I, 115-16.
22. Ibid., II, 97.
23. Ibid., p. 106.
24. The Counter-Case of the U.S. of Ven., II, 194, 195.
25. The Case of the U.S. of Ven., II, 114.
26. Ibid., p. 119.
27. Ibid., p. 305.
28. The Counter-Case of the U.S. of Ven., II, 203.

29. The Case of the U.S. of Ven., II, 185.
30. Ibid., p. 213.
31. Ibid., III, 37.
32. Humboldt, op. cit., III, 22-23, 77, 85. The quotation is from the last reference. In addition to the various works cited in the previous chapters of Book II, the following publications contain important information on missionary effort in Venezuela: Angel Altolaguirre y Duvale (ed.), Relaciones geográficas de la gobernación de Venezuela... (Madrid, 1908); Froilán Rionegro (ed.), Relaciones de las misiones de las antiguas provincias españolas hoy República de Venezuela (Seville, 1918); Cayataño de Carrocera, La orden franciscana en Venezuela (Caracas, 1929); Joseph Strickland (ed.), Documents and Maps of the Boundary Question between Venezuela and British Guiana... (Rome, 1896).

CHAPTER XIII

1. Izaguirre, op. cit., I, 16-18.
2. Zamora, op. cit., p. 22.
3. Francisco Xeres, "A True Account of the Province of Cuzco," in Clements R. Markham, Reports on the Discovery of Peru (London, 1872), pp. 54-56.
4. Francisco Alvarez de Villanueva, Relación histórica de ... los pp. Franciscanos en las Indias (Madrid, 1892), pp. 15-16.
5. David Rubio, Los Agustinos en el Perú (Lima, 1912), pp. 17-18.
6. Torres Saldamando, op. cit., p. ix.
7. Olivia, op. cit., pp. 152-54, 157-58, passim.
8. Borda, op. cit., I, 41.
9. Noticias auténticas, p. 173; José Chantre y Herrera, Historia de las misiones de la Compañía de Jesús en el Marañón español (Madrid, 1901), pp. 21-27.

10. Borda, op. cit., I, 41-42; Chantre y Herrera, op. cit., passim.
11. Rodríguez, op. cit., p. 38.
12. Ibid., pp. 153-54.
13. George E. Church, Aborigines of South America (London, 1912), pp. 168-70.
14. Rodríguez, op. cit., pp. 224-25.
15. H. J. Mozans, Along the Andes and Down the Amazon (New York, 1923), pp. 379-97. This is a charming and valuable work.
16. Pastoriza Flores, History of the Boundary Dispute between Ecuador and Peru (New York, 1921), p. 5.
17. Rodríguez, op. cit., pp. 23-28, 163-64.
18. Church, op. cit., pp. 157-58.
19. Mariano H. Cornejo and Felipe de Osma, Arbitraje de límites entre Perú y el Ecuador. Documentos anexos a la memoria del

Perú, 7 vols. (Madrid, 1905), III, 226, 229-32.

20. Figueroa, *op. cit.*, p. 189.
21. Rodríguez, *op. cit.*, p. 204.
22. *Ibid.*, p. 89.
23. *Op. cit.*, I, 130.
24. Ricardo García Rosell, *Conquista de la montaña* (Lima, 1905), pp. 11-12.
25. Rodríguez, *op. cit.*, pp. 49-50.
26. *Noticias auténticas*, pp. 174-77.
27. Clements R. Markham (ed.), *Expeditions into the Valley of the Amazon* (London, 1859), p. 52, n.
28. *Noticias auténticas*, p. 180.
29. Rodríguez, *op. cit.*, p. 89.
30. *Noticias auténticas*, pp. 190-91; Maúrtua, *op. cit.*, V, 286.
31. *Noticias auténticas*, pp. 184-85.
32. Alvarez de Villanueva, *op. cit.*, p. 16.
33. Markham (ed.). *Expeditions into the Valley of the Amazons*, pp. xx-xxi.
34. Maúrtua, *op. cit.*, V, 328; Marcós Jiménez de Espada, *El Río Putumayos y Marañón* (Madrid, 1890), *passim*.
35. Markham (ed)., *Expeditions into the Valley of the Amazons*, pp. 51-55.
36. *Ibid.*, p. 60.
37. Borda, *op. cit.*, I, 51.
38. *Journal of Father Samuel Fritz*, p. 51.
39. Rodríguez, *op. cit.*, pp. 90-91.
40. *Noticias auténticas*, p. 202.
41. Markham (ed.), *Expeditions into the Valley of the Amazons*, pp. xvii-xix.
42. Torres Saldamando, *op. cit.*, p. 194.
43. Rodríguez, *op. cit.*, p. 357.
44. Acosta, *op. cit.*, I, 15.
45. Figueroa, *op. cit.*, pp. 56-62.
46. *Ibid.*, pp. 68-70.
47. *Ibid.*, pp. 75-76, 77.
48. Maúrtua, *op. cit.*, II, 121.
49. Rodríguez, *op. cit.*, p. 161.
50. Figueroa, *op. cit.*, p. 17.

51. *Noticias auténticas*, pp. 274-280.
52. Markham (ed.), *Expeditions into the Valley of the Amazon*, p. xxxvii.
53. Maúrtua, *op. cit.*, II, 72-73.
54. *Ibid.*, p. 59.
55. *Noticias auténticas*, pp. 274-80; Diego de Córdova Salinas, *Crónica de la religiosísima provincia . . . del Perú de la Orden de S. Francisco . . .* (Lima, 1651), Chaps. XXXII to XXXIV; Amich, *op. cit.*
56. Markham (ed.), *Expeditions into the Valley of the Amazons*, p. xxxvii.
57. *Cartas edificantes*, XVI, 99.
58. Markham (ed.), *Expeditions into the Valley of the Amazons*, pp. xxxix ff.
59. Rodríguez, *op. cit.*, 265, 311.
60. Figueroa, *op. cit.*, p. 161.
61. *Ibid.*, p. 165.
62. Raynal, *op. cit.*, IV, 415-16.
63. Rodríguez, *op. cit.*, p. 165.
64. *Ibid.*, p. 172.
65. Izaguirre, *op. cit.*, VI, 49.
66. Rodríguez, *op. cit.*, p. 168.
67. Raynal, *op. cit.*, IV, 419-20.
68. Rodríguez, *op. cit.*, p. 264.
69. Figueroa, *op. cit.*, pp. 144-45.
70. *Ibid.*, p. 94.
71. Juan and Ulloa, *op. cit.*, p. 356.
72. Rodríguez, *op. cit.*, p. 25.
73. Chantre y Herrera, *op. cit.*, pp. 176-80, 303-7, 575-83.
74. Paul Radin, *The Story of the American Indian* (New York. 1927), pp. 360-61; F. W. Up de Graff, *Head Hunters of the Amazon* (New York, 1923), pp. 272-83.
75. Rodríguez, *op. cit.*, p. 95.
76. Lockman, *op. cit.*, II, 462.
77. Figueroa, *op. cit.*, pp. 95-96.
78. Rodríguez, *op. cit.*, p. 289.
79. Markham (ed.), *Expeditions into the Valley of the Amazons*, pp. xxxiv-xxxv.
80. *Memorias de los virreyes*, II, 5.
81. Borda, *op. cit.*, I, 76.
82. Juan and Ulloa, *A Voyage to*

South America, 2 vols. (London, 1806), I, 371.

83. *Journal of Father Samuel Fritz*, p. 97.

84. Juan and Ulloa, *A Voyage to South America*, I, 391.

85. *Journal of Father Samuel Fritz*, pp. 97-98.

86. *Ibid.*, p. 65.

87. *Ibid.*, pp. 68-69, 80.

88. Borda, *op. cit.*, I, 71.

89. Cornejo and Osma, *op. cit.*, III, 221.

90. Juan and Ulloa, *Noticias secretas de América*, pp. 363-65.

91. Figueroa, *op. cit.*, pp. 294-96.

92. *Noticias auténticas*, pp. 78-79.

93. *Op. cit.*, pp. 578-83. This author gives an excellent exposition of the government of the missions and the daily life of the converts (pp. 584 ff.). See also Padre Antonio Astrain, *op. cit.*, *passim* for summaries of Jesuit effort in Maynas and other fields of Spanish America.

94. Raynal, *op. cit.*, IV, 418-19.

95. Maúrtua, *op. cit.*, VI, 24.

96. Izaguirre, *op. cit.*, VIII, 51-52.

97. Church, *op. cit.*, pp. 168-70.

98. Maúrtua, *op. cit.*, VI, 25.

99. *Ibid.*, VI, 26.

100. José Pardo y Barreda, *Arbitraje de límites entre el Perú y el Ecuador. Documentos anexos al alegato del Perú*, 2 vols. (Madrid, 1905), I, 182-83.

101. Mozans, *Along the Andes and down the Amazon*, p. 458.

102. Maúrtua, *op. cit.*, VI, 295.

103. *Memorias de los virreyes*, VI, 129.

104. Joseph Hipólito Unánue, *Guía política, eclesiástica y militar del virreynato del Perú, para el año 1793* (Lima, 1793), pp. 200-7.

105. Wissler, *op. cit.*, pp. 252-55.

106. [Mozans], *Along the Andes and down the Amazon*, p. 452.

CHAPTER XIV

1. *Cartas edificantes*, VII, 7.

2. Raynal, *op. cit.*, IV, 235.

3. Robert Southey, *History of Brazil*, 3 vols. (London, 1819), III, 200-1.

4. *Cartas edificantes*, VII, 95.

5. Maúrtua, *op. cit.*, VII, 8.

6. *Ibid.*, X, 1.

7. Southey, *History of Brazil*, III, 198, 199.

8. Markham (ed.), *Expeditions into the Valley of the Amazons*, pp. xxxix-xl.

9. Southey, *History of Brazil*, III, 205-6.

10. *Ibid.*, p. 206.

11. *Cartas edificantes*, VII, 108-9.

12. Lockman, *op. cit.*, II, 450.

13. Quoted in *ibid.*, I, 99-100.

14. Eguiluz, *op. cit.*, p. 57.

15. Lockman, *op. cit.*, II, 160-61.

16. Maúrtua, *op. cit.*, X, 34.

17. Southey, *History of Brazil*, III, 208-9.

18. Church, *op. cit.*, p. 103. Padre Altamirano's book, *Historia de la Misión de Mojos*, was published in La Paz in 1881 (M.V. Ballivián, ed.).

19. Eguiluz, *op. cit.*, p. 62.

20. *Op. cit.*, X, 34-42.

21. G. Desdivises du Dezert, "Les Missions des Mojos et des Chiquitos de 1767 à 1808," *loc. cit.*, p. 406.

22. Maúrtua, *op. cit.*, VI, 23; VII, 46.

23. Charlevoix, *op. cit.*, II, 94.

24. Southey, *History of Brazil*, III, 169-70.

25. Church, *op. cit.*, p. 94.

26. Southey, *History of Brazil*, I, 352.

27. Church, *op. cit.*, p. 94.

28. Charlevoix, *op. cit.*, II, 125.

29. Juan and Ulloa, *A Voyage to South America*, II, 164.

30. *Ibid.*, II, 170-71.

31. Fernández, *op. cit.*, I, 35.

32. Pablo Hernández, *El extraña-*

NOTES

miento de los Jesuítas del Río de la Plata y de las misiones del Paraguay (Madrid, 1908), p. 162.

33. Martin Dobrizhoffer, *An Account of the Abipones, an Equestrian People of Paraguay*, 3 vols. (London, 1822), p. 162.

34. Hernández, *op. cit.*, p. 166.

35. Moses, *Spain's Declining Power in South America*, pp. 121-23.

36. Church, *op. cit.*, p. 206.

37. Lorente, *Historia antigua del Perú*, pp. 188-89.

38. Southey, *History of Brazil*, III, 166.

39. *Ibid.*, III, 163.

40. Dobrizhoffer, *op. cit.*, I, 125-26.

41. Markham, *op. cit.*, pp. xiv-xv.

42. Church, *op. cit.*, pp. 216-18. See also pp. 206-15.

43. Southey, *History of Brazil*, III, 167.

44. Church, *op. cit.*, p. 209.

45. Muriel, *op. cit.*, p. 209.

46. *Ibid.*, pp. 219-223; Church, *op. cit.*, pp. 222-23.

47. Quoted in *ibid.*, pp. 223-24. Padre Tomajuncosa's report will be found in Pedro de Angelis, *Colección de obras y documentos relativos a la historia antigua y moderna de las provincias del Río de la Plata* (Buenos Aires, 1836).

48. *Green Hell. A Chronicle of Travel in the Forests of Eastern Bolivia* (London, 1931), pp. 19, 162, 225.

CHAPTER XV

1. R. H. Whitbeck, *Economic Geography of South America* (New York, 1926), pp. 357 ff.

2. Southey, *History of Brazil*, I, 221-24.

3. Griesinger, *op. cit.*, p. 128.

4. Robertson, *op. cit.*, p. 110.

5. Southey, *History of Brazil*, II, 251-52.

6. Marcos Jiménez de la Espada, *El Iza o Putumayo* (Madrid, 1880), p. 9.

7. Muriel, *op. cit.*, pp. 241 ff.

8. Robertson, *op. cit.*, p. 140.

9. Jarque, *op. cit.*, IV, 23.

10. Quoted in *ibid.*, p. 14.

11. D'Azevedo, *op. cit.*, I, 208-9.

12. H. Boehmer, *Les Jésuites* (Paris, 1908), pp. 181-82.

13. J. Fred Rippy, *Historical Evolution of Hispanic America* (New York, 1932), pp. 120-22.

14. Page, *op. cit.*, p. 476.

15. *Cartas edificantes*, VII, 411.

16. Charlevoix, *op. cit.*, I, 314-15.

17. *Ibid.*, pp. 371-72. A convenient discussion of the Paulista raids on the Paraguay Missions will be found in R. B. Cunninghame Graham's *A Vanished Arcadia* (New York and London, 1901), pp. 51 ff.

18. *Ibid.*, pp. 328-29.

19. *Ibid.*, pp. 409-10.

20. *Ibid.*, p. 254.

21. *Ibid.*, II, 118.

22. *Ibid.*, I, 385.

23. Muriel, *op. cit.*, p. 14.

24. Dobrizhoffer, *op. cit.*, I, 161.

25. *Noticias auténticas*, p. 78.

26. Southey, *History of Brazil*, III, 331.

27. *Ibid.*, pp. 348-50.

28. Hernández, *op. cit.*, pp. 164-66.

29. Charlevoix, *op. cit.*, II, 106.

30. Southey, *History of Brazil*, III, 347.

31. Borda, *op. cit.*, I, 69.

32. Rodríguez, *op. cit.*, p. 378.

33. Borda, *op. cit.*, I, 72.

34. *Journal of Father Samuel Fritz*, p. 96.

35. *Ibid.*, p. 107.

36. *Ibid.*, pp. 120, 125, 126.

37. *Ibid.*, p. 92.

38. *Ibid.*, pp. 32, 68.

39. *Ibid.*, pp. 84, 86.

40. *Ibid.*, pp. 150-51, 152.

NOTES

41. *Ibid.*, pp. 154-55.
42. *Ibid.*, p. 113.
43. *Ibid.*, p. 119.
44. *Ibid.*, pp. 119-20.
45. Southey, *History of Brazil*, III, 142-43.
46. Borda, *op. cit.*, I, 72-75.
47. *Journal of Father Samuel Fritz*, p. 127.
48. *Ibid.*, p. 81.
49. *Ibid.*, p. 128.
50. Figueroa, *op. cit.*, appendix, pp. 331-32.
51. *Ibid.*, appendix, pp. 294 ff.
52. *Ibid.*, appendix, pp. 367-70.
53. Southey, *History of Brazil*, III, 365-66.
54. *Ibid.*, pp. 364-65.
55. Borda, *op. cit.*, I, 72-75.
56. Raynal, *op. cit.*, IV, 420, 421.

57. Gumilla, *op. cit.*, pp. 261-62.
58. Juan and Ulloa, *A Voyage to America*, I, 369.
59. Borda, *op. cit.*, I, 217-18.
60. Cornejo and Osma, *op. cit.*, II, 117-118.
61. Muriel, *op. cit.*, pp. 262-64.
62. Robertson, *op. cit.*, p. 143.
63. Griesinger, *op. cit.*, pp. 559-60.
64. Muriel, *op. cit.*, pp. 23-42; Moses, *Spain's Declining Power in South America*, pp. 73-96.
65. Griesinger, *op. cit.*, pp. 561-63.
66. Robertson, *op. cit.*, pp. 149-50.
67. Mozans, *Along the Andes and Down the Amazon*, p. 452.
68. *Op. cit.*, p. 285. Father Pablo was merely quoting with approval the editor of *Noticias secretas*.
69. *Relaciones de mando*, p. 223.

CHAPTER XVI

1. Quoted in Astrain, *op. cit.*, II, 305-6.
2. Figueroa, *op. cit.*, p. 40. Quoted from a letter by Father Lucás de la Cueva.
3. Rivero, *op. cit.*, p. 10.
4. Humboldt, *op. cit.*, II, 389-90.
5. Rivero, *op. cit.*, p. 119.
6. Figueroa, *op. cit.*, pp. 217, 218.
7. *Journal of Father Samuel Fritz*, pp. 60-61.
8. *Cartas edificantes*, XIII, 314.
9. Quoted in Lockman, *op. cit.*, I, 98-99.
10. Rivero, *op. cit.*, p. 134.
11. *Journal of Father Samuel Fritz*, pp. 134-35.
12. Figueroa, *op, cit.*, pp. 220-27.
13. Lockman, *op. cit.*, II, 440-41.
14. Humboldt, *op. cit.*, II, 411.
15. Rivero, *op, cit.*, p. 185.
16. Fernández, *op. cit.*, I, 65.
17. Mozans, *Through South America's Southland* (New York, 1916), p. 441.
18. Gumilla, *op. cit.*, p. 317.
19. Humboldt, *op. cit.*, I, 272.
20. Figueroa, *op. cit.*, pp. 187-88.

21. *Ibid.*, pp. 191-92.
22. Lockman, *op. cit.*, II, 463-64.
23. *The Counter-Case of the U.S. of Ven.*, III, 52.
24. Rivero, *op. cit.*, p. 133.
25. *Ibid.*, pp. 32-33.
26. Maúrtua, *op. cit.*, X, 1.
27. Rivero, *op. cit.*, p. 117.
28. Figueroa, *op. cit.*, p. 274.
29. Depons, *op. cit.*, I, 242.
30. *Journal of Father Samuel Fritz*, p. 56.
31. Rivero, *op, cit.*, pp. 163-64.
32. *Ibid.*, p. 249.
33. Figueroa, *op. cit.*, pp. 229-30.
34. *Ibid.*, pp. 26-27.
35. *Cartas edificantes*, XIV, 45.
36. Astrain, *op. cit.*, III, 167.
37. Depons, *op. cit.*, I, 234-35.
38. Juan Pérez Bocanegra, *Ritual formulario e institución de curas, para administrar a los naturales de este reyno los santos sacramentos* (Lima, 1631), pp. 130-79.
39. Figueroa, *op. cit.*, pp. 328-29.
40. *Ibid.*, pp. 19-20.
41. Rivero, *op. cit.*, pp. 89, 90.
42. Humboldt, *op. cit.*, II, 362.

43. Gumilla, *op. cit.*, pp. 293-94.
44. Cristóbal de Acuña, "A New Discovery of the Great River of the Amazons," in Markham (ed.), *Expeditions into the Valley of the Amazons*, pp. 84-85.
45. Borda, *op. cit.*, I, 103.
46. *Journal of Father Samuel Fritz*, pp. 71-72.
47. Rivero, *op. cit.*, p. 164.
48. *Ibid.*, pp. 142, 143.
49. Figueroa, *op. cit.*, p. 28.
50. Gumilla, *op. cit.*, p. 149.
51. *Ibid.*, pp. 149-50.
52. Rivero, *op. cit.*, p. 161.
53. Gumilla, *op. cit.*, p. 121.
54. *Relaciones de mando*, p. 227.
55. Humboldt, *op. cit.*, I, 309.
56. Figueroa, *op. cit.*, p. 148.

57. Humboldt, *op. cit.*, II, 248.
58. *The Counter-Case of the U.S. of Ven.*, III, 73-74.
59. *Ibid.*, p. 70.
60. Juan and Ulloa, *A Voyage to South America*, I, 410-11.
61. Rodríguez, *op. cit.*, pp. 169-70.
62. Figueroa, *op. cit.*, pp. 228-29.
63. Raynal, *op. cit.*, IV, 418.
64. Rivero, *op. cit.*, pp. 69-71.
65. Figueroa, *op. cit.*, pp. xiii-xiv.
66. Borda, *op. cit.*, I, 51-54.
67. *Ibid.*, pp. 57-58.
68. Lockman, *op. cit.*, II, 468.
69. Gumilla, *op. cit.*, pp. 367-68.
70. Figueroa, *op. cit.*, pp. 65-66.
71. *Ibid.*, p. 200.
72. *Relaciones de mando*, pp. 311-12.

CHAPTER XVII

1. Rivero, *op. cit.*, pp. vii-viii.
2. F. García Calderón, *Latin America, Its Rise and Progress* (London, 1913), p. 56.
3. Oliva, *op. cit.*, p. 120.
4. W. R. Wheeler and W. E. Browning, *Modern Missions on the Spanish Main* (Philadelphia, 1925), pp. 193-94.
5. Caulín, *op. cit.*, pp. 208-9.
6. Zamora, *op. cit.*, p. 243.
7. Lodares, *op. cit.*, I, 64-68.
8. *Ibid.*, pp. 150-51.
9. Zamora, *op. cit.*, p. 397.
10. Rodríguez, *op. cit.*, p. 184.
11. *Journal of Father Samuel Fritz*, pp. 56-57.
12. Figueroa, *op. cit.*, p. 96.
13. *Ibid.*, p. 269.
14. *Ibid.*, pp. 152, 269.
15. *Ibid.*, p. 267.
16. Rodríguez, *op. cit.*, pp. 24-25.
17. Lodares, *op. cit.*, I, 29.
18. Acosta, *op. cit.*, II, 525-26.
19. Figueroa, *op. cit.*, pp. 136-37.
20. Eguiluz, *op. cit.*, pp. 48-49.
21. Jaguars were called *tigres* in South America.
22. Charlevoix, *op. cit.*, II, 114.

23. Fernández, *op. cit.*, I, 143-44.
24. Eguiluz, *op. cit.*, p. 49.
25. Rivero, *op. cit.*, p. 120.
26. Lodares, *op. cit.*, I, 81-82.
27. Figueroa, *op. cit.*, p. 273.
28. Zamora, *op. cit.*, p. 218.
29. Gumilla, *op. cit.*, pp. 527, 528.
30. Zamora, *op. cit.*, p. 212.
31. Rivero, *op. cit.*, p. 384.
32. *Ibid.*, p. 93.
33. Rodríguez, *op. cit.*, p. 307.
34. Caulín, *op. cit.*, pp. 203-4.
35. Rivero, *op. cit.*, p. 24.
36. Ruiz Blanco, *op. cit.*, p. 87.
37. Fernández, *op. cit.*, II, 53-54.
38. Figueroa, *op. cit.*, pp. 182, 185-86.
39. Rodríguez, *op. cit.*, pp. 92-93.
40. Acosta, *op. cit.*, II, 298, 299.
41. Caulín, *op. cit.*, pp. 417-18.
42. Figueroa, *op. cit.*, p. 52.
43. *Relaciones históricas de las misiones de padres capuchinos de Venezuela*, p. 53.
44. Rivero, *op. cit.*, p. 98.
45. Zamora, *op. cit.*, p. 209.
46. Juan B. Ambrosetti, *Supersticiones y leyendas* (Buenos Aires, 1917), p. 123.

47. Rivero, *op. cit.*, p. 106.
48. These fabulous events are told in Figueroa, *op. cit.*, pp. 375-76.
49. Caulín, *op. cit.*, p. 106.

50. *Journal of Father Samuel Fritz*, pp. 61-62.
51. Rivero. *op. cit.*, pp. 134-35.
52. Acosta, *op. cit.*, II, 531-32.

Chapter XVIII

1. Torres Saldamando, *op. cit.*, p. 31.
2. Rivero, *op. cit.*, p. 153.
3. *Ibid.*, p. 153-54.
4. E. Boyd Barrett, *The Jesuit Enigma* (New York, 1927), p. 21.
5. *Relaciones de mando*, pp. 294-95.
6. *Recopilación*, I, 70.
7. Raynal, *op. cit.*, III, 329.
8. Gage, *op. cit.*, p. 8.
9. Mary Wilhelmine Williams, *The People and Politics of Latin America* (Boston, 1930), p. 190.
10. William Warren Sweet, *A History of Latin America* (New York, 1919), pp. 122-23.
11. García Calderón, *op. cit.*, p. 55.
12. Gage, *op. cit.*, pp. 17-19.
13. Juan and Ulloa, *Noticias secretas de América*, pp. 347-49.
14. Lea, *op. cit.*, pp. 515-16.
15. Zamora, *op. cit.*, p. 208.
16. *The Counter-Case of the U.S. of Ven.*, III, 52-53.
17. *Recopilación*, I, 58 and II, 236.
18. *Ibid.*, I, 72.
19. Muriel, *op. cit.*, p. 424.
20. *Memorias de los virreyes*, I, 72.
21. Gage, *op. cit.*, p. 23.
22. Moses, *Spain's Declining Power in South America*, pp. 128-30.
23. Juan and Ulloa, *Noticias secretas de América*, p. 336.
24. *Ibid.*, p. 338.
25. *Ibid.*, pp. 335-36.

26. Charlevoix, *op. cit.*, II, 47-48.
27. Koebel, *op. cit.*, p. 144.
28. *The Counter-Case of the U.S. of Ven.*, III, 60.
29. Groot, *op. cit.*, I, 270, 271.
30. Borda, *op. cit.*, II, 136-40.
31. *Ibid.*, pp. 123-24.
32. Depons, *op. cit.*, I, 355.
33. Astrain, *op. cit.*, III, 161.
34. Juan and Ulloa, *Noticias secretas de América*, p. 343.
35. Depons, *op. cit.*, I, 234.
36. Acuña, "A New Discovery of the Great River of the Amazons," *loc. cit.*, p. 84.
37. Lodares, *op. cit.*, III, 340.
38. Juan and Ulloa, *Noticias secretas de América*, p. 289.
39. Eguiluz, *op. cit.*, pp. 50, 51.
40. *Ibid.*, p. 51.
41. Charlevoix, *op. cit.*, I, 278.
42. Muriel, *op. cit.*, p. 382.
43. *Ibid.*, p. 379.
44. For this account see Humboldt, *op. cit.*, II, 213-14.
45. *Ibid.*, III, 88.
46. Borda, *op. cit.*, I, 28-29.
47. Griesinger, *op. cit.*, pp. 577, 580.
48. W. C. Cartwright, *The Jesuits: Their Constitution and Teaching* (London, 1876), pp. 139-41.
49. Barrett, *op. cit.*, p. 297.
50. *Relaciones de mando*, pp. 228-29.
51. Humboldt, *op. cit.*, II, 509.
52. *Ibid.*, pp. 201-2.
53. Depons, *op. cit.*, I, 351.

Chapter XIX

1. Nuix, *op. cit.*, pp. 297-98.
2. This statement is made in Zamora, *op. cit.*, p. 25.

3. Mozans, *Through South America's Southland*, p. 483.
4. *Noticias auténticas*, p. 229.

5. Lockman, *op. cit.*, pp. 456-57.
6. Desdivises du Dezert, "Les Missiones des Mojos et des Chiquitos de 1767 à 1808," *loc. cit.*, p. 409.
7. *The Counter-Case of the U.S. of Ven.*, III, 58-60.
8. Joseph Luis de Cisneros, *Descripción exacta de la provincia de Benezuela* (Madrid, 1912), pp. 12-13.
9. *The Counter-Case of the U.S. of Ven.*, III, 140 ff.
10. *Ibid.*, pp. 125-26.
11. Humboldt, *op. cit.*, III, 19, 25.
12. Caulín, *op. cit.*, p. 8.
13. Borda, *op. cit.*, II, 143-44.
14. Maúrtua, *op. cit.*, XII, 283.
15. *The Counter-Case of the U.S. of Ven.*, III, 57.
16. *The Case of the U.S. of Ven.*, II, 345-46.
17. Charlevoix, *op. cit.*, I, 265-66.
18. *The Counter-Case of the U.S. of Ven.*, III, 53-54.
19. Barrett, *op. cit.*, p. 211.
20. Borda, *op. cit.*, II, 48-50.
21. Humboldt, *op. cit.*, II, 48-50.
22. Torres Saldamando, *op. cit.*, p. 38.
23. The following books written by Colonial ecclesiastics on the native languages are in the Duke University library:
Arte de la lengua Quichua compuesto por el Padre Diego de Torres Rubio de la Compañía de Jesús, Lima, 1619.
Arte y vocabulario de la lengua Quichua general de los Indios de el Perú, que compuso el Padre Diego de Torres Rubio de la Compañía de Jesús, y añadió el P. Juan de Figueredo de la misma Compañia, Lima, 1754.
Arte de la lengua Quechua general de los Indios de este reyno del Pirú. . . . Compuesto por el Doctor Alonso de Huerta, clérigo presbytero de la dicha lengua . . . , Lima, 1616.
Declaración copiosa de las quatro partes más esenciales, y necessarias de la doctrina christiana . . . por el eminentíssimo Cardinal Roberto Belarminio de la Compañía de Jesús . . . Traducida de lengua Castellana en la general del Inga por el Bachiller Bartolomé Ivrado, Lima, 1649.
Padre Diego González de Holguín, S.J., *Arte y diccionario Quechua-español*, Lima, 1608.
For additional citations of books not in the Duke library, see José Toribio Medina, *Bibliografía de las lenguas Quechua y Aymará*, New York, 1930.
24. Rivero, *op. cit.*, pp. viii-ix.
25. Gumilla, *op. cit.*, pp. 318-19.
26. Fernández, *op. cit.*, I, 64.
27. Lockman, *op. cit.*, II, 167.
28. Torres Saldamando, *op. cit.*, pp. 180-81.
29. García Calderón, *op. cit.*, p. 56.
30. Ambrosetti, *op. cit.*, pp. 77-79.
31. Dobrizhoffer, *op. cit.*, I, 120.
32. Pallarés and Calvo, *Noticias históricas . . .* , p. 23.
33. Caulín, *op. cit.*, pp. 34-35.
34. *Ibid.*, p. 21.
35. *Noticias auténticas*, p. 107.
36. Charlevoix, *op. cit.*, I, 193.
37. Gumilla, *op. cit.*, p. 491.
38. Charlevoix, *op. cit.*, I, 20.
39. Dobrizhoffer, *op. cit.*, II, 290, 303-11.
40. Rodríguez, *op. cit.*, p. 337.
41. Borda, *op. cit.*, I, 219-20.
42. Gumilla, *op. cit.*, pp. 390-91.
43. *Ibid.*, pp. 457-58.
44. *Ibid.*, pp. 490-91.
45. Borda, *op. cit.*, II, 46-48.
46. Blanco, *op. cit.*, p. 31.
47. Caulín, *op. cit.*, p. 91.
48. Rodríguez, *op. cit.*, p. 374.
49. Rivero, *op. cit.*, p. 15.
50. Humboldt, *op. cit.*, II, 270.
51. Dobrizhoffer, *op. cit.*, I, 282.
52. Charlevoix, *op. cit.*, I, 322-23.
53. Ambrosetti, *op. cit.*, pp. 93-94.
54. Dobrizhoffer, *op. cit.*, I, 301-2.
55. Father Pedro Lozano, *Descripción chorográphica del terreno, ríos,*

arboles, y animales . . . del Gran Chaco (Córdoba, 1733), p. 38.
56. Charlevoix, *op. cit.*, I, 24-25.
57. Dobrizhoffer, *op. cit.*, I, 258-59.
58. *Ibid.*, pp. 255-56.
59. Acosta, *op. cit.*, I, 148.
60. Lozano, *op. cit.*, p. 39.
61. Charlevoix, *op. cit.*, I, 26-27.
62. *Ibid.*, p. 24.
63. Dobrizhoffer, *op. cit.*, I, 290.
64. Charlevoix, *op. cit.*, I, 192.
65. Zamora, *op. cit.*, p. 10.
66. Carvajal, *op. cit.*, p. 205.
67. Dobrizhoffer, *op. cit.*, II, 292.
68. *Noticias auténticas*, pp. 105-6.
69. Figueroa, *op. cit.*, pp. 203-14.
70. Gumilla, *op. cit.*, p. 409.
71. Zamora, *op. cit.*, p. 55.
72. Charlevoix, *op. cit.*, I, 21.
73. *Ibid.*, p. 22.

74. Dobrizhoffer, *op. cit.*, II, 293.
75. Figueroa, *op. cit.*, pp. 213-14.
76. Zamora, *op. cit.*, p. 55.
77. Dobrizhoffer, *op. cit.*, II, 291.
78. Carvajal, *op. cit.*, p. 176.
79. Zamora, *op. cit.*, p. 57.
80. Gumilla, *op. cit.*, pp. 449-51.
81. Humboldt, *op. cit.*, II, 503.
82. Carvajal, *op. cit.*, p. 246.
83. Dobrizhoffer, *op. cit.*, I, 243-44.
84. Rodríguez, *op. cit.*, p. 377.
85. Caulín, *op. cit.*, p. 13.
86. Gumilla, *op. cit.*, pp. 28-29.
87. *Journal of Father Samuel Fritz*, p. 104.
88. Gumilla, *op. cit.*, pp. 292-93, 500.
89. Acosta, *op. cit.*, I, 7, 82, 85, 96, 106.

<h2 align="center">CHAPTER XX</h2>

1. Bolton, "The Mission as a Frontier Institution in the Spanish-American Colonies," *loc. cit.*, p. 43.
2. Priestley, *op. cit.*, p. 127.
3. Groot, *op. cit.*, I, 67, 101, 102.
4. Quoted in Charlevoix, *op. cit.*, I, 245-46.
5. John A. Mackay, *The Other Spanish Christ* (London, 1932), p. 40.
6. Juan and Ulloa, *Noticias secretas de América*, p. 353.
7. Ambrosetti, *op. cit.*, p. 147.
8. Mackay, *op. cit.*, p. 93.
9. Rubio, *op. cit.*, p. 38.
10. Humboldt, *op. cit.*, I, 299-300.
11. Rivero, *op. cit.*, pp. 60-61.
12. Gumilla, *op. cit.*, p. 63.
13. Rivero, *op. cit.*, p. 103.
14. *Ibid.*, p. 111.
15. Humboldt, *op. cit.*, I, 201-2.

16. Depons, *op. cit.*, I, 238-39.
17. Sebastián Lorente, *Perú bajo la dinastía austriaca* (Paris, 1870), pp. 328, 347.
18. Page, *op. cit.*, pp. 224-25.
19. For account of this tale see Ambrosetti, *op. cit.*, pp. 124-25.
20. Izaguirre, *op. cit.*, IX, 60-62.
21. Mozans, *Along the Andes and Down the Amazon*, pp. 451-53.
22. *The Case of the U.S. of Ven.*, III, 118-19.
23. Koebel, *op. cit.*, p. 136.
24. Grubb, *op. cit.*, p. 19.
25. Ambrosetti, *op. cit.*, pp. 79-90.
26. Church, *op. cit.*, p. 124.
27. Mozans, *Through South America's Southland*, p. 447.
28. Browning, *op. cit.*, pp. 49-50.
29. K. G. Grubb, *Amazon and Andes* (New York, 1930), pp. 42-43.

INDEX

394

395

Vespertina Solemnitas